Great Baddow Oral History

Compiled by

Allen Buckroyd

With the help of his dedicated team from
Baddow and Galleywood U3A

Great Baddow Oral History

Compiled by: the Oral History Team of the Baddow and Galleywood U3A, comprising:
Allen Buckroyd (Team Leader)
Brian Barker
Pauline Cutmore
Hugh Cutmore
Vera Evans
Mike Nel
Ken Nickol
Sylvia Tingey
Norman Tingey
Ann Whalley

Edited by: Allen Buckroyd and Ann Whalley

© Baddow & Galleywood U3A Publications 2003

ISBN 0-9546650-0-7

First Published in 2003 by: Baddow & Galleywood U3A Publications.
Telephone 01245 478417 E-mail: allen.buckroyd@hemscott.net

Printed by: PressXpress, Fox Meadow, 23 Courtauld Road, Braintree, Essex CM7 9BD

Cover Photo: View of St. Mary's Parish Church from Galleywood Road

The printing and publication of this book has been made possible by funding from the Local Heritage Initiative, which is a partnership between the Heritage Lottery Fund, Nationwide Building Society and the Countryside Agency.

Local Heritage *initiative*

 Heritage Lottery Fund

 Nationwide

 The Countryside Agency

Additional publications by Allen Buckroyd:
Great Baddow Walking Guides 1 to 4

Foreword

The Parish Council is delighted to see the publication of an oral history of Great Baddow, celebrating memories of life in the village in the last century. We all find it fascinating to hear recollections of Great Baddow before modern developments brought so much change and now, thanks to the initiative of the local U3A's oral history team, these memories have been recorded and preserved.

Great Baddow is one of the largest villages in the country, and it says much for our community spirit that most residents still regard it firmly as a village and very distinct from the town of Chelmsford. As a Parish Council we strive to maintain this community spirit; helping to increase knowledge and awareness of life in Great Baddow in the last century is as much a part of this as looking to provide facilities for the future. We were therefore very pleased to be able to make a small contribution towards the cost of this publication and to the earlier costs of gathering the information.

Having had the opportunity to preview some of the early chapters, I am sure this book will bring back many memories to long standing residents and provide us all with a greater insight into village history. Above all this book is a pleasure to read and one you will not want to put down - congratulations to Allen Buckroyd and his team for their dedication and enthusiasm in bringing it to fruition.

Chris Shaw

Chairman, Great Baddow Parish Council

Preface

"One of the Sweetest Villages in the Kingdom"

Reference to "the village" of Great Baddow may give rise to a wry smile in some people, who regard it as a suburb of Chelmsford. Yet some of the local residents still talk of "going to the village" when off to the shops, to a meeting in the Village Hall, or to the library. If you stand by St.Mary's Church and look across to the White Horse pub and the old parade of shops with its Georgian 3 bay windows, thought to be unique in Essex, you might just go so far as to agree with a quotation in an Essex history of the 18th century which said, "Great Baddow is remarkable for being one of the sweetest villages in the Kingdom".

Despite extensive development and expansion there is still much of historic interest and beauty, and even the modern shopping area on the Vineyards site has received accolades within the county. The site was redeveloped in the late 1960s when most of the changes in the village started. Until then the village looked as if it had been little altered for hundreds of years.

The Aim of the Book

This book aims to recall some of the history of the village, based on the lives of people who have lived here in the last century. This will retain for posterity the reminiscences and memories of Gt. Baddow residents, which would otherwise be lost. Perhaps this will foster a greater civic pride in the village. This book does not pretend to be a definitive history of Great Baddow; it does not deal with the volume of written material that exists in various other sources; we have only interviewed a relatively small number of residents who might have something worthwhile to record. The group of contributors was chosen in 2001 after a number of requests for volunteers were made locally. BBC Essex was kind enough to interview me 'over the airwaves' asking for interested parties to get in touch and that resulted in the generous group of people who gave their time and memories.

The Basis of the Book

We have recorded interviews with a wide variety of current and former residents of the village, some of whom have lived here all their lives, and using their memories we have tried to build up a composite picture of everyday life in Gt.Baddow. Lest we be accused of wishing the village had remained in a pre-war time warp we have also looked briefly at life as it is today through the eyes of some of our younger villagers. This will give to the reader a sense of continuity and a comparison between 'then' and 'now'.

Structure

The book is divided into subject headings, such as early family life, schooldays, wartime reminiscences, work and leisure. We have touched on health issues, local legends and village characters. Some of the quoted entries stand alone, but some are linked together where the topics are similar. Additional data is included where needed to provide an overall picture.

We have included the personal opinions of residents about local issues, but we have endeavoured to avoid contentious matters that might upset persons of a sensitive disposition. We have tried to confirm the 'facts' as far as possible, but by its nature an oral history is based on personal reminiscences and opinions that cannot always be verified. The editing team has tried to exclude any entry that might upset a person mentioned in the text, or their successors. Throughout the writing of this book the intention is to inform, educate and entertain, to provide a sense of 'belonging' to a village that has a long and distinguished history.

We are indebted to the residents who consented to being interviewed, and to those who provided written reminiscences and precious photographs, many of which are reproduced in the following pages. A list of contributors is included at the end of the book.

The verbal statements of our contributors are indented or in inverted commas. The word '(photo)' in parenthesis indicates that a photograph relevant to the preceding text is included in this chapter.

Maps

Several maps relating to Great Baddow have been included to provide an overall view of the village, and to give an idea where some of the long lost houses were situated. A list of the main buildings has also been added, with the reference number of the house as per the maps.

No	House	No	House
1a /b	Baddow Hall & Baddow Hall Farm (D)	27	Peculiar People's Chapel
2	Kings Head PH	28	Chantry School (L)
3	Jasper Jeffery's House & School (L)	29	St Mary's Church (LB)
4	Parish Hall	30	Village School
5a /b	Manor Farm (old (D)& new)	31	The Vicarage (L)
6	Beech House (L)	32	White Horse block (L)
7	Manor Lodge, Place &Cottage (L)	33	George & Dragon PH (D)
8	Baddow Lodge (D)	34	Baddow House (L)
9	Meadgate Farm	35	Branwoods
10	Carpenters Arms PH	36	RC Church (ex RAF Hut)
11	Star PH	37	Baddow Place (L)
12	Whitehouse Farm (D)	38	Adstocks
13	Beehive PH	39	Pound House
14	Noakes Place (D)	40	Baddow Court (L)
15	Blue Lion PH	41	Brewery
16	Yew House (Youse) (L)	42	Pitt Place
17	Rothmans (L)	43	Pontlands (L)
18	Vineyards House (D)	44	Baddow Research
19	The Limes (L)	45	Newport House
20	United Reformed Church	46	Seabrights Farm/Barn
21	Red House/Brick Walls (L)	47	Gardiner's Farm (D)
22	Carters Bakery/Shop (Daces)	48	Lathcoats Farm (L)
23	Well House Farm (D)	49	Abercorn Nurseries
24	Foxholes (D)	50	Great Sir Hughes
25	British Restaurant/ Old Library	51	Little Sir Hughes
26	Bell Inn (D)		

Notes:

D = Demolished   L = Listed, Grade 2   LB = Listed, Grade B

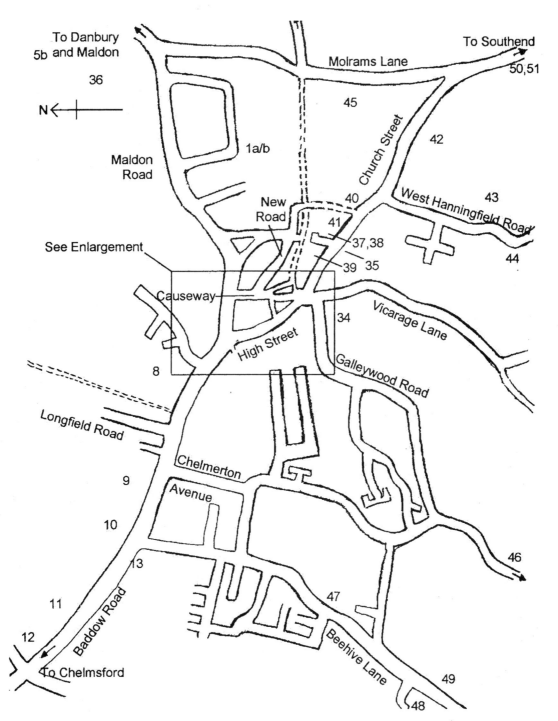

Note: *See associated key to identify numbered buildings*

Great Baddow Village
around 1940

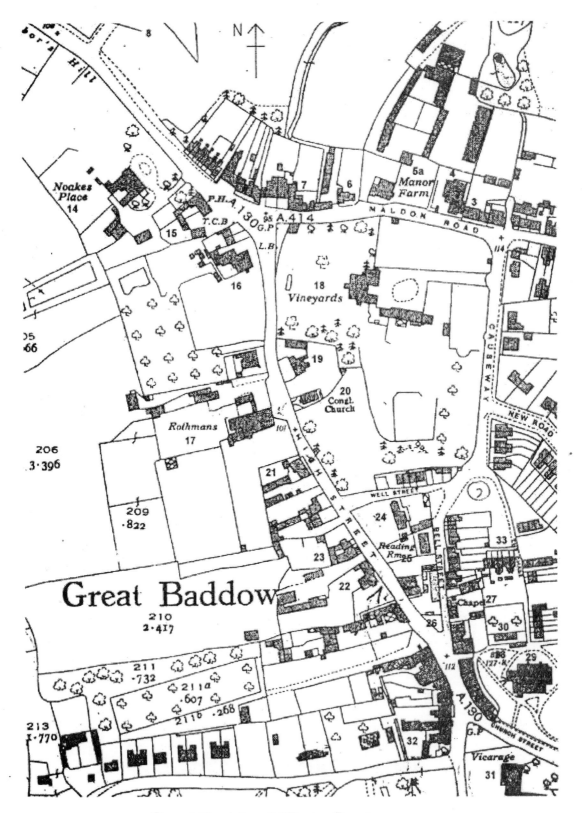

Great Baddow Village Centre

Beehive Lane (not to Scale)

BEEHIVE LANE

DEADMANS LANE

LATHCOATS FARM

ABERCORN NURSERIES

SAWKINS AVENUE

Marconi's Social Club

Gardiner's Farm

WESTBOURNE GROVE

BEEHIVE LANE

DORSET AVENUE (1937)

AVENUE ROAD

ST PAULS

LOFTIN WAY (1937)

WINCHELSEA DRIVE (1937)

GIRL'S HOME

COTTAGES OCCUPIED BY GRAVEL PIT WORKERS

GRAVEL PIT

Mr TIPPING'S TAXIS
Mrs BROWN (layer out)

GRAVEL PIT

ELIZABETH VILLA, named after wife of Robert Jackson, owner of pit

Isolation Hospital

COTTAGES OCCUPIED BY GRAVEL PIT WORKERS

TOWER GARAGE

Stables

Garden

Mr WHITING

BEEHIVE INN

Walter Jackson's Engineering Sheds

Mr BOREHAM'S Butchers Shop

OLD ARMY & NAVY INN

Mrs SMITH Greengrocer

Mr WRIGHT Butcher

Mission Hall

BADDOW ROAD

CHELWATER

WATER TOWER

Mrs BOREHAM General Store & P.O.

ENTRANCE to MARKET GARDEN

MAFEKING VILLA

STAR P.H.

Great Baddow Oral History

"One of the Sweetest Villages in the Kingdom"

Contents

Chapter 1 - Setting the Scene

Introduction

Throughout his life farmer Reg Spalding of this parish wrote a journal, a perpetual diary. In it he described a casual walk through the village in 1900. We will use this to set the scene for the oral history of Great Baddow.

Southend Road or Church Street

Reg: Let us start early in the morning from Ladywell Corner where Southend Road meets Molrams Lane.

Near there at Brookside Dairy Mr Cordell is milking his cows before starting his round. Mr Cordell, a Quaker, who used to farm Reeds farm on the Roxwell Road, lives at the Grove. Then we go past Pitfield House where Mr Boghurst Fisher lives. (Ed: I think this is the crumbling edifice now called Pitt Place. It used to generate its own electric power via a wind generator and had a large pond in the back garden, complete with rowing boat). (Photos 1-1 & 1-2). Then we go to the corner of West Hanningfield Road.

On the left is Pontlands where we find Mr Thomasin Foster, who was known as The Squire. I meet his manager Ruben Stock working with the cattle. Then I pass Baddow Court where Mr.Smithers, a stockbroker lives.

Next I pass Baddow Brewery which is quite a big brewery owned by Crabb, Smee and Veley. (Photo 1-3 shows the old building and photo 1-4 shows the staff in 1899). They brew a very strong beer. They keep 17 heavy horses to deliver the beer. The time now is 6 am and the brewery is in full swing. A pair of horse wagons loaded with beer barrels is coming out to start the deliveries. Mr Veley lives at Adstocks, next to the Brewery. The Crabbs live next to Adstocks at Baddow Place. Mr Crabb, who is a little eccentric, is starting out with an apple tree and a spade. He will plant a tree in an area called "Crabb's Folly" owned by the Brewery in West Hanningfield Road. After he had planted many trees there he built an apple house, which is (supposedly) still there. Then he dug up all the apple trees. Further on the opposite side is a long line of trees. It is on what is known as "a slang" just a piece of waste land between the farm hedge and the road. His sisters are very religious, but they look down on the poor, and they only give away religious tracts, not money. If the children do not bow and scrape before them one of the Miss Crabbs will go to see their parents about it. In the apple room at the top of their house they have a text saying "Keep thine hands from picking and stealing". In the kitchen they have another saying, "Obey your masters". The Crabbs own the church 'living', (the advowson) and if the vicar's sermon lasts less than 40 minutes he too is severely criticised.

Crossing the road I pass Houghtons, the residence of Mr. Prior Johnson and his sisters. Once the family had been very rich; his father had built Lilystone Hall in Stock. He used to farm Gt. Sir Hughes but lost all his money owing to the farming depression in the 1880s.

Branwoods[1] is the same side of the road as Houghtons. Here lives Mr Herman Hicks, a Stockbroker, who grows beautiful orchids. He always has one in his buttonhole as he sets

---

[1] Knocked down in the 60's to make way for the flats in Seabrook Road

off to London. Then I pass Mr Bush the blacksmith busy at his forge (at the corner of Baddow Place Avenue). He is shoeing a hunter. He buys corn drills at sales and repairs them for resale. His nickname is "Paint and Putty Jack". I pass one of the village butchers, Downeys. Mrs Downey used to call out "All meat, no bone!" and the local village lads would reply "All bone, no meat!"

Lower down Church Street on the right I pass Pound House where the Jackson Brothers are the local wheelwrights. They build the good drays used by the brewery. Next door the Miss Stannards manage the Post Office[2]. They are busy getting out the first post round. The ponies that bring the mail from Southend pick up letters and parcels from all the small post offices on the way.

Also on Church Street on the same side are the small houses called Friars Hall belonging to King Edward VI Grammar School in Chelmsford.

Lower down is St.Mary's Church. Mr Harnden is the clerk, Mr Mallet the lay reader. The church has been renovated. All the narrow pews have been taken away and the galleries taken down. A special pew used to be allotted to Meadgate Farm, who have to pay 1 shilling for the Sunday Bread Dole which are loaves of bread left in the Church porch for poor widows. Another pew belonged to Gt. Sir Hughe's estate, which has to pay 2s-0d a week to be spent on bread to be distributed to the inhabitants on St.Thomas's Day. On Gt. Sir Hughe's land was a field called Charities Field, which had to pay £5-4s-0d each year for bread to be distributed on St.John's Day, December 21st. This farm when it was bigger had to pay the parson 1 guinea a year in 4 equal parts to preach a sermon on Good Friday.

On the North side of the church is the old village school. The headmaster is Mr.Turnage. It is a church school erected in 1837 at the time of the General Education Act.
Opposite the Church on Church Street is the vicarage inhabited by the Rev Alfred Noel Colley, who is a very devoted parson. (Photo 1-5).

Vicarage Lane

Turning sharp left I am in Workhouse Lane[3]. On the left a little way up the road are some almshouses. During the wars against Napoleon the old inhabitants say that their fathers remembered a big camp of German soldiers. At the same time there was a bigger camp in Chelmsford.

Galleywood Road

I will divert now along Galleywood Road, where a little way along on the left is Baddow House owned by Mr Bristowe a stockbroker (Mr De Zoete, a former owner who was a benefactor in Baddow was Chairman of the Stock Exchange). Mr Bristowe maintains the Baddow Cricket ground on his land. The tram[4] is called "The Gentlemen of Gt. Baddow Tram". It is kept in order by Mr. Ockendon, the Baddow coal merchant. He cuts and rolls it with his horse, which wears leather boots over its shoes. It is the only horse that I have seen with one of its forefeet exactly the same shape as its hind foot.

---

2 Now Gerrard's hairdressers
3 Now called Vicarage Lane
4 I think this refers to the contrivance pulled by the horse, possibly a roller. The dictionary gives one meaning of tram as the shafts of a cart. Alternatively, from the sense of the entry it could be the cricket pitch itself, which resembles a tramway.

During World War One Baddow House was taken over by the Government as a Prisoner of War Camp for German soldiers. They were very good workers. I employed two and used to collect three more for Mr Fleming at Barnes farm. I used to take them home at 6 p.m. and deliver them at the front of the house and get a receipt for them, then drive round the back and bring them back to the farm to do some more work.

Beyond Hollywoods further along Galleywood Road is a small meadow belonging to St. Mary's church. It is let by auction in the vestry at the Easter meeting. I think it is about two and a half acres. Mr Bristowe has just bought and pulled down two old houses on the corner of Galleywood Road next to the White Horse pub, so as to double the width of the road. (This accounts for the two missing house numbers at the bottom of Galleywood Road). You do not need to go far down Galleywood Road to feel you are in the country. (Photo 1-6).

High Street

Let us return to the High Street, occupied mainly by shops with accommodation above. Jutting right out into the street is the Bell public house, owned by Baddow Brewery. It has overhanging top storeys. On the bell sign is written in Latin, "Vivos voco morticos plango" my first Latin[5]. (Photo 1-7).

Bell Street

On the right is a road leading to Maldon Road, called Bell Street. Two paces up there on the right is the shop belonging to Mr. Russell the village plumber and builder.
By the left side of the entrance to the builder's yard is an entrance to the village Tithe Barn. An old man, John Gunn, lives in it. His grandfather or great grandfather used to be the Tithing Man. On one side of the entrance are bundles of tithing sticks. When a farmer had cut his corn or hay he had to stand his corn up in 'traves'[6] and his hay in 'cocks' and he could not cart any away until the Tithing man had come to the field with his sticks. He could start anywhere in the field to put a stick into a trave or cock, but once he had started he had to keep on and select every tenth one (for the church). This was to prevent the farmer making the tenth one smaller each time. The corn or hay selected by this method was stored in the Tithing Barn[7]. Some bundles of tithing are still in the barn (can they be located 100 years on?). This practice was stopped by the Tithe Act of 1835. To save trouble many of the parsons used to try and guess the size of the crop and bargain with the farmers (for the cash equivalent presumably, to save them having to sell the produce).
(Photo 1-8 shows even older premises of Mr Ruffell).

Further along Bell Street is Slut's Hill[8], in the middle of which stands one of the village pumps. Another name for this road is Cucking or Ducking Stool Lane as at its lower end on the right side is the remains of the old ducking pond. On the left at the top of the hill is the old village lock-up. It is not very big but heavily built of oak. I don't think P.C Wright uses it very much.
Opposite are the Almshouses with their pretty dormer windows. They are occupied by nine old inhabitants, who share one lavatory in the middle, known as a 'pail closet'. In the block of almshouses are two from which the Church Clerk Mr. Hornden collects 1s-0d each (5p) rent per week.

---

5 This means: "I summon the living; I lament the dead". A bell and a public house could both be said to do this.
6 Trave is an obsolete word, and the Shorter Oxford Dictionary defines it as an enclosure of bars in which a restive horse was held while it was shod. The sense of the paragraph above suggests corn in bales or sheaves, but obviously the amounts were variable, allowing for some cheating by farmers.
7 This barn has been renovated and is now Russell's Restaurant. During the mid 20th century it was used to store plumbers items, building material, timber etc for Mr Russell and his successors.
8 Now called Pump Hill.

The Chase

Leading from there is a small road leading up to the North side of St.Mary's Church, The Chase. On the right side is the George and Dragon Public House. Further up on the same side there used to be a Chapel of St. John the Baptist which had been dissolved at the Reformation.

Coming back to the end of Bell St, I come into The Causeway, leading to Maldon Road. On its left side is another village pump. Further along is the back entrance to The Vineyards mansion.

Maldon Road

Opposite the Causeway in Maldon Road is Miss Turnage's school[9]. Turning right I go towards Maldon. On my left is Mr Lynn the village builder. His ancestor constructed the culvert under the main street leading from Brookhouse Farm to the lower end of Manor Farm[10].

On the left in Maldon Road I pass the King's Head Public House kept by Tom Shorten. Just opposite is John Lewis Sparrow's blacksmith's shop[11]. He is a very clever worker in wrought iron. He showed me some gates he was making (for I think Danbury Palace) with his trademark, a little wrought iron sparrow in the corner. He is a staunch liberal and leader of the local chapel. I think Mr Sparrow's shop belongs to St.Mary's church.

On the right hand side of the road, further on is the entrance to Baddow Hall where Mrs Gilmore lives. Baddow Hall Farm is on the land of Baddow Hall and can be reached from the entrance between the Brewery and Baddow Court and through the Bringey.

Coming back along Maldon Road, just past Miss Turnage's school is Jasper Jeffery's school. This is now closed because of shortage of funds. A Mr.Sharman, now dead, was the last master. It (presumably the charity) owns Pynings Farm at West Hanningfield.

High Street

Now I go back to the Bell Public House and walk down the High street. After passing Mr Liddiard's shop, going towards Chelmsford I pass Dyne's[12] which is the residence of Mr Charles Burgess Snelling, who is a freeman of the City of London and a jeweller. At one political meeting a man asked him why he (Snelling) was rich while he was poor. Mr Snelling replied "When I was young I graced my own parlour; you adorned the brewer's parlour".

Next to Dynes is Mr Henry Carter, who farms at Gt.Seabrights. Mr Carter has a bakery behind the shop here in the High Street[13], a milk business and sells corn and hay.

Henry Carter has a big family who all work for him. He is a chapel man and on Sundays drives a waggonette with nearly all the family on board. He wears a top hat, and because he has a long beard he is known as "Nanny Goat Carter" and because he is very tight in his dealings (he probably has to be) he is also called "Hungry Carter".

---

9 Later Baron's Store, now Copsey's Dental practice

10 Which at the time of writing the journal was next to Beech House at No 7 Maldon Road. It moved to the location near the waterworks on the outskirts of Baddow when Tyrells Way was built in the early 1970s. Brookhouse farm was owned by the Carter family, situated behind Carter's Bakery in the High Street.

11 Site now occupied by Kingham's flats.

12 I think this must have been next door to Essex Carpets, where there is now an Osteopath practice.

13 Now a Design Office next to Dace's piano shop.

Lower down on the opposite side of the road is Foxholes[14]. This is a very old and pretty house, which is occupied by Mr Charles Richard Finch who is Registrar of Births and Deaths. He has a very fine collection of cut glass.

Opposite (on the High Street) is a house, yard and meadow occupied by Mr Aldred Senior, who sells antiques. His son Fred is a dealer in cattle, whose drover is called Tiggy Newman. He sleeps rough, but is a good drover. Next I come to The Hollies where Mr Martin Sparrow lives. He is the vet or horse doctor. (Photo 1-9).

At the back of his house live Mr Collins and his two sons George and Tom. Mr Collins senior drives a big grey horse pulling a horse bus to Chelmsford 8 am, 12 p.m. 2 p.m. and 5 p.m. George helps him and drives a brougham for private use, weddings and funerals. Tom draws the carrier's cart to Chelmsford twice a day. They are very honest and staunch members of the 'Peculiars'[15].

Further down I pass Mr Edward Finch's butchers shop and slaughterhouse. The joints were large for the big houses, and if one of them ordered a joint of beef about 7 lbs. Finch was liable to send one of 10-12 lbs.

On further is Rothmans, latterly the residence of the Pledger family. I pass quickly as I am told there have been two suicides there in living memory. Some of the windows have been blocked up as in the Hollies, owing to the Window Tax. A Mrs Finch formerly lived at Rothmans. Opposite Rothmans is the Congregational Chapel, which is always well attended. (Now the United Reformed Church).

Next down is the new Percival House, built by the retiring Doctor Hart in the garden of his old house, The Yews. Dr. Lyster has just taken over from Dr. Hart and now he lives in the Yews.

Next door to the chapel Mr Smee, who is a partner in Duffields the lawyers, occupies The Limes. He is a big church worker. The entrance to Vineyards mansion is next, owned by Mr.D.Cecil Gibbs, of soap fame. Formerly it was the home of the Rev Bullen, who was the vicar before Rev Colley. Rev Bullen's mother was the owner of the house and she also owned the living of the church at the time.

Tabors Hill and Baddow Road

After the Blue Lion Public House we can see The Cedars or Noake's Place behind the trees[16]. (Photo 1-10) Mr. Sewell, who had something to do with wines, lives here. He is a big man who hunts quite a lot and has two big horses to carry him (one at a time).

Going up Tabors Hill on the right I see Baddow Lodge, where Mr Watney of brewer fame lives. (Photo 1-11). This estate pays the vicar one guinea (= £1.05) to preach a sermon on Good Friday.

Bounding this estate is a footpath to Barnes Mill across Baddow Meads called Loves Walk (or the Twitten). Just past Loves Walk I pass two high houses where James Brittain Pash had opened the Home School before it moved to Rainsford End[17].

---

14 Replaced by town houses in Pump Hill.
15 The Peculiar People were a religious sect, explained in the chapter on Religion.
16 Replaced by the Buckleys development in the 1960s, named after Mr Buckley a consultant who lived at The Noakes in the 1950s. The name lives on in Noake's Place playing field.
17 Now 2 blocks of flats between Longfield Road and Chelmer Lea.

Then I pass the lane leading to Meadgate Farm, owned by my father Mr Henry Spalding. Meadgate farm can be traced back to the Reformation. It had belonged to the Free Chapel of St. John the Baptist, which was situated on the right side of The Chase leading to St. Mary's Church, Gt. Baddow. The farm was called by several names: Pierce at Mede, Pierce atte Vignes, Piers, The Free Chapel Lands, Oldberries and finally Meadgate. Henry VIII took it from the Chapel of St.John the Baptist and somehow it came to belong to the Petre family. They gained 3,000 acres in Essex for their diligence in suppressing the monasteries.

Further down Meadgate Lane we find the Baddow Meads. Years ago there was a Baddow Mead's Fair on Turning Out Day[18]. A tent was erected and beer served.

Now I have returned to the top of the lane and turn right towards Chelmsford.

Beehive Lane

Along Beehive Lane there are two gravel pits, Coplands and Jacksons.

Baddow Road

Opposite Beehive Lane is the Carpenter's Arms Public House and behind it is the water tower 90-ft high. (See sketch)

A pump from a spring or well beneath fills a large tank on top. The first day it was filled it burst and Mr Mildred who managed it heard a noise. He looked out of the door and was knocked down and nearly drowned by the cascade of water. Lower down Baddow Road are the Engineering Sheds of Mr Robert Jackson, where he carries out an engineering business. His chief business is hiring and repairing steam engines. (They were the chief source of portable power on the farm before tractors). Then on the left-hand side I pass the entrance to Mr Potter's gravel pit. On my right hand side is the Star Public House and lastly, just inside the Chelmsford/Baddow boundary in the White House lives Mr Robert Cooke, the leading sportsman of Essex[19]. Behind him is Whitehouse farm, which is farmed by Elijah Sorrell. The borough boundary goes right through the farmhouse. Mr Sorrell lives in the East Side in Baddow and is entitled to free water because the water tower is on Whitehouse farmland in Baddow. His tenant however is on the West Side in Chelmsford, and has to have his water piped through after dark to avoid paying Chelmsford RDC for the water.
When Elijah Sorrell retired he had 1,000 gold sovereigns in a sugar box beside his chair, which made into a bed at night. He told me when I suggested he put it in a bank "When I looks after anything for anybody I charge them for doing it. The Bank takes it and pays me for looking after it. Taint logic!"

Self-Contained Entity

You will see from this walk that Great Baddow was almost a self-contained entity around 1900. There were schools, blacksmiths, carpenters, builders, wheelwrights, grocers, bakers, several farmers, a few public houses, undertakers, and gravel pits. There was a post office, sweet shop, brewery, boot-maker, church, chapel, Peculiar People's Hall, a bus, a carrier, veterinary surgeon, upholsterer, milkman, cattle dealer, and a thatcher. Based at Sandon was Mr.Belcher's threshing machine driven by David Green who lives on the left-hand side of the path leading to St.Mary's Church.

---

18 This was the last Saturday in August when cattle were turned out onto the Meads to graze. Presumably the fair was held in a different part of the Meads to where the cattle were.
19 Church of the Latter Day Saints is on the site of the White House.

Alms Houses

Some of the inhabitants are very rich but some are suffering great poverty. To me as a young lad this was very puzzling, but I'm afraid it was taken as a matter of fact by most people. There were three sets of almshouses. The main ones were at the top of Sluts Hill (Pump Hill). They were very small ones with dormer windows. [Ed: We think these faced down the Causeway, with their backs towards the Church]. At the left of the entrance were two who used to pay the Parish Clerk one shilling [=5p] per week rent. On the right were four houses. Some had an inhabitant upstairs and another downstairs. In one Lottie Banks was up top and Mrs Marsden downstairs. When they had a disagreement Lottie used to empty an ewer of water on her floor which ran through the floorboards into Mrs Marsden's living room.

Poverty was very sad then. All the people could get was 3/6d per week from the Parish. (This is equivalent to 17.5 p in today's money, though you could buy rather more with that sum then). They even had to go and collect the money themselves. Each week mother used to send us with ¼ lb. of tea, ¼ lb. rice, ¼ lb. sugar and ¼ lb. of butter and very often a big rice pudding (to give to various poor parishioners). At Christmas enough red flannel for ladies to make a petticoat was supplied. One Christmas Lottie Banks went round the parish wearing hers outside.

There were almshouses on Maldon Road, opposite the Kings Head Public House. [Ed: These were thatched cottages, and were replaced by houses dedicated to Canon Kingham in the 1980s]. (Photo 1-12) There were also three on the left side of Workhouse Lane [later renamed Vicarage Lane]. They were the best at the time. (Photo 1-13) Once upon a time there were also two adjoining the vicarage opposite The White Horse.

For some reason poverty was looked on as a crime. I have known good hardworking men have an illness or accident so that they could not work. After they had used up their life savings they were taken up to the Workhouse (Spike) and one was put one side and the other the other side.
[Ed: I wonder what 'Spike' means in this context? Was the stigma of poverty marked with a spike? Perhaps he meant that in the Workhouse men were on one side of the building and women the other side, which was the usual arrangement? Spike is also used in connection with Union].

To show how hard up some people were, there was an old man called 'Donkey Soup', so called because when his family were starving he cut up a dead donkey and used it for meat and soup.

Peter Emery told me that he had once kicked up a frozen turnip and eaten it because he was so hungry.

Beating the Bounds

I well remember 1902, I think it was, when they beat the bounds of the parish. They always took some small boys with them and they were spanked at each marking post or tree to make them remember the spot.
[Editor's note: Interestingly, Writtle still has boundary posts marked on their village map. I wonder whether Baddow has such posts?]

Conclusion

Reg Spalding's journal, which was an ongoing diary that he kept for many years, is an important historical document and much of it has been recorded in this book. It is intended to set the scene of the life in Great Baddow early in the 20th Century. Later chapters will record the changes that have occurred since this time, to produce the village that we recognise today. This chapter is concluded by several old photographs of the village. (Photos 1-14 to 1-20), and two family groups of around 1883, the Carter family (photo 1-21) and the Jackson family (photo 1-22). Note that photo 1-14 shows soldiers on the green during the First World War. Note that photo 1-15 of the green in 1910 also shows the Bell pub which was demolished in the late 1920s or early 30s.

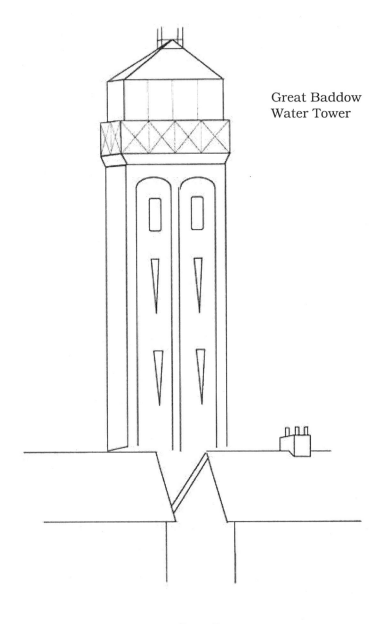

Great Baddow
Water Tower

Photo 1 - 1 Pitt Place c.1920

*Photo 1 - 2
Rear of
Pitt Place*

Photo 1 - 3 The Brewery

Photo 1 - 4 Brewery Staff c.1899

Photo 1 - 5 The Vicarage

*Photo 1 - 6
Galleywood Road*

Photo 1 - 7
The Bell Pub

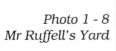

Photo 1 - 8
Mr Ruffell's Yard

Photo 1 - 9
The Hollies
(Red House)

Photo 1 - 10
Noake's Place

Photo 1 - 11
Baddow Lodge

Photo 1 - 12
Alms Houses
Maldon Road

Photo 1 - 13
Vicarage Lane
Alms Houses

Photo 1 - 14
Village Green
c. 1916

Photo 1 - 15
Village Centre
c. 1910

*Photo 1 - 16
Church Street*

Photo 1 - 18   Tabors Hill

Photo 1 - 17   West Hanningfield Road

Photo 1 - 20   Cottage in Detail

Photo 1 - 19   Cottages in The Chase

Photo 1 - 21 The Carter Family c. 1883

Photo 1 - 22 The Jackson Family c.1883

Chapter 2 - Village Life.

Introduction

The subscribers to our oral history have given us an insight into Great Baddow village as it used to be in the first half of the 20th century. It was a relatively small village around 1900 and at that time the parish of Great Baddow included Galleywood. Together the two communities grew and prospered until by 1972 the parish was believed to be the largest parish in the country. It was decided at this time to divide the area into two parishes, and the Clerk of the Great Baddow Parish Council advised that in 2002 the tally for the Electoral Roll was approximately 10,000. This of course excludes children, so this number equates to a population of approximately 16,000.

In the early 1900s the parish was largely agricultural. There were approximately 21 farms then, providing direct work for several hundred villagers who were employed as farmers, cowmen, pigmen and horsemen (who did the ploughing). There were several market gardens too, providing a living to entire families on a relatively modest acreage. In addition the farms provided indirect employment for blacksmiths, harness makers, carriers, hirers and drivers of traction engines and threshing machines.

The impression we have gained through this project is that the village of Gt.Baddow remained much the same for several hundred years until WW2. Hitler's bombs damaged many buildings, but it has changed much more significantly in the last 50 years as a result of a vast programme of expansion. From a small agricultural village it has expanded into a large suburb of Chelmsford, but it has managed to retain much of its village character. Many fine old buildings have been destroyed in the name of progress, but thankfully an equal number still remains.
This chapter attempts to rekindle memories of bits of the village that were familiar and well-loved in days gone by.

Various residents have described the village based on their childhood memories, covering the period from the 1920s to the 1950s. Most of the village of Great Baddow is described, on a street by street basis. Details of shops that were around in this period can be found in the Shops & Businesses chapter. We have also included local legend concerning tunnels.

Molrams Lane

Reg Bush was born in Gt.Baddow but has strong links with Sandon (and has written a book about that village). He starts us off at the Sandon end of Great Baddow:
> Molrams Lane around 1920 was a grassy lane, overhung on both sides by trees, with none of the houses you can see these days. It marked the boundary between Baddow and Sandon, each Parish Council being responsible for maintaining their side of the road. For many years no maintenance occurred as the councils couldn't agree who should do what.

Dora Norrington:
> Just through the village (going towards Southend) there was a big house called The Grove [1] and a farm called Grove Farm. By the side there was a walk and they called it

---
[1] Apparently Sir Richard and Lady Redmayne lived there around 1940.

Ladywell Grove. At the top of Ladywell Grove was a big brick house, a very dull house. It was a huge place with a flat roof and a huge garden. They said that a Russian and his wife lived there.[2] I don't know whether the house is still there. I think that Ladywell Grove is there because Great Baddow tennis club had their clubhouse the other side of the walk. The path came out at the church at Sandon. It was a nice meadow to go through, full of peggles[3], which you don't ever see now. It used to be a lovely Sunday walk.

Church Street

Dora Norrington told us about one of the Crabb sisters of Baddow Place:
> Miss Crabb was a very frail lady. One day she met my grandmother, in Great Baddow, and said, 'good morning Jackson and bow to me when you say good morning to me'. My grandmother said, 'I bow to no one but my maker'. After that grandmother ignored her. Miss Crabb was a very proud lady, who tried to rule Great Baddow. The villagers got fed up with her. After all, who was she? One day Miss Crabb said to my grandfather, 'Jackson, will you hold my horse and cart?' She wanted to go into Miss Burdles, the sweet shop. She gave him a shilling. He kept the shilling for years as Miss Crabb had given it to him. He only did it for fun.

Mr McIntyre (now in his 80s) told me that his family moved to Gt.Baddow in 1928 and owned Baddow Court until the war started. The army took it over for the duration of the hostilities and made a bit of a mess of it. During World War Two Mr.McIntyre's family moved into the coachman's house, called Baddow Court Cottage. This is now a café.

Jesse Pryke senior was offered Baddow Court and bought it from Mr.McIntyre senior in 1945. Later the land behind Baddow Court was sold to a local builder who built Smither's Drive, and the builder himself lived there. (Photo 2-1).

Jesse Pryke junior, (now semi-retired) told us:
> Baddow Court was a lovely old house on many different levels, with fine wide staircases, which was converted into flats. However in the 1980s the Council declared it unsafe, saying walls should be added, staircases changed, metal fire escapes added and fire doors put in to satisfy some new regulations. This was unfeasible, so the people were re-housed and the house stayed empty for several years.
> Gavin Suttle bought Baddow Court from me and converted that into luxury flats.

> Where Baddow Place Avenue is was a garden to one of the big houses. Just before that it was Chestnut cottage. Reg Bush's granddad was the local smithy (1 of 2 in village). There was a huge horse chestnut in their garden.

Dora Norrington referred to Mr Bush the farrier. She used to love to watch him at work. "The smell was lovely when the shoes were put on the hooves," she said.

A big house called Branwoods stood where Seabrook Road was built. (According to Dora Norrington the Seabrook family[4] occupied Branwoods in 1939).

---

2 This would have been Aylmer Maud and his wife. They were British, but they spent many years in Russia. Aylmer Maud was born Ipswich 1858 and spent 23 years in Russia, rising to become director of the Russian Carpet Co. He met Louisa Shanks in Russia and married her. They returned to England in 1897. Aylmer died in 1938 in Ladywell House. Their claim to fame was the translation and illustration of most of the works of Tolstoy from Russian to English.
3 Peggles are cowslips
4 A fine coat of arms is placed on the garages at the end of Seabrook Road, which may relate to the Seabrooks. The Latin inscription means 'The end crowns the work'.

West Hanningfield Road

This road leads to Pontlands hotel (called Pondland on the Chapman & André map of 1777), to the Marconi Research Labs, built in 1937, with the addition of the radar tower moved here from Canewdon after WW2. Apparently this is the only surviving tower of the former Home Radar used to give advance warning of enemy aircraft approaching from the continent.

On a map dated 1919 an army camp occupied the area between West Hanningfield Road and Vicarage Lane, now the Maltings estate.

Galleywood Road

Jesse Pryke gave us first hand knowledge of Baddow House, which his father owned for a time. He said:

> Baddow House was bought by my father (also called Jesse) in 1938 just after I was born. Previous owners were Carter's Seeds who used the gardens to test their seeds.
>
> In those days a big house wasn't practical and no one could afford to live in a house like that. It was only men like my father who converted big houses into flats who could make money out of big houses at that time. We moved into the house in 1939. My father converted it on a modest scale for ordinary people to live in, just as you would for council flats.
>
> Luxury flats came later, after I left there, when Gavin Suttle bought Baddow House from me. He was an architect, and he drew up the plans and had it converted. (Photo 2-2).
>
> There were lakes and watercourse behind Baddow House, formed from the stream. During WW 2 my father employed Italian POWs, from a camp at Writtle, to dig out the bed of the stream, remove bamboo, roots and other rubbish, which clogged the stream. This stream was 4-5ft wide in summer and a 10-ft raging torrent after winter rains. My elder sister swam in this stream and there was a 6-ft waterfall in the line of the stream 2 houses back from the junction between Vicarage Lane and Galleywood Road (photo 2-3).
>
> We kept pigs and goats and used Copsey's abattoir behind Rothmans when necessary. There were greenhouses sunk into the ground containing vines in this garden. We grew apples, pears, nuts and roses. My father had a rose in his lapel every day.
>
> I remember there were only two old houses in Galleywood Road on the other side of the road from Baddow House. The rest was all fields.

Peter Newman lived with his aunt and uncle in Galleywood Road around 1947. He said:

> I often visited Hollywood Farm, known as 'Mutton Hall'. Two Miss Wheelers lived at Hollywood farmhouse. A Mr Davis lived in High Chimneys, near Hollywood Farm. A Mr Eagle, parish councillor lived in Galleywood Road, in a house made of white stock bricks. A Mr Pearce also lived there; he played cricket for Essex. There was a gap then Miss or Mrs Bly, then Estric Playing Fields. Mr.Sewell, owner of Cambridge Motors in Chelmsford lived on the right hand side of Galleywood Road. The cowman at Gardiner's Farm bought a cottage facing Deadman's Lane. In the lane Mr Carter's brother had a home for nurses.

High Street

Les Sparrow:

> I was born in Well House Farm, which was where Foxholes Road now meets the High Street. (Photo 4-3). We had a well in the house and a well up the garden. A stream ran down beside what was then Carter's shop, now Daces. There was a well and a spring

in that area, now overgrown. Over to the right where the flats are now in Foxholes Road there was a well that was the deepest one of the lot. That part of Baddow is all on water, there's water everywhere down there.

Waterton's yard was where Reynard's Court flats are now situated, with a terrace house behind the Hollies, then Well House Cottage and Well House.

Mr. Copsey apparently bought Well House for the development of Foxholes Road; he built houses in the road about 1963 and some of his employees lived there.
(Photo 2-4 is a view along the High Street to Manor House and Manor Place, taken in 1966).

Jesse Pryke added to our knowledge of this area. He told us:
The warehouses opposite Daces' piano shop were formerly part of the cellar of Bell Inn, which stood where Bell Street and the High Street join. The pub had a rounded frontage to match the shape of the road. The yard behind the Bell Inn on Bell Street was subsequently used by Essex County Council (ECC) to store tools and materials when they were working in the village. This yard then became a car park for the old library, now for the Bell Centre (which is rented by the Parish Council from ECC). The last licensee of the Bell Pub was Mrs Alice Neish mentioned in 1912 on the essexpubs website. Baddow Brewery who owned it was not closed until 1928.

Derek Hurrell told us that one of the reasons the Bell pub had to go from the corner of the High Street and Bell Street was because it caused traffic hold-ups. When the hay wagons passed they left lots of hay attached to the pub and to Liddiard & Tanner's.
(Photo 2-5 shows the closeness of the two buildings).

Richard Carter remembers that the carts and the horses for Carter's bakery were kept behind Brook House, and latterly they had vans.
I remember a petrol pump there. My grand mother had a kitchen garden and a green house there where she had a vine and grew the most delicious grapes. Above the Post Office the loft was made into a restaurant in the late 40's or early 50's. It provided lunches, and I remember the odd party held up there.

Pump Hill

Harry Clayden advised us that there used to be people named Samms at Foxholes. They were tailors, with a little shop in old Baddow Road, Chelmsford, opposite the entrance to the back of the Regent. It was an outfitter's for country sports, horse riding. His daughter had a dance company.

Dora Norrington recalled that at one time a family called Ward lived in Foxholes. She thought that Simon Ward (who played the young Churchill on TV) is of this family. Simon's brother was an antique dealer. On top of Pump Hill is the cottage that became Ducking Stool Cottage, so named because of the pond at the top of the hill where a little green is, where it is reputed witches were ducked. (Photo 2-6).

James Hodgson told us that in the early 1600s it was at the village pond that the Witch Finder General Matthew Hopkins and his associates managed to capture and kill so very many women by ducking them in the pond when they were accused of being witches. This was a typical no-win situation: if the woman drowned she was innocent; if she survived she was guilty and was tried as a witch at the local assizes. Matthew Hopkins was based in Manningtree and his witch finding has a particularly obnoxious history for Essex and indeed in East Anglia when many innocent women were murdered in this way. (There is an official map showing the sites in Essex where witches were 'dealt with'. This does not mention Gt. Baddow specifically, but Chelmsford is mentioned very often as the site of trials so perhaps Gt. Baddow witches are included in their tally).

Roy Walls' memory is of a pond at the bottom of Pump Hill, which is mentioned in a book on witches. "I'm told this was filled with water, and drunks were thrown in".

Den Harvey was asked where the actual pond was in relation to Ducking Stool Cottage. He said:
> The pond was on the little green opposite. There is a little tiny piece of green opposite. I understand that's where it was, even though it appears to be a bit of a slope.

He was certain about a well down near the bottom of Pump Hill because he fell down it when he was a kid. It was in the grounds of the big old house called Foxholes. He added:
> Just inside the gates to Foxholes, on the left going down, was a well covered over by a big flagstone. As kids we moved it away and I fell in. This was pre-school. I remember my mum taking me to Mrs Ambrose who lived in the first house up Pump Hill on the left going up. I remember her stripping me off, standing me in the sink, washing me down and cleaning me up. I can't remember there being a well on the other (north) side of the road, because the big Plane tree was there in a little tiny spinney.
> At Carter's you could walk under the road, as there was a big culvert, all the way to the Blue Lion. It picks up the stream behind Manor House. As kids we used to go frog hunting through there with torches. We got access to it behind Carter's, now Dace's the piano shop. There is a fence that is boarded in. That used to be a little place where people parked their bikes. If you went down over the back and got in the stream, you could walk down the old culvert.

Jim Hurrell told us that on the site of the Ducking Stool Cottage garage was a metal cage, which his father told him was the village lock up demolished in 1950, or 60s.

Bell Street

Bell St. was much as it is now with a Reading Room where the slate club[5] met during WW2 for billiards and cards, and there too was the back entrance to Foxholes.

Den Harvey: I was born at number 2 The Munnions. You could walk through number 1 and 2 into Bell House in the attics. You could walk from one end of the block to the other. There was no such thing as fire breaks in those days. You could go over the top or underground as we had a tunnel as well to the Carpet shop.

There is also a belief that you could walk through in the lofts from the carpet shop through to the White Horse.

---

[5] The Slate club existed before the NHS to allow people to save up a little each week to provide financial help when they were sick. Any left over at Christmas was shared out. Records were kept on a piece of slate.

Maldon Road

Bert Hunt:
>Down Maldon Hill, past the Parish Hall, and along the drive by Beech House, No 5 Maldon Road, a path led to a large farm called Manor Farm. The farm barn was directly behind the Parish Hall. The path was one of the routes used by local boys to reach the river Chelmer, used for swimming in summer, as we see in the chapter on Leisure.
>
>Where the small parade of shops is opposite the Kings Head were thatched almshouses, 4 or 5 of them. Where Crescent Road and Jeffrey Road now meet was the entrance to allotments, no houses. There was a hedge there which was kept clipped and when I went to Baddow School that way in the summer time you could climb on top of the hedge and walk on top all the way to New Road without touching the ground.
>
>The owner of Baddow Hall was Mrs Gilmore and in my first recollection of her she had a coach and horses. She used to come into the village in her coach. She was a nice lady.
>Baddow Hall was a grand old house. (Photo 2-7). It had a big iron fence all round it and a shrubbery in the front in a lovely setting with the farm at the back. We used to play in the field at the front. It was a very good field for mushrooms. On the parkland, which now backs onto Jeffrey Road, was a former gravel pit. Further on was Baddow Hall Farm.

Jim Hurrell referred to part of the lease on his house, on Maldon Rd. It is dated 1st August 1902. It mentions Mrs Gilmore as tenant of Baddow Hall and gives a description of the house, stabling, gardens, orchard and 21 acres of grassland, entrance lodge and plantations. Hall Farm comprised 75 acres, 1 rod, and 38 poles of arable and pastureland together with a bailiff's cottage and agricultural buildings in occupation of Mr James Smith. The allotment field and hall field adjoining the above consisted of 18 acres, 2 rod, 13 poles. This probably covered all the land from Molram's Lane to the Causeway.

Dora Norrington:
>Baddow Hall was a big house and there was a path attached to it, a beautiful path on which we were allowed to go to play. The owners had a son who was in the 1st war and lost a leg. It "turned" his brain. We used to hide from him if we saw him while we were playing. He was perfectly all right though. He would never hurt anybody, as he didn't really know where he was.
>
>The Gilmores who owned Baddow Hall had a farm nearby. There was a footpath through to Molrams Lane. The Bringey[6] was between Baddow Court and the brewery. You went up there, turned right, went over a stile and across the field towards Molrams Lane. The farm was just there. The name of the people who had the farm was Bearman. I was friendly with Isobel, their daughter.

Ruth Brooker added a little about the Lynn family of builders who lived opposite the paper shop in Maldon Road:
>Miss Lynn used to ride a bike with a barrel on the back of it. It was an old home-made wood barrel and she carried all sorts of things in it. She wore a scruffy old mac and a cap, her face was weather-beaten, and her hair was cut short, just like a man.

---

6 According to Mr.Hodgson Bringey is derived from the word, possibly Saxon, which refers to a moneyer. A man who made money, and probably defaced money to make more money.

Facing down the Causeway is a group of cottages currently painted yellow reputed to be the oldest houses in the village, dated 15th century. The one nearest Baron's former shop was called Olspar, named after Olive Sparrow (Les Sparrow's mother) who once lived there. (Photo 2-8).

Causeway

Dora Norrington:
>William Jackson owned all that property at the corner of Maldon Road and the Causeway. There was a house attached to the paper shop, which my cousin had (now the RSPCA charity shop). Next door to that was the bungalow where Florrie Twitchet lived, called Vineyards Lodge. My other cousin married and they lived there. The two sisters lived side by side.
>The large Vineyards Lodge garden was owned by my uncle, Samuel Jackson. He built Causeway House in the garden around 1914. The bungalow still had quite a nice bit of garden left. Opposite was one of the village water pumps, but no water came out as I recall.

Bert Hunt: Vineyard's Lodge was thatched in my young day, and it was the Lodge to the Vineyards House, and the person who lived there was a member of the staff of the Vineyards. It subsequently became a private house. Opposite the Lodge was the back entrance to the Vineyards, with an avenue of lime trees either side of the drive. I think two of these lime trees are left in the car park today. A little further along was an alcove let into the 7-ft high brick wall and there stood one of the village water pumps. It was used a lot when I was a boy, but it gradually got into disrepair. Next to Vineyard's Lodge was Causeway House and the other big house next to it, Westbourne House.

The entrance to New Rd was there, then you had the Causeway Cottages on the left. Facing dead ahead was a fork to the Chase where there were two old, thatched almshouses, very primitive.

Ruth Brooker:
>There was a Mr Mills, who was nicknamed 'Tin Tacks', who bought a house on the left of the Chase. He came from London and did not know how long he would stay so he tin-tacked his wallpaper on so that he could take it away with him if and when he moved. He also built a wheelbarrow in his kitchen, but had to take it to pieces to get it outside. He always had good clothes as his brother was a valet and used to give him his clothes.

New Road

New Road only contained 6 houses then (in the early 1920s), the rest was allotments.

The Vineyards

The Vineyards mansion was built in 1740, and there was a fine article about it in Country Life dated January 1911 (a copy of which can be seen in the Essex Record Office). An earlier building called Vynezerd was mentioned in 1421. (See photos 2-9 & 2-10)
Christine Vernon also mentioned the old Vineyards, (which would still be there during her childhood at The Hollies). One previous owner was David Cecil Gibbs, father of Armstrong Gibbs b.1896, who was a composer. Several of his tunes were played on the wireless during WW2. This family was connected with Gibbs toothpaste, being soap and chemical manufacturers. Armstrong's mother died when he was two. A Miss Hart brought him up.

He went to a prep school, then Winchester. Later he lived in the 'Cottage in the Bush' in Danbury (near the top of The Ridge at the entrance to Lingfield Common). The High School sang with Armstrong Gibbs and he was a member of Danbury Music Society, which enjoyed much success in Essex singing competitions.

Colleen Yaxley remembers that swallows flew all around the Vineyards area during the day and bats swooped around at night. She recalls walking through all the leaves in the autumn. You could never see the Vineyards house in those days.

Derek Hurrell added that the Vineyards was a magnificent building, with a super 12 foot high brick wall all around it, and some beautiful trees in the garden.

Les Sparrow:
> I think of the Vineyards having the main entry from the Causeway, though there was also an entry from the High Street. There was large wall around Vineyards, down Maldon Road, along the High Street, up Pump Hill and back along the Causeway.

Dora Norrington added a little story about the Vineyards.
> To get to The Vineyards you went down a long drive. The vineyards included all the ground right round Pump Hill to the Congregational Chapel. We used to jump over the wall because there were banks and banks of daffodils. We picked daffodils until we got caught one day and got into trouble.
> I remember the Vineyards house. I was about twelve when I was asked if I would sell flags for the lifeboats. I had a box and a tin. I knocked on the door of The Vineyards and the cook came to the door. I asked if she would buy a flag. She went to ask the "governor". He gave me a shilling for two flags. Then they let the dog out and I have never run so fast in my life.

Jesse Pryke:
> The Vineyards had been a hotel until the early 60s but had been empty for some time when the auction took place. Sadds, the timber merchants from Maldon, were the owners, now long gone.

Doug Shinn was elected to the Parish Council in 1958, as one of the four representatives of Rothmans Ward. He was Chairman of the Parish Council 1960-1 and a Member of Great Baddow Parish Council 1967-73. As an ex Parish Councillor, he was able to add more about the redevelopment of the Vineyards.
> The Vineyards used to be a hotel. Planning permission for development was sought, perhaps in 1959. There was considerable public concern. In 1960 the Parish Council organized an open informal public meeting on this subject in the Parish Hall. The Deputy Planning Officer of Essex County Council attended and answered questions. Eventually a vote indicated that, of perhaps 180 people present, 12 declared themselves broadly in favour of the project. Nearly everyone objected to the proposed height of the buildings. In the final, accepted, application this height was considerably less. Detailed information about the development, and many other matters, may be found in the records of the Councils.

A local resident, Dennis Byatt of the Causeway told me how he fought long and hard against the development of the Vineyards complex and many of his objections were recorded in the local papers at the time. In 1961 an article showed the former manager of the Vineyards

Hotel, Miles Humbert, who looked after the place for fourteen and a half years up to 1961, when he and his family moved to Oxfordshire. During its time as a hotel it was often used by visiting Marconi engineers. The building was occupied by troops during World War Two. After Mr. Humbert and his family left the building was left vacant such that it deteriorated badly.

The Planning Committee records in the Essex Record Office record some of the ramifications of the approval process, which went from Chelmsford Borough to Essex County Council to the Ministry of Housing. The planning application started in early 1962 and despite public protests was eventually approved. The plans were toned down slightly, but apart from the Vineyards mansion itself the development ruined many fine trees (even some 'protected' by preservation orders, see photo 2-11) and a beautiful garden. However the parade of shops now form the retail hub of the village.

John Parkinson remarked that Derek Walden the architect of the Vineyards development has a lot to answer for.

Doug Shinn was also involved in his capacity as a Parish Councillor with respect to the Baddow bypass. He said:
> In 1958 there was no Great Baddow by-pass. Traffic at rush hour times crawled along Baddow Road. The Parish Council was anxious to promote the by-pass as far as it could. In 1959 another Parish Councillor, and myself, called on farmer Reg Spalding in order to discuss the project. He said that the Councils had been talking about the by-pass since 1925 and had made very little progress! As we now know the by-pass was constructed just a few years later.

Tabors Hill and Baddow Road

As we pass The Blue Lion we see that like the old sign the new pub sign has ' a lion rampant azure'. This is believed to be from the arms of the Mildmay family. This many-branched family for 4 centuries held much land in and around Chelmsford and elsewhere in Essex. In the 17th century a Thomas Mildmay was Lord of the Manor of Gt.Baddow, owning Baddow Hall and Great and Little Sir Hughes. The Mildmays also had the advowson of St.Mary's Church from 1547 to 1554, when it was sold to John Sammes (according to Richard Pusey in "Essex Rich and Strange").

Opposite the Blue Lion we see Ebenezer Cottages, Holly Cottage and Valley Cottages, all of which date back to the 1850s. Several of them are listed buildings of historical importance, though they started life as quite humble dwellings. (Photo 2-12).
Mr and Mrs Willsher lived at 1 and 2 Valley Gardens. Mrs Willsher was chauffeur to Dr Lyster and gained the car in the doctor's will.

Apparently Baddow Road had lots of big houses belonging to professional men and wealthy shopkeepers. In the 1920s those who went to London daily travelled to and from the station in hansom cabs.

In the Buckleys is one such house, named after a Mr.Buckley who owned Noakes Place (also called Cedar Lodge at one time). You can just make out the gateway to the house next to the Blue Lion. The photo 1-10 in Ch.1. shows the house and photo 2-13 shows the ponds as they were.

Pre-war Baddow Lodge was occupied by Mr Britten, who was Chairman of the Gt.Baddow Parish Council from 1925 to 1932. He took a prominent part in the extension of the Parish hall in 1928. Britten Crescent is named after him. The map in the Preface shows the location of Baddow Lodge and many other extinct mansions.

Jesse Pryke added a note:
> After I married in 1958 I bought Oldbury House, No. 401 Baddow Road, which I had attended as a school when quite young. Oldbury Avenue was built later. Tony Appleton, who is another Baddow old boy and holder of the lordship of the manor of Gt.Baddow, lives nearby.

Dora Norrington's grandfather, Solomon Jackson, built Cannon House in Baddow Road, near the entrance to the Recreation Ground. Solomon acquired a cannon from the Boer War, which decorated the driveway for many years. However, when in WW2 the call went out for metal to be melted down into modern guns and tanks, Dora's Uncle Herbert Jackson, then in ownership, gave the old cannon for the cause. "The family was furious!" Dora said.

Reg Spalding made a note in his journal that Longfield Road was originally a very long field on which he grew potatoes. Apparently it was very difficult to plough.

Between Longfield Road and Chelmer Lea is a large building that was converted into luxury flats a few years ago. In a previous life this building, then called Albert Buildings, was 2 separate establishments known as The Essex Industrial School and Home for Destitute Boys. (Photo 2-14). This was founded in 1872 by Joseph Brittain Pash. It provided food, accommodation and care, provided an informal uniform and taught the elements of crafts such as horticulture and shoemaking. Once old enough, boys were placed in trade locally or in London though they could still live in the home. The photo shows it in its modern state. Nearby is a wall with an interesting ownership carved into it concerning a Mr Greenwood (who was one of the farsighted group of people who developed New London Road in the mid 19th century). (Photo 2-15).

[Joseph Brittain Pash was father of Ellen Louisa Pash (1871-1903) a (so-called) Golden Girl, who obtained a degree when women generally were not allowed to go to university].
A Dr. Bodkin of Baddow Road owned a plot on Baddow Meads (according to Betty Spalding) Dr William Bodkin, was father of 8 children. Dr Ernest Bodkin, born 1895, is also mentioned in records. Also Dr.Herbert Bodkin, born 10.4.1881. William was father of Nora Helen Bodkin (1878-1974) and Amy Maud Bodkin (1875-1967) who were also 'Golden Girls'.

Betty Spalding told us about the land owned by Meadgate Farm, She said:
> My knowledge of this area started with the coming of the Baddow bypass. In fact the bypass was scheduled many years before in the 1920s. In anticipation at this time the Spalding family bought a farm at Beccles and another one at Bures because they believed this bypass was coming. When I married Reg and came to live here in 1965 it was pegged out but not started. They started soon afterwards. We did not know about the housing estate that was also planned; this was a sudden decision, and the planning was done incredibly badly.

Chelmerton Avenue

The houses along Chelmerton Avenue were built from the 1920s. It is possible that Chelmerton Avenue takes its name from Chelmerton Villa, which appears on the official map of 1873 and was situated on Baddow Road opposite Chelmerton Avenue. On the map of 1897 Chelmerton Lodge is mentioned in this position. In the deeds of number 365 Baddow Road, built in 1914 it refers to number 367 next door as Renmark Lodge, formerly Chelmerton Lodge. (Photo 2-16 is dated around 1900). Chelmerton Villa is next door (Photo 2-17 shows the modern house, which appears to have been two houses in the past).

Back on Baddow Road, nearly opposite the path to Meadgate Farm is a house called Bartletts, where Eileen and Dennis Hance live. (Bartletts was built by Mr Howard, builder, who lived there originally. He was churchwarden at Gt.Baddow church for 25-30 years).

Before the Hances bought it, it was a home for young unmarried mothers and their babies.

When we interviewed retired Magistrate Eileen Hance, she showed us the Great Baddow Staff, made in George III's reign, which the Village Beadle used to carry. (Photo 2-18). Dennis Hance's great-grandparents lived in a cottage next to the church (house now demolished). The great grandfather was the 'parish clerk' and the Hances still have his account books where he entered all the accounts for the village. He might also have been the beadle. His surname was Dennis (hence Dennis Hance's Christian name). Dennis Hance's mother would walk from Coval Lane in Chelmsford to visit her grandparents in Great Baddow, which was 'in the country' then. Sometimes they would use a pony and trap.

Apparently the recreational grounds opposite Longfield Road were all fields pre-war. Many of the terrace houses in Baddow Road were built between 1900 and 1910. On the South side behind these houses were the gravel pits, which were all still working in the 1920s. On the East side of Beehive Lane were the disused pits, which were known as Snow's Gravel Pit. Some little workshops were built in there and some are still there.

Beehive Lane Area

We were advised by one contributor:

> There was a water tower now the parking site for the dustcarts (or Refuse Collection Vehicles if we wish to be politically correct) in Chelwater, opposite the British Legion Hall. The water tower was over a borehole, belonging to the Rural District Council. They owned all that allotment area. The nearby spring fed many streams, which created boggy ground lower down (in what is now Meadgate Estate). There were water meadows covered with marsh marigolds. The authorities said it would never be built on because it was so damp.

Presumably Tower Garage was named after the water tower, as were Tower View cottages at the bottom of Beehive Lane. Mr Greygoose was in charge of the water tower and lived in a house opposite. Apparently the views from the top were magnificent. (See drawing in chapter 1).

Dora Norrington has first hand knowledge of Baddow Road and Beehive Lane, having lived there for most of her life.

> The first gravel pit in the area was behind where Tower Garage now is in Baddow Road (the garage owned by Messrs Jones). There was a cake and milk shop next door towards Beehive Lane, next to a row of cottages.
> Howards of Portland House had the pit, extracting sand and gravel with shovels and wheelbarrows.

Beehive Lane

On the right hand side of Beehive Lane (going up) were 2 larger houses, 1 owned by Dora Norrington's Uncle Robert Jackson. He started a gravel pit, and the workers lived on the opposite side of Beehive Lane. He had 5 daughters and 1 son, Walter Jackson, who used the engines for extracting material. The pit stretched almost to Princes Road. (See photo in chapter 7)

Peggy Bradley told us more about Beehive Lane. She said:

My maiden name was Tipping and my father ran a taxi service. We first came to Beehive Lane when I was a year old, which was in 1921. My mother told me that it was just a muddy lane, with the mud up to the axles of the pram, as she tried to push it up the lane. Over the years I have lived in five different houses in Beehive Lane, so I know it fairly well.

To get to and from school we used Baddow Road most times. Sometimes if we were staying at Hampton, which was the Duffield's house, where my father was chauffeur for a while, we would cut across the fields, by the White Horse, around Gardiner's Farm and into the garden.

I do remember the last house my father bought, number 22 Beehive Lane. I was about 14 or 15 when we moved there. That looked over Jackson's gravel pit, with the footpath going up the side, on the left as you go down Beehive Lane. It faces what is now Winchelsea Drive. The footpath at the side led to the Isolation Hospital.

At one time we lived in a bungalow in Deadman's Lane, which had a large garden, big enough for a tennis court as well as flower borders and a large area of gravel as you went in through the gates. We had chickens at the end and a vegetable garden at the side. We had about a three-acre plot of land there. Mr Taylor used to use part of it to grow strawberries and sometimes some flowers for seeds.

She added the colourful note that in Beehive Lane there was Sergeant Pink, Mr Snow, Mr White, Mr Green and Mr Brown.

Clive Barker said:

The bloke who lived on top of the pit was old man Tipping. He had a taxi business. If ever you went sliding down the slope of the pit, he was the one who always chased you.

Don Brown added more about the pits.

One pit was called Gardiner's Pit. Mr Gardiner then sold the area to Mr.Snow, who built himself a bungalow at the corner of Winchelsea Drive and Beehive Lane. There were steps down to the pit where the garage to number 30 stands. Mr.Snow had a carpentry business and trained Mr.Frost. He had a shop next to Elnaugh's in Baddow Road. Mr.Chris Steele rented a house over the shop, and Mr.Snow gave him a plot in the pit when he set up a building business. Mr.Steele managed the pit, then bought it. His daughter Christine Goldstone has now inherited it. Sand and gravel from the pit was used around 1914 to build Marconi's New Street.

A Mr.Loftin built Loftin Way in 1937 on land owned by Lord Darlington. He built himself a house on the corner with Beehive Lane (probably the North side). Previously there had been a farm there. There used to be allotments where St.Paul's church is now. St Paul's church was in Baddow Road then (on the site of the Mobil garage below the Beehive, in a corrugated iron building). They started building Sawkins Avenue and Dorset Avenue was built in 1937. Gard the builder built 12 houses there before starting Winchelsea Drive. Mr Gard senior chopped wood there (on the site of the Cabin) for firewood bundles, which he sold to the shops. Gards lived in Navigation Road. They now own the wood yard beyond the Army & Navy Public House.

At a recent exhibition in Oaklands Museum a poster dated around 1979 was included about Carl Graham Fischer Lloyd, Animal tamer and trainer of Loftin Way Gt.Baddow. He handled lions, tigers, elephants, leopards and bears. He settled in Chelmsford in 1983.

Dora Norrington:
In Baddow Road after the Mission Hall we find the turning to Baddow Isolation Hospital ; this turning was the parish/borough boundary line. You always knew where the boundary line was because on the Chelmsford side the road was tarmac but on the Baddow side it was all potholes.

Where we find the Church of the Latter Day Saints there used to be a large house called the Whitehouse built by a Mr Wilson. Behind this house was White House Farm, hence the name given to the modern road in this area, Whitehouse Crescent.

In those days Baddow Road went straight across the Army and Navy; there was no pub there then, nor the roundabout nor Princes Road. Marriages' Mill and the river was there, and that was the area of Baddow Road known as 'the iron railings', near the old Baddow Road which branches off Parkway. The iron railings there were the fences between Marriages Mill, the Meads and Baddow Road and every year that area flooded.

The Army & Navy pub used to be in Baddow Road, opposite the doctors' surgery, now Hadler's motorcycle shop. The site of the current pub used to be fields belonging to Grays, who owned the big house opposite Marriage's mill. They were related to Grays the brewers.

Local Legend

An item we found fascinating was local legend about ghosts and underground tunnels. At least one tunnel is based on fact but some stretch the imagination a little.

Jim Hurrell told us about the tunnel under the High Street from the Carpet Shop, which has been authenticated by Mr Nutbeem, who owns the Carpet Shop. He explained that the tunnel goes between the cellar of the Carpet Shop and the Munnions, where there is another bricked up doorway in the cellar).

Jim: My uncle at one time lived in Tanner's, the grocers - which is now the carpet shop - and he said that in the cellar was a bricked up doorway facing the church said to be a subway into the church. These properties go back to pre-Reformation - old monastic buildings attached to church. No one has investigated to my knowledge.
After the 1958 flood during the repair of the culvert some old medieval drains were found leading into the culvert. There are no maps, so no one knows where they lead.
From the carpet shop to the White Horse was thought to be one building. My grandfather

working on repairs said he could walk from one end to the other through the loft space. Den Harvey described the other end of the tunnel.

The Munnions was a very old place. According to legends and stories it goes back to the 1400s. The same time as the first figure in the church, so I am told. I was told it was part of the old monastery. I believe Munnions stands for kitchens in the monastery. There used to be a tunnel in mum's kitchen that went under our house (number 2 The Munnions) and joined up with number 1 The Munnions and Bell House. It also went under the road and across to Miss Bryant's general provision shop, which is now the Carpet Centre. This was the escape route for the monks when the soldiers came (after the Reformation, presumably). They took off one of the old doors in mum's house, years ago, which was boarded over. When they took the boarding off the door was seen to have four peepholes in it about the size of old penny pieces, which had been filled in. It was supposed that anyone hidden there could see who was coming.

You could walk through from number 1 and 2 into Bell House via the attics. There was no such thing as fire breaks in those days. You could go over the top or underground as we had a tunnel as well.

Numerous things have been found about the place. The oldest thing I found was a 1754 shilling in the garden.

Alan Willis has long had an interest in local history and provided stories of village ghosts. He said:

A ghostly apparition stalks rooms of the White Horse Inn and is affectionately known as 'Albert' by the owners. Here stood an alehouse in Tudor times, on land that belonged to the Church.

There were tunnels running from the church to 16th century cottages adjoining. A monk became trapped here and died. An opening in the pub cellar can be seen to have been bricked up.

The ghostly figure of a monk gliding slowly down the south aisle of the church has also been seen to disappear through the west wall heading in the direction of the cottages.

Cromwell's soldiers sitting around the fire in the old alehouse on a winter's evening were told of the goings on, and no doubt had their own ideas of who the ghost was.

Recent work at St.Mary's Church failed to reveal any evidence of a tunnel there.

Less easy to corroborate was a report about the passageways throughout the whole building from Skinners to the White Horse. Ray Walls reported:

I believe, but I'm not sure that the house called Dynes in the High Street (next to Carter's bakery) used to be a nunnery. I have been told that there was a passageway in the roof, which led from Dynes through the roof space of Skinners to the White Horse. This was where the nuns used to take their evening walk. During the last war a stairway was uncovered but it did not lead anywhere, which means that the house had been altered at some time. (This is a similar story to that of the staircase in the Munnions opposite, which Jesse Pryke mentioned, which sounded more first hand and more authentic). Also a very large brick fireplace was uncovered in the sitting room. A woman who used to live there told me that they used to feel a 'presence' in the room that seemed very kind and peaceful. Behind the iron bars that can be seen close to the pavement were the punishment cells.

Friar's Hall was where the friars lived. I have been told that there was a passageway leading from there to the nunnery.

(Ed: I think that Friar's Place was beyond the church, which is some distance from the Carpet Shop, a bit far for a tunnel. However, there are likely to be drains that follow this route, which might stack up with Jesse Pryke's story when he had the shop next to Dale Hire). Jesse said:

> The shop has a cellar, and it may be an old wives' tale but there was talk of a tunnel. When we lived at Baddow House we used to have a big wall round the garden and the river went down a waterfall, and under Galleywood Road. The river was open but dropped lower into Dr Wallace's garden at 4 Galleywood Rd. Then it went underground under Carter's bakery, under the High Street, came up and was visible in the Vineyard's garden, then went under Maldon Road. Then it was visible as it is to this day as it flows down to Baddow Meads. We had a flood in the DIY shop on Church St caused by water coming up through a hole in the floor when it rained heavily, so perhaps our 'secret passage tunnels' are only entrances to drains.

Even less likely was a story from Ray Wall's mother about Foxholes. Mrs Wall says there is no evidence for this, so it was recounted with some trepidation.

> A very old house called Foxholes, which has now been demolished, stood in Pump Hill. Ann Boleyn used to visit. There was a tunnel that went from there to a house in Little Baddow. King Henry VIII so it is said used to visit Ann Boleyn through this tunnel when he used to visit Little Baddow. It has also been said that the tunnel was used for moving troops around. In the case of Friar's Hall tunnel and Foxholes tunnel nothing has been found to indicate that tunnels were there.

[Ed: Most of the tunnel story relating to Foxholes seems highly unlikely, especially the idea that a tunnel could go to Little Baddow. It would be very close to the water table, through very unstable soil. Henry was a very big man, fat and middle aged at this time, and it is doubtful he would suffer the indignity of crawling through a tunnel. Also we know that Henry had bought New Hall, Boreham from the Boleyn family in 1517, so that is a more likely place for a tryst. By coincidence, in the book 'Boreham History, Tales and Memories of an Essex Village' edited by Eleanor Burgess and Mary Rance, a chapter entitled 'the Changing Face of New Hall' by Sister Mary Stephen refers to the period of ownership by Henry VIII starting in 1517. It states: "Underground we have a network of tunnels the Tudor drainage system, not to be confused with the rumours of tunnels linking New Hall with Springfield Place in Boreham and *even across the river to Little Baddow*".

There is much better evidence for the tunnel from Munnions to the Essex Carpet shop. The latter was owned by Henry VIII, being part of the Manor of Gt.Baddow, given to Katherine of Aragon in the divorce settlement. He could easily have visited Ann Boleyn there].

Dora Norrington believed there was a tunnel from the White Horse to the church.

> My friend, Billie Chew, lived at the White Horse with her aunt. Her parents died when she was young. We used to go into the cellars and try to find where the tunnel went. It was used years and years ago when people were 'up against the churches'. They used to hide in there. The tunnel was supposed to have gone to the church. I think the White Horse tunnel was found.

Other residents have heard rumours of a tunnel between Baddow Brewery and nearby houses Adstocks, Baddow Place or Houghtons, which it is believed were formerly owned in the 19th century by one or more of the founders of the Brewery, Messrs Crabb, Smee or Veley. It was suggested that the tunnel(s) enabled them to carry their takings home in safety, free from the threat of mugging.

Conclusion

This deals with most of the geography of the village. Following chapters deal with the daily life in the shops, schools and work places. Perhaps you will now shiver a little as you walk past the buildings housing the Baddow ghosts!

Photo 2-1
Baddow Court

Photo 2-2
Baddow House

Photo 2-3 Baddow House Pool

Photo 2-4
Manor House and Manor

Photo 2-6   Ducking Stool Cottage

Photo 2-5
Side View of The Bell PH

Photo 2-7   Baddow Hall

Photo 2-8
Oldest houses
in Baddow

*Photo 2-9
Vineyards
Front Entrance*

*Photo 2-10
Adams Ceiling*

Photo 2-11 Tree Slaughter

Photo 2-12
Ebenezer Cottages
c. 1900

Photo 2-13   Noakes Ponds

Photo 2-14 Albert Buildings

Photo 2-15 Greenwoods Wall

Photo 2-16 Chelmerton Lodge

Photo 2-17
Chelmerton Villa

Photo 2-18
Beadle's Staff
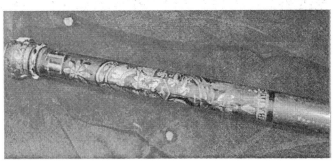

Chapter 3 - Shops & Businesses

Introduction

Various residents have described the Baddow shops that they remember from their youth. Since many of their contributions overlap I will only include the contributor's name for the more personal recollections. These records will be described street by street.

High Street

Starting logically at number 1 near the Blue Lion, we have Radio & TV shop of Alan Thomson, who provided some detail:

> The building dates from about 1780 and was originally two shops. Thomson's shop was converted in 1959 from Rose Stores, a greengrocers run by Mrs Spencer-Phillips, the wife of young doctor Spencer-Phillips, and was doubled in size in the early 1990s. (Photo 3-1) The business was founded in September 1959 with a partnership between Mr James Miln Thomson (previously of Waltham Abbey) and his son Mr Leonard Miln Thomson.
>
> James Thomson was born in Scotland but moved to Waltham Abbey when he was three years old. His father, who worked for Nobel (the explosives manufacturer and giver of prizes) as an industrial chemist, was asked to convert the explosives factory in Waltham Abbey from gunpowder to cordite (nitro-glycerine).
>
> (Leonard Thomson worked for Ferguson, the radio manufacturer, in the late 1930s; was in telecommunications in the RAF during the 1940s and then worked for EKCO, the television manufacturer, in the 1950s when television production commenced. E.K. Cole, the founder of EKCO, lived in Great Baddow at 'Hampton House' in Beehive Lane and also at 'The Grove' Southend Road).

> Alan Thomson the current owner came to Gt.Baddow in 1958 (just before the great flood) and joined the family business in 1970 after working for the Plessey Telecommunications Company, and lives next door in the grounds of Yew House. The business has grown and now employs 14 people.

'Rothmans' combines a fine private house and a business. The latter is now an Indian take-away but was recently a coffee-house. (Photo 3-2). Previously it was Copsey's butcher's 2nd shop, with a fishmonger next door. Les Sparrow provided the facts:

> Mr Copsey senior was usually in the cash desk and always wore a bowler hat. They were also meat wholesalers. Their abattoir was behind the shop in the area now occupied by garages and a children's playschool.

> Opposite the new library we have a Building Society & what used to be the Midland Bank, now an Estate agents. Copsey's original shop was here. There were several buildings behind the shop and at the side was the slaughterhouse for small animals. He used to kill mainly pigs, not so much the big animals. On Tuesdays, which I think was pig-killing day, you could buy jugs of blood for black pudding. Several people used to go there then.

Another contributor said that Copsey's 1st shop was a grocers in late 50s, early 60s. It had a tiled floor with COPSEY'S written in tiles. The two modern shops were built in 1970s.

Travelling up the hill past Well House was Mr Henry Carter's, who farmed at Gt.Seabrights. Mr Carter had a bakery behind the shop here in the High Street, a milk business and sold corn & hay. He had a big family who all worked for him. Carter's former shop is now Dace's piano shop.

They baked all their own bread and cakes. Deliveries were made locally and also further afield. Iris Easter's father started working for them in 1937 and delivered bread by pony and cart. He returned, after the war, and delivered by van. There was a little hand-barrow too, which was used for very local deliveries. Mr Fred Stoneham trundled this around. He was a dear little man who came from Galleywood. Two sisters, Eve and Flo Easton managed the shop. They lived in a house called Lamberths, which was next to Well House. Mr & Mrs Carter, who owned the shop, lived in a house behind the shop.

Les recalled that if you had no facilities at home for baking cakes at Christmas, say, you could take along your cake mixtures and Carter's would cook them for you. You could have them iced, or just cooked. Loads of people used to take them along.

Richard Carter remembers:
"As a young boy I remember visiting the bakery business quite often, when I stayed with my grandparents. I used to go into the bake house, in the evening, when the dough was being first mixed. Then it was put into large bins so the yeast could make it rise. Then it was put through various machines, to slice it up into smaller bits, and then put into tins to make the loaves of bread. The bread would rise during the evening and then the bakers would come in early, in the morning, and bake the bread in coke ovens, later replaced by gas ovens. I can remember the long poles, with spade ends, with which they put the loaves of bread in and out of the ovens. It was sold immediately in the bakery shop, or delivered round the village by horse drawn baker's carts. They were a number of these baker's delivery carts. (Photo 3-3). I remember as a young child riding around with the baker delivering the bread. The smell of the new bread is something wonderful you never forget.

The carts and the horses were kept behind Brook House, and latterly they had vans. I remember a petrol pump there. My grandmother had a green house there where she had a vine and grew the most delicious grapes.

The Post Office came relatively towards the end of their business career. The Post Office was put into that pair of shops on the High Street. It occupied what had been the office for the business. Miss Gray was my grandfather's secretary, who used to do the bookkeeping. She was moved to an office upstairs, and the Post Office was downstairs, until the Post Office business was sold to Martins in the Vineyards. The corn shop, which was a shop that sold dog food and things like this as well as corn, was latterly converted, and I helped convert it into a baker's shop. Above it the loft was made into a restaurant in the late 40's early 50's. It provided lunches, and I remember the odd party held up there.

Next to the bakery was a grocery store which had a café downstairs and a restaurant upstairs".

Les Sparrow:

Next door[1] were the premises of Messrs Liddiard[2] who has a very high-class provision and clothing business, wholesale and retail. He goes as far as Burnham and Bradwell with his van or his cart. He also cures a lot of bacon and ham. He is noted for his hams. (Photo 3-4).

He was the family grocer. The shop front has not altered at all. It was originally Tudor, that is 15th or 16th century. When you went inside the shop you went down a step and there was a big long counter on the left hand side with an array of shelves up to the ceiling behind the counter and right at the top huge metal containers, green and gold, containing tea, coffee, sugar. They weighed a ton to lift down from the shelves. In front of the counter, set at an angle of 45° were all the glass-topped biscuit tins. You could choose your biscuits through the glass. There were no packets of sugar in those days; sugar was in large sacks, later in wooden boxes. As boys we loved to get hold of these boxes as Tate & Lyle boxes could be made into a lovely truck. Butter was not pre-packed; you had a quarter or a half a pound because the money didn't go too far in those days to cover the necessities. Whatever cut of bacon you wanted was cut off on the bacon slicer while you waited. If you wanted butter, the amount was taken out of a barrel onto the counter, patted into a block using the wooden patties. "What would you like Mrs Sparrow - Wheatsheaf, Rising Sun?" You could have a pat of butter with a stamp on it. Produce was in jars, sacks or boxes. They had broken biscuits for sale some days, which the children could buy cheaply.

At some point in time around the 1940s this shop became Bryant's shop. This was a lovely old shop. Mr Bryant and his daughter Polly served in the shop. Apparently they sold sweets but many could not buy them very often because of rationing.

The story goes that Miss Bryant fitted an old Ostermilk tin, less top and bottom, into the ceiling of the shop directly over the till. She would then sit upstairs above this 'spying tube' and observe any 'adverse cash flow'.

On the opposite side of the road next to the Munnions was Liddiard's & Tanner's wholesale grocers' warehouse, with sugar and other goods stored in bulk. (This was formerly the warehouse of Sutton's Seed Merchants). On the top floor there were two doors which opened to allow use of a gantry to load goods from a horse & cart underneath for storage. That is still there but I think it's sealed up now.

Next to the Carpet Shop was a house called Skinners. At one time it had a board on the front saying, 'Bunty's Tea Rooms'.

Bobby Jackson was a village character who also lived just past the Carpet Shop in a little shop that had been a general store but became a cobbler's. He was a man of diminutive stature, who had to stand on a box to see over the counter. He was the butt of many jokes and laughs in the old days, but he was a very nice chap and a good cobbler. For working shoes you couldn't beat him, but he had no finesse for ladies' shoes.

Opposite the White Horse Mr. Burlong and Mr Read kept two shops. Next to Sutton's, going towards the church, was Downing's the saddlers - brothers who were lovely gentlemen. Mr Downing could do anything with leather. His brother was the harness maker at Danbury. Each Monday morning a third brother who worked with him

1 Now the Essex Carpet Centre
2 Mr Liddiard was the uncle of Dora Norrington, who told us that at some time he sold the business to Mr. Tanner. However it does appear to have been known for some years as Liddiard & Tanner, presumably a partnership.

harnessed up their white pony and went round the local farms taking repaired harnesses and collecting broken harnesses and especially collars to be repaired. He charged 10s-0d a year to keep a collar in repair.

Next door was a bootmaker who was a first rate stitcher. Mr Bristowe of Baddow House called in there one day and to his astonishment saw a pair of his best shoes which he had taken to the foremost shoemaker in London. He was told that the London firm always sent their best shoes to be stitched here in Baddow.

Next door was Mr.Overall, an upholsterer who was a master of his craft.

Shops that used to back onto the church, now demolished, include Mr. Frith - shoemaker, repairer and upholsterer - a very quiet man but good at his trade. Lastly before the church was Mr Rust who had a little sweet shop. He was always wearing a trilby. The choirboys used to get their sweets there. The shop was underneath and at the rear were steps up to living quarters. They were all little cottages. (Photo 3-5 shows the shops after 1930. Note the Bell pub has disappeared).

There were two wool shops in the village at one time - one on the Maldon Road, which used to be Hurrell's shop originally; the other between Bryant's shop and the White Horse. They both used to be very busy. The shop by the White Horse named Geraldine's (owned by the daughter of Mr.Radford, the newsagent) was just one little room in a house really. It had a great stock of wool and cottons in there.

Church Street

There were some wooden cottages past St Mary's church, a whole row of them, where the modern houses now are. It is thought these small houses were called Friars Hall belonging to King Edward VI Grammar School in Chelmsford.

Les Sparrow continued his description of shops there.

Where Gerrard's hairdresser is now was Miss Stannard's, which was a post office at one time, from which the postman used to operate. Mr. Westrip was the postman pre-war, and a Mr. Trimnall. Early in the morning they were busy getting out the first post round. The ponies, which bring the mail from Southend, pick up letters and parcels from all the small post offices on the way. Reg Bush remembered delivering telegrams to outlying houses and being paid sixpence a time.

Later the Post Office was moved to a private bungalow near West Hanningfield Road & still later (in the 1950s or 60s) to Carter's shop.

Westrip's shop was a sweet shop in 1967, known to local children as the 'black shop' because it was painted black.

At one time the Gt.Baddow Telephone Exchange was at No 45 New Road, according to Bert Hunt. The new Telephone Exchange is on Church Street opposite West Hanningfield Road).

Jesse Pryke opened a DIY shop here that he and his wife ran for 8 or 9 years (1982-90), before they sold it to Gerrard's, who have been there ever since. The Pryke's bought the shop from Ashdown's. Jesse said:

The shop is over 100 years old, dated 1880ish. Lawrie Russell's daughter Jill lived 3 doors from my shop towards the Church. I knew her fairly well; I knew all the family. I asked her if she would work for us and she worked in the shop for about 7 years. She used to work in her dad's shop when he first opened, so she knew the business inside out.

Next door to Jesse Pryke's former DIY shop is now Dale Hire, formerly Jackson's garage and filling station. That was quite a hive of industry pre-war, mainly motorbikes, some with sidecars, but not many cars about. Several people remembered going up there to get petrol in cans. Petrol was 11.5d normal, 1s-1d for posh/super, per gallon (equivalent to 5p in today's money). Pre-war the Jackson Brothers were the local wheelwrights. They built the good drays used by the brewery.

Petrol was fed from a pump in the yard via swinging an arm over the pavement. (Photo 3-6).

As you pass by a small shop (number 31) in the block of cottages just past Gerrardo's restaurant, note above the window 'Taber, Dealer in Coffee, Tea, Tobacco and Snuff'. The owner discovered this ancient lettering during recent repainting.

Reg Bush's father's parents owned the Baddow Smithy on Church Street on the corner of Baddow Place Avenue. They did not follow the practice in Sandon on Sundays when the forge became the barber's shop!

A large chestnut tree was on this corner (hence the name Chestnut Cottage), but it was blown down on Queen Elizabeth II's Coronation Day in 1952.

Two old ladies lived in a little cottage near the forge and sold home made sweets & cakes. Nearby was one of the village butchers, Downeys.

Baddow Brewery was started in the mid 1800s by Messrs Crabb, Smee and Veley. It brewed strong beer and cider and eventually closed in 1930. The building was subsequently used as a furniture factory and showroom, offices, and retails sub-aqua equipment. (Photo 3-7).

The owner of Baddow Court pre war was a Mr McIntyre who had a chicken farm alongside the Bringey. In fact the current antique business uses the old chicken sheds.

On the opposite side of Church Street we now have a variety of small businesses where there was once another chicken farm before WW2. During the life of the Brewery the building nearest Church Street housed the dray horses, and the tethering rings and drainage channels are still there.

The wooden building, until recently the offices of Essex Radiators, was once the headquarters of the Baddow Fire Brigade. This area was also used by Munnion's coach builders (formerly of Springfield Road, Chelmsford) to build fire engines. (Photo 3-8).

This area now houses a garage, a dance studio, a monumental mason and numerous small businesses.

The former Woodworkers houses a computer company, and a tile and carpet company. Note the architectural features on the wall nearest the road showing King Edward VII and Queen Alexandra.

Retracing our steps we come to Bell Street.

Bell Street

Two paces up there on the right is the shop which belonging to Mr. Russell the village plumber and builder, now called Russell's delicatessen. Les Sparrow said:

That was a cottage in the early days. The Fords lived there. Mr. Russell turned it into his plumbing and hardware shop in 1906 having acquired it from a Mr Ruffell. As the local builder he just operated from the yard originally. The shop didn't exist in the early days. Mr Russell started it as a hardware shop and his wife used to run it with his daughter Gill.

The old barn was originally thatched and used to store building material. The roof was changed to corrugated iron to reduce the likelihood of fire damage in WW2.

Harry Clayden told us:

> I had an offer from a Great Baddow gentleman, whom I had known for years, to become manager of his hardware shop in Great Baddow. This was Russell's hardware shop. My wife and I worked there hoping, one day, that we could buy the business. It didn't plan out quite like that.

All the Munnions block was owned by Mr Russell and rented out. Around 1985 the daughters of Mr. Russell sold the block of property to Mr. Johnny Flack. He found the old barn at the top of the yard and wanted to restore it. He asked advice from the Council who got excited and listed it on a grade 2 preservation order, as it is a 14th or 15th Century Essex barn. Mr Flack was allowed to convert it and it is known as Russell's Restaurant named in memory of the Russell family. It used to be a shed for storing timber, but must have been a farm barn originally.

The restaurant was sold to a Halstead man called Barry Watson who moved to No 2 The Munnions, the house in the passage that goes up to the graveyard and the Church. Jesse Pryke went there to assist when he was converting it. They uncovered a staircase, which apparently went nowhere, but they found an upstairs room. It was really old; the area is believed to be 600 years old if not more. (Apparently old Mr Russell had blocked it off in the early 1900s, soon after he acquired it from a Mr Ruffell. Interestingly they only had to change two letters on the nameplate when the business changed hands). Mr Flack had the house done up so that he could use it.

The Causeway

The Vineyards Shopping Parade was built around 1968, despite many objections raised at the time. These days it forms the focal point of retail activity in the village, now that the majority of the other shops in this chapter have disappeared. It currently includes a Chemist, Clothing Cum Haberdashery, Greengrocer, Butcher, Stationery cum Post Office, Card Shop, Betting shop, 2 Banks, Supermarket, Hardware & General Store, Baker, Fish & Chip shop, Chinese Restaurant and Take Away, and lastly a Hairdressers. In competition with other shopping parades around Chelmsford it has recently received 'best kept shopping area' awards. (Photo 3-9).

Another branch of the Jackson family operated a thriving business in New Road, just off the Causeway. They combined a taxi business with a successful nursery. Les Jackson sold plants. If you were going to put them outside he would never let you have them until the end of May. He would not let them out of his sight until then. He was always very amusing. He always wore the same bib and brace overalls, wellies and a woolly hat. (He was said to have been buried in this garb). According to Derek Hurrell, if he didn't like the look of a customer he wouldn't sell them anything.

His father was Silas Jackson. He was quite a character and drove an Austin taxi. It was big and black and he always wore a trilby. He was very just so in his dress.

Maldon Road

Let us start again at the Blue Lion corner in our shopping trip down Memory Lane. We are looking at the CNC Tooling, the specialist engineering business at Manor Place Cottage adjoining Valley Cottages and Manor Place. In the 1940s it was occupied by a hairdresser called Dilys, which used to be a real old fashioned hairdresser with the hot tongs and all the old wires. Then it became a sweet shop. Nat West Bank occupied the premises before they moved into the Vineyards in 1968.

Les again:

> The establishment that is now Tony Pennack's funeral parlour was once Carter's green grocers, general provisions and stores, and it was owned by the same family who owned the bakers shop in the High Street. The Carters themselves referred to it as the Lower Shop.
> Mr Atterbury was manager of this shop at the bottom of the hill, then after his wife died and his tenancy came to an end he took over the shop that became Baron's stores. He had that for a number of years. He lived there as well so I imagine he owned it too.

> Carter's grocers eventually became a Chemist shop, possibly in the 1950s. John Parkinson, the owner, later joined Mr Lawson in this Maldon Road shop. He built a new shop front to replace the bottle glass front of the 1512 building. John said that this is a historically interesting property, which was a tannery in early 18th century. Two old wells were found at the back of the premises. John ran the chemist shop alongside Same's chemist shop on Vineyards (when that opened in 1968) until John sold out in 1990. Moss Pharmacy is now the chemist on the Vineyards and the old shop is now owned by Tony Pennack.

> Going up from Carter's on the left hand side was Sid Pennack's funeral furnishers & builders, still in the Pennack family. Just past number 5 Maldon Road, Beech House (so named because of the beech trees opposite) was the entrance to Manor Farm. The farm gateway now leads through to Tyrell's Way.

The old farmhouse was replaced in the 1950s, when the two farm cottages in Maldon Road near the fire station were built. The old farmhouse was pulled down and three houses plus a parade of shops was built in their place. These now comprise a Locksmith, Dress shop, and Off Licence. Then we have the Parish Hall and Jasper Jeffery's, which in its time has been a school, a café and an antique shop and is now a private house. The barn belonging to Manor farm used to back onto the Parish hall, I understand.

Baron's store had two different sides either side of the front door, with greengrocery on the right side and grocery on the left. It was described as a 'very old fashioned grocer's shop that sold everything'. Baron's is now the local dentist. (Photo 3-10 is a painting by Alan Beedham).

Now we are at the RSPCA charity shop opposite; it used to be a paper shop belonging to Mr Radford, the local newsagent and a hard working man. He also had one at 266 Baddow Road. Later Martins owned it.
Prior to being a paper shop this corner housed a cycle shop and petrol station, owned pre-war by William Jackson. One can imagine that stopping here for petrol would cause a bottleneck, but traffic was much lighter then. The area was known as Jackson's Corner.
John Jackson supplied the photograph of the corner shop with one or two petrol pumps outside. (Photo 3-11).

Behind the old houses on the left between Baron's and the Kings Head was a building business owned by the Lynn family.

Next we have the King's Head itself. (Photo 3-12). Reg Bush's grandparents on his mother's side were licensees of the Kings Head at one time. Prior to 1900 the licensee was listed as James Patten, bricklayer then Albert Taylor, carpenter. It would seem that in times gone by a publican had to have a 'day job'.

Den Harvey recalled:
> I frequented the King's Head before I should have done. In those days if you were sixteen, and behaved yourself, you could go in to have a drink. Ted Taverner was the first landlord that I can remember there.

Opposite the Kings Head was the old family sweet shop. Several interviewees described the shop thus:
> Run by a dear old lady named Mrs Sandford but locals used to call her Dirty Dick. Her husband wore thick rimmed spectacles. The boys would go in for the cordial bottles, with the split tops. You would get three old pence on returns (i.e. the empty bottles). They would put them on the counter, while she was on her way into the shop from the backroom. In reality they had only picked them up off the floor; they hadn't taken them in with them. She had black hair, which was going grey. She used to put black ink on it to disguise the grey.

At number 42 Maldon Road lived Mr & Mrs Wills. He was a shoemaker and cobbler.

Mr B Clark, a local amateur archaeologist stated that:
> The two premises shown front onto the Maldon Road virtually opposite the Kings Head Public House were built immediately post war, in a cheap utilitarian form of construction. The building on the right, 52 Maldon Road, consists of a pair of hairdressing salons; gentlemen and ladies respectively. Mr Digby first occupied the premises as hairdresser and ran the business for over 30 years until he retired. Now trading as Vogue, it continues with hairdressing up to the present day.

Muriel Plowright told us that her family kept the hairdressing shop many years ago.

Ronnie Crowe's outdoor sports shop used to be Hurrell's the grocer and green grocer. They used to deliver groceries every week. People used to bring the order in and he would deliver. There were two brothers Ernie and Jack Hurrell. They ran the business from 1936 until 1956. It is claimed that this was the first supermarket in the district.

Mr Clark added:
> Ronnie Crowe's Gun and Tackle Shop is built in essentially the same style and, at the same time as the Green Grocers and Hairdressers opposite. As a long established business in an essentially rural area, even with the imposition of increasingly stringent restrictions on firearm ownership and use, both sport and clay pigeon shooting remains popular. Fishing too remains a popular hobby, under less restriction than shooting and with support from across the community.
> The shop itself is a veritable Aladdin's Cave of supplementary equipment needed to support the two activities of shooting and fishing.

We're past Ronnie Crowe's and we are now at number 63. This is owned by Mr Terence Hill, a bespoke tailor. Let us now retrace our steps to the Blue Lion again for a walk up Baddow Road.

Baddow Road

Next to the Blue Lion was a shop, between Thompson's and the Blue Lion. Alan Willis's family lived there for two or three years about 1930. Alan's father was apprenticed to a shoemaker and had a business there for a time. Alan lived there until he was about five. That building was demolished and is now the car park for the pub.

Opposite the Blue Lion we now have Robert Michael Interiors. Previously that was the Co-operative grocer.

There do not appear to have been any shops between the Blue Lion and the Carpenter's Arms.

Una Matthews told us that her grandfather, Mr Hockley, had been publican at the Carpenter's Arms in Baddow Road. He had been one of a large family who farmed near Dunmow. When farming hit hard times in the 19th century he'd made his own way and become landlord. He was also an undertaker and made coffins at the Carpenter's Arms and was a friend and rival of grandfather Pennack. (Photo 3-13).

Harry Clayden informed us that:
> A Mr Cottis who was a baker lived just opposite the Beehive in the shop that is now the glass shop, at the corner of Chelwater and Baddow Road. They used to call him the Midnight Baker, mainly because he was subject to 'delays' in the local public houses, hence many people got their bread rather late.

According to Dora Norrington he made lumpy bread, which he delivered around the village in a basket covered with a green cloth. He always ended up at Bobby Jackson's shop, then visited the White Horse! Mr Cottis married Robert Jackson's daughter.

> Also in that area was Spooner's Yard. Spooners was a Baddow family who had a haulage business, with traction engines which used to go round the farms and also they were hired to the County Council for road works.

> It is understood that traction engines were kept on Mr Jackson's land off Beehive Lane in the quarry. Mark Spooner was the Steam Plough Contractor and Argent Bulcher ran the threshing machines. The Spooner brothers built two large houses near the Carpenters Arms and in the back yard they kept their threshing machines. David Green drove one and Mr.Lodge the other. At harvest time they would be seen driving off at 5 am. and they did not come home until the harvest was finished. They towed a caravan behind each machine that was stocked up with enough provisions to last until they had finished.

The first account of shops here near the Beehive Lane junction stated that:
> The former tyre shop opposite the Carpenter's Arms (now developed into the Co-operative Funeral Service) used to be three shops. Hugh Wright was a butcher and he had several shops and his own slaughterhouse. Next was Mrs Boreham, mother of Dora Norrington. Mr. Smith had the third shop and he was a greengrocer. He is remembered with a bowler hat and moustache. In Beehive Lane itself, next to the Beehive, is now a florist; it used to be a dairy run by Walter Whiting, and was a butcher's in the 70's.

Dora Norrington's account goes thus:
> "Grandfather Jackson owned 3 shops in Baddow Rd, on the corner with Beehive Lane. Mr Cook the tailor & Mrs Barker were retiring. He suggested my mother (Mrs Boreham)

start a business, but he was very mean & despite her being a widow he still charged rent. Mother ran the middle shop as a general store. Later mother was asked by the GPO to start a post office & telegraph office. People wanted to use a phone, so one was put in the house. She rented the shop next to BEEHIVE LANE corner to butcher Mr Wright. He had butcher's shops in the town and he was the Mayor of Chelmsford at one time. He paid £30 for the rent once a year but we had an awful job to get it. He was supposed to be rich.

He didn't live there; he lived in the town where he had more butcher's shops. He employed a manager in the Baddow Road shop. We used to invite him into our house to have a warm at the fire, because he was frozen in the winter. We kept an eye on his shop for him. The third shop was greengrocer's run by Mrs Cook then by Mr Smith"

Running the PO was hard work because although the grocer's shop opened from 8 am to 9 p.m. the PO open hours were limited to 9 am until 5 p.m. However people expected to be served at the PO counter after hours if the grocery part was open. Then there were telegrams, which had to be phoned to head office in Chelmsford.

We also sold stamps, dealt with pensions on Friday (10/- a week) and parcels. People came with their parcels from Danbury. We always had a word; mother was very friendly so we knew everybody's troubles, and their children's details.

In the shop we had to weigh everything. 1 hundredweight sacks of sugar were divided into 1lb blue bags for 2d. There were also some 2lb bags, not many, costing 3d. There was no profit on sugar. We had a case with drawers containing sultanas, currants, demerara sugar and Quaker oats, all loose. Customers bought many goods in ¼ lb quantities. They were hard times.

We bought sweets for the shop from Hawkes Brothers, who had a factory in New Street in Chelmsford. These were delivered by van every Thursday. Dora selected the sweets required, which went into jars.

However, speciality peppermint humbugs came from a Mr Hardy. His shop in Moulsham Street was about half way up Moulsham Street. He had a little place out the back where he made his humbugs. He didn't make all his sweets but he made wonderful humbugs. They were square and quite big. They were lovely. He had a straw bag with 6 jars of humbugs. He fitted three on one side and three on the other. He carried them from Moulsham Street up to us. We bought six at a time. They were very cheap at four pence a quarter. People would come from Danbury to buy a pound of humbugs. I had to walk down to Moulsham Street to order them. (We weren't on the phone then). It didn't matter how hot the summer was or how cold it was he came with his straw bag of humbugs.

When he delivered to us mother made him a cup of tea, as he used to be so tired. We used to invite him in to our room at the back of the shop. She would pay him cash and he would go straight over to the Beehive Inn. He would spend every penny and then go rolling home. He was such a nice old boy. Hawkes Brothers tried their hardest to get the recipe out of him and offered him lots of money for the recipe but he refused to sell, so the recipe for those humbugs died with him.

In our grocery shop we sold butter, margarine and lard. Not a lot of butter was sold as people ate margarine. We had great packs of butter and we had two little wooden pats. You cut it and then you patted it. Then we had a little roller that went along the top with a nice little pattern on it. We would wrap it up in greaseproof paper first and then in brown paper afterwards.

We used to cut perhaps two ounces of margarine and I always put the little roller over the top. There wasn't much to put over. I've may have those rollers and pats somewhere in the shed even now.

To keep the butter and milk etc in the hot days we had a cellar and it opened up from the corner of the shop and it was cool enough down there. Outside there were gratings for the air to get in and we used to make ice cream in the cellar. There was a little wooden thing that you put the cream in and you turned and turned the handle until it became ice cream, and you patted it round with salt. One day a lady came into the shop and said "Mrs Boreham you taste this ice cream" and we did and it tasted of salt. The salt had gone into the ice cream, so we had to throw it all away. The hours we turned this handle! We did quite a trade in the summer.

The butcher had a cellar as well where he kept his meat. Mr Wright used to deliver on Monday afternoons from the butcher shop in the town when all the chops etc were ready. Sometimes a boy would bring up the meat from the town on a bicycle.

Another thing we sold was vinegar and that used to come in a barrel. I used to have to lift this barrel of vinegar onto a frame and we used to serve half a pint of vinegar at a time, and people brought their own bottles. It cost 3d a pint and 1d for a half pint. We had some beautiful eggs from a man who kept a farm in Beehive Lane and we used to have a big basket where we kept the small eggs 1d and large eggs 2d. We used to have great big stone jars in the cellar full of eggs as people often wanted them at Christmas for puddings and they were cheaper that way.
People were very poor. Many of them worked in the gravel pits where the pay was bad and every penny was precious.

We used to get our biscuits from McVities straight from the factory. They were kept on a long counter and we had to weigh all the biscuits from bulk. Their traveller used to come round periodically and mother gave him the order. All the travellers were such gentlemen. However, when delivery was made, you paid the traveller before you had the biscuits, so you had to check that what had been delivered was what we had ordered. The biscuits came by van. We were motorised then. Pat-a-cake biscuits some were called.

About 1939 when I was not very well and expecting a baby, we sold the shop to a non-Chelmsford man.

Some years earlier Dora Norrington's uncle kept The Rodney PH at Little Baddow, but wanted to be a butcher. So Dora's father worked as a butcher with his brother, in a shop in Baddow Road (now a hairdressers), nearly opposite the Star public house. (Photo 3-14). He killed his own pigs & sheep in the yard at the back. After a while Dora's father left his brother at the butchers and set up as a Market Gardener on the opposite side of Baddow Road based in a house called Mafeking Villa. No such name exists now, but the houses east of the Star all date from the early 1900s so it was probably one of those.
The orchards & garden produce were very successful, with produce sold in London. They employed 2 or 3 men plus women from nearby cottages who picked gooseberries & strawberries.
Clive Barker mentioned another business in Baddow Road:
    Steele's the builders, a well known building company, are still at the entrance to the
    Isolation Hospital (now demolished and replaced with a housing development). They

have been there since the late 1800's.

Robert Norrington told us:

My brother-in-law Gerald worked in an old established grocer's shop called Porter & Howards. It closed in the 1950s. Hadler's motorbike shop is now on this site. I worked at the Co-op and I got him a job at the Co-op and eventually he became the manager of the off-licence in Beehive Lane.

Going back many more years this building was The Army & Navy public house.

Apparently a Mrs Cooper ran a wholesale grocery business in Baddow Road, between the current Army & Navy and the old A & N (which as stated above was Porter & Howards). Currently there are two businesses in this position, one of which sells tills and computers, the other selling in-car audio and alarm systems.

Lower down, past the turning to the hospital towards Chelmsford on the right hand side, was the abattoir belonging to Harrison and Barber. All the cattle and horses were slaughtered there. The allotments used to be there but that area is now the Baddow by-pass.

Conclusion

We have looked at Gt.Baddow as it used to be before the days of Tesco's and Sainsbury's. At that time the village was largely self-sufficient. Villagers often thought of Chelmsford as alien territory and only ventured there when forced, for clothing and furniture perhaps.

Photo 3-1
Thomson's Shop

Photo 3-2
Rothman's Shop

Photo 3-3
Carter's Delivery Van, with
Charles Partridge, baker's
roundsman. c. 1909

Photo 3-4
Liddiard & Tanner's
Wholesale Grocers Shop

Photo 3-5
High Street Shops
post 1930

Photo 3-7   The Brewery

Photo 3-6   H. Jackson's Garage

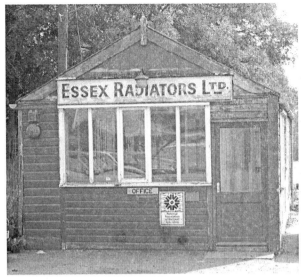

Photo 3-8
Essex Radiators

Photo 3-9
New Vineyards

Photo 3-10
Baron's Shop

Photo 3-11
Maldon Road
Garage

Photo 3-12
Kings Head PH

Photo 3-13   Carpenters Arms

Photo 3-14
Boreham
Butcher's
Shop

Chapter 4 - Family Life

Introduction

How has family life changed in the living memory of Gt Baddow residents? It is interesting to compare the childhood, courtship and married life of our interviewees with those of today, and note how the day to day routine has altered.

Love, marriage & courtship

Most of the first meetings of couples we were told about were as random as today's romantic encounters. Colleen Yaxley met her future husband at the Shire Hall, at a football dance, though neither of them were football supporters. She said:

> He was meant to go on his motor bike to see his sister, but it broke down. He came back to Chelmsford to see somebody else, but she wasn't there. So it was me that he met. At the time I had a different boy friend. My grandparents didn't like that situation at all. They didn't know who Bob was, but when they did meet him they said he was a 'very decent chap'. That changed every thing.

Rosemary Hill literally bumped into her husband in 1948, on the dodgems, at the fairground in Chelmsford.

> I was with my friend and Roland was with his friend and we bumped into each other on the dodgems, and that was how our romance started. Roland was a Braintree chap. The four of us went around for a while then the other two split up. We've just had our 50th wedding anniversary.

The Great Baddow Minstrels brought Les Sparrow & his wife together:

> I met my wife at the rehearsal of the Great Baddow minstrels at the home of Mr Cocker in 6 Avenue Road. Mr Cocker was a pianist and I was at this rehearsal and I noticed a young face and thought it was just a new person joining the group. I asked who she was and was told it was Mr. Cocker's daughter. I wrote her a letter to see if she would go to the pictures with me, (her father was very strict). Eventually she said yes and we went to the Odeon and saw Spencer Tracey's 'Boys Town'. We had fish and chips on the way home. In those days you could have two seats at the pictures and two small portions of fish and chips for half a crown. And that's how we started. After we got engaged the war came and I went overseas and Joan joined the WRAF.

Friends also played their part in introducing people. John Parkinson's friend Derek Powell introduced him to Betty at the Grove Lawn Tennis Club and things blossomed from there.

But surely few can beat John Jackson's uncle, Will Furness? He got married in 2001, aged 92, to someone he'd known for years and who had been his district nurse. She was "a bit of a lass" aged 81! After he'd been married a few weeks, he received a brochure for prams. John said, "I asked him whether he was going to buy one, but he said he wasn't sure."

We are all romantics at heart. How well we understand Richard Carter.

> Soon after I took over Manor Farm, a neighbour Reg Spalding, came up to me and said "Richard, what ever you do you must not cut down the tree on the Baddow Meads. Your father told me that it was right by that tree, on a stack of hay, he got engaged to your mother". For that reason I have never cut it down.

Weddings

Although Dora Norrington was married as long ago as 1926, in Gt. Baddow church, by the Rev Colley, she has vivid memories of the day.

> I got married from the shop (at the corner of Baddow Road and Beehive Lane). It had to be a Wednesday afternoon. The post office wouldn't let you close any other time. It was their early closing. I had my presents all arrayed in the room upstairs over the shop. It was our lounge. I've still got my wedding dress. It was white satin and it had a little train. It was very tight fitting with little buttons and the sleeves came down to a point over my hand. Bond's made it. It had a cowl neck and had a spray of orange blossom from the shoulder. I carried a bouquet of red roses.
>
> I had seven bridesmaids. They wore the same satin as I had, but in cream. Bond's made them all. They had red jackets, red shoes and little halos of red and white satin with pearls. They carried bouquets of coloured sweet peas.
>
> I had a very big reception at the County Hotel. The traveller for MacVities, who make biscuits, said they would make the wedding cake, with three tiers, and they made us a present of the bottom two tiers. (See photo 4-1 of the Boreham/Freeman wedding in 1905, and photo 4-2 of Dora's family. The line up from the left is Dora's mum, then Esme, Nell and Edith, called Ciss. John and Dora are in front.)

Peggy Bradley was married in 1941, in Gt Baddow church, so it was more difficult, with wartime rationing. She bought the material for her dress in Chelmsford market and had it made. She did have a cake, soaked in brandy, which an uncle had made in London as he had a restaurant. Her father (who had a car hire firm) supplied the cars:

> My husband-to-be hadn't got anything to do that morning, so he was asked to clean the cars ready for the wedding. My husband and I were both in the fire service at that time, so we had quite a lot of people at the wedding. We had a guard of honour, with the firemen hanging their hatchets over our heads. They congregated at the White Horse, at Gt Baddow, so there were several fire engines in case the siren went and they were called out. It was the same day, 23rd December 1941, as Dr Spencer-Phillip's daughter was married, just before us, so the church was already decorated. We didn't have to buy any flowers.

Les Sparrow was married on June 9th 1945. That was the first wedding in Baddow church, after the war, to have the bells rung because during the war the bells could only be rung if there was an invasion. Les:

> We were never charged for the bells, because ours was the first wedding after the war. The reception was held in the Parish Hall and with rationing you had to make do, so everyone 'clubbed in' even though we had engaged a catering firm.

Although many venues, such as Hylands House, are now licensed for weddings, Gt Baddow church continues to be the preferred choice of many village couples.

Childbirth

Talking to people about family size, we could trace the gradual reduction in the number of children born during the century. D. Hurrell's great aunt Louise was one of ten, but he himself has only two daughters. Robert Norrington was the youngest of seven, but went on to have just two sons. Eileen Hance also had two sons, whilst she was one of eleven children (with a twelfth who died in the first week).

St.John's hospital, where D.Hurrell was born in 1936, has seen the birth of many Gt Baddow residents. The alternative was often Brooklands Nursing Home. Here it was that Les Sparrow's wife gave birth to Geoffrey in 1947, staying there two weeks (the minimum stay at that time).

Many others like Den Harvey in 1944 were born at home.

Mr. & Mrs. Sparrow's second son Peter was born on 28th May 1951 at home, 64 Loftin Way. The midwife was called Nurse Gotobed (really!). The first thing she said to me when I asked what I could do to help was, "go into the kitchen and make me a cup of tea". I wasn't allowed to witness the birth. I was told to stay in the kitchen until I was called.

Dora Norrington also gave birth at home when she was expecting twins at the age of 51:
I was very innocent in those days. I'd already had three boys and a miscarriage. We took the children on holiday to Walton-on-the-Naze. We had some friends who had a small hotel. They invited us there for a fortnight. We had a very enjoyable holiday. The weather always seemed nice in those days. We came home and I didn't feel at all well. My husband said we have had a lovely holiday and you ought to feel on top of the world. I just didn't. I thought 'I know the signs!' The district nurse came in. She was awfully nice. She came regularly. One day I had a lovely fire going. She asked me to lie down on the rug so that she could examine me because I was very big. She said, "You've got a baby there." She visited me every week and I got bigger and bigger. One day she said that she believed that there were twins! I said "there can't be!" I wanted to have them at home. The district nurse couldn't see any reason why I couldn't. Dr Pirie was my doctor, and he brought a friend of his in to advise him. He was the consultant at St John's Hospital.

Dora was following a family pattern! Her great grandmother and grandmother had both given birth at home and, curiously, had both been pregnant at the same time. Dora:
A gypsy visited my great grandmother when she was expecting the baby. The gypsy was selling pegs, as they used to in those days. Great grandma bought some pegs from her. The gypsy said "I am going to tell your fortune. When your baby is born there will be something missing". It upset my great grandmother so much. When the baby was born initially they couldn't find anything wrong with him. When she was bathing him she noticed that, when he opened his eyes wide, there was a little half moon piece missing from one eye.

Housing

Much is said about the difficulties young couples face nowadays finding a house, but many people we interviewed seem to have started married life living with in-laws or renting.

Les Sparrow and his wife lived with parents before renting a house in Loftin Way at 30s (£1.50) per week plus rates.

Once married Eileen and Dennis Hance lived with his parents, Eileen said:
Things were a bit desperate as we had the two children, and we did want our own house. Dennis saw that Bartletts was up for sale, and asked me to get the details. When we viewed the house we knew it felt right.
Eileen & Dennis Hance bought Bartletts on Baddow Rd in 1959 for £3,500.

Kathleen Stevens was married in 1959 and lived in rented rooms in Galleywood before buying a caravan in Temple Grove, between Galleywood & Stock. Four years later they obtained a Marconi flat in Rothmans Avenue, since Mr Stevens was a Marconi employee.

It is fascinating to see what people paid for their homes. Robert Norrington was the first to live in Winchelsea Drive, which was not a made-up road in 1937. He paid £560 for the house - £25 deposit and monthly repayments of £2.50 for twenty five years. His brother said he was "stupid to have a mortgage round his neck".
"I've never regretted it, and wouldn't change it", he told us.

When interviewed, Kath & Don Brown were still living in the house in Winchelsea Drive that they moved into the day they married in 1939. It cost £595 & was built by Johnny Gard who also built part of Dorset Avenue.

Facilities

Surely few can match Les Sparrow's childhood home. He said:
> I was born in Great Baddow in July 1919 in the Old Well House Farm which stood at the entrance to where Foxholes Road now is. It was an old Tudor house with three wells, one inside the house and two outside. It was a nice old house with oil and gas lamps, no electricity, a big kitchen range in the living room with a water tank at one end for hot water and with two ovens. There was a host of crickets underneath which used to chirp at night when the fire was damped down! It had a large inglenook fireplace in the lounge with a turn-spit on the side in those days where you could hang produce. I mainly remember fish or kippers being hung on it, though at Christmas they used to use it. It burned 6 ft logs, which would burn right up the chimney and gradually get lower and lower. We would put the logs on at Christmas and the fire would not burn out until New Year's Eve. Upstairs were one inch board floors, slopey old floors everywhere and thick oak doors. I remember my bedroom, which was in one of the back rooms that overlooked the farmyard. It had a big old wardrobe alongside the door, which moved across the floor whenever any one banged a door in the house. It would sidle along the sloping floor until it covered the door and I couldn't get out. I remember my grandfather once had to get the ladder out, climb in through the window to push the wardrobe back and rescue me. (Photo 4-3).
> There was a collection of old furniture in the lounge. There was a huge sideboard, about 10-ft long. There were oil lamps and chandeliers on the side. In the wintertime, the farm workers came in and we ate our hot evening meal. Later we damped down the fires. Granny would put three soft Essex red bricks in the oven, heated up ready to take to bed wrapped up in flannel to make the bed warm.
> The main timber, which ran right through the house, was reputed to come from The Armada. It was a big old carved timber beam, which had all sorts of lovely carvings on it. It ran through two rooms and out the other side. It was a well-built creaky old house, always on the move, and it made noises. My Grandma used to say: "It's talking to you. There's nothing to worry about". In the warm weather the timbers used to creak as it cooled down at night.

Yet in their way prefabs (prefabricated houses erected during and after the war as emergency housing, many still standing!) were as well loved. Janet Chilvers moved to the prefabs on the Maltings with her parents and they stayed ten years:
> They were such lovely places. There was a lovely atmosphere on the Maltings. Everyone was very friendly and neighbourly. There was a long living cum dining room. The kitchen was very big and you could eat in there. It had a bathroom and toilet, which

was marvellous, plus hot and cold water. It must have been coal fired but I can't quite remember. We had just the one fire in the main room, but no heating in the bedrooms.

Compared with the facilities described by many older residents, the prefabs must have seemed like a palace. The lack of heating in most homes is their abiding memory, with freezing cold bedrooms. Sadie Gemmell said:

> I wonder how we survived! The toilet was outside, at the bottom of the garden, reached at night with the help of a torch.

Dora Norrington admitted they had 'means' upstairs:

> There was no separate bathroom. In the bedroom were washstands, with bowls and jugs of water. Daily we washed in cold water. We had to wash every morning before we dressed. Sometimes it was bitterly cold. We rather liked to leave our neck, but mother used to inspect us. Friday night was bath night, when a big tin bath was brought into the kitchen and filled with hot water boiled in saucepans. We all had the same bath water. The big ones made sure they got in first. My brother and I were the last ones in. Our hair was washed at the same time. I had such a lot of hair and it was curly. Mother used to bank the fire up. We only had coal and wood fires. I had to kneel in front of the fire to dry my hair. (Photo 4-4)

Janet Chilvers was luckier when living together with her parents at her grandparent's house. As the baby of the family she was allowed first dip, but everyone was vague as to when their parents bathed. Janet said, "I can't remember my parents ever bathing in front of me ".

Janet also spoke about the fact that the front room was rarely used. It was laid out as a sitting room, an old fashioned "best room" which many of us can remember. (Photo 4-5). Even in the 1940s there was no electricity in Janet's house, just gas lighting.

Sadie Gemmell even remembered using candles for light, then small hand lamps. The main lighting in her house in the 1920s was by oil, with the wicks being trimmed daily. She could still recall the thrill of turning on an electric switch for the first time!

Florence Hardwick also has memories of oil lamps. If we got excited, my mother's cry was, "mind the lamp." She was terrified it might be knocked over. We had candles as well. I once set light to the curtains with a candle. I'd stood the candle on the windowsill. My father was very quick and put it out.

Housework

Given the dearth of facilities in people's homes until relatively recently, it is no wonder that housework took so long, especially the washing.

Colleen Yaxley described it:

> In the kitchen was a brick copper for the washing. This was lit every Monday morning, the only wash day of the week. Everywhere was steamed up and newspapers covered the floor.

Florence Hardwick sums up a typical woman's week:

> Washing was always done on a Monday. Mother heated the water, in the copper, and it was washed in a tin bath, and then put in the copper to boil. It was brought out, rinsed, and then put on the line. Tuesday was ironing. Wednesday and Thursday were bedrooms and housework. Friday was shopping day.

Mary Parsons tells us a mangle was used to wring clothes in their house, but it had no screw top to tighten rollers, it had a 28lb weight each side on a hook to provide pressure. These were taken off at the end and stored. (Photo 4-6).

Les Sparrow remembers wash days:

Washing, come hell or high water was always on a Monday. I remember going to school, and the washing was out all over Baddow. You could go out in the village and it was like Empire day, a Flag Day. Everybody's sheets and blankets were out by 11 o'clock if it was a fine day. If it was a bad day, when you came home there was wet washing hanging everywhere, up in the kitchen, all over. You had to climb your way through it. Though my help can't have been welcome Grandma would remark, "before you go out to play I want you to put this lot through the mangle". The mangle was outside, so I would take the cover off, and my friend of those days, would say, " we'll get through this quickly". He turned the handle and I pulled the washing through from the other side, because it was very hard to turn. Sometimes sweaters would come out six inches wide and six foot long!

Most cooked on a coal-fired range, which - as Sadie Gemmell told us - had to be black-leaded every day.

Dora Norrington spoke of her home over the shop at the corner of Beehive Lane:

First of all when we went there was only an old range to cook on. (Photo 4-7). My mother said she couldn't use it so she bought a gas cooker. Nothing like they are today. It was just the top and a single oven. I was always in the shop and mother did the cooking but we had a young person in to do the housework upstairs. We had three bedrooms and a lounge over the shop that had an open fire that was lit at weekends. In the room at the back of the shop we had a coal or log fire and we had to keep running in there to warm our hands.

Spring-cleaning was a ritual recalled by Les Sparrow:

After the threshing was done, usually early in the year, on a fine day hopefully, I remember the spring-cleaning taking place, starting with the chimney. When granddad wanted to sweep the chimney he put two bales of straw up the chimney and set light to one of them and it went straight up the chimney and that was the chimney sorted out. Nobody bothered about smoke in those days, and every one in the village was on coal. Then Granny started going right through the house from top to bottom, with everything taken out except the really big furniture. The carpet was put on the washing line and beaten with a bamboo beater.

Some people were lucky and had a maid to help with all this work. Dora Norrington's relative Ada had a "maid of all work" to help her on Gardiner's farm in Beehive Lane, whilst Dora's mother had a young girl to help with housework in their shop in Beehive Lane. Sadie Gemmell's mother had a live-in help, though Sadie said they were hard to get hold of because of the war. One wonders what their lives were like, when Colleen Yaxley described how "the maid was in a shed, which seemed to me to be full of spiders."

After the day's work most men seem to have maintained a vegetable patch. D. Hurrell spoke about his father:

My father's gardening routine amused me. He always put his runner beans in on May the 12th every year. He thought there was some magic about it. I found the reason latterly. In Chelmsford on May the 12th, since the Middle Ages, there was a fair. People would have the day off and put their runner beans in. It was rather like putting your potatoes in on Good Friday. They didn't have annual holidays then, so on their day off they looked after their own garden. May 12th is still called runner bean day in our household.

Meals

Meal times were more formal than nowadays. Les Sparrow said they kept regular hours in those days, there was a set routine throughout your school life and throughout your home life. There was no question of having your breakfast piecemeal; the whole family sat down at one time, apart from when they were at the farmhouse.

Sadie Gemmell's family was also strict:
> Giggling at the table was not allowed. Father would be furious. We always sat down to all meals together. Father was very prompt. Mother was concerned if he was not home on time.

There was not the variety we enjoy now, though many supplemented their food by not only growing vegetables, but also keeping chickens, making jam and bottling fruit.

In Sadie Gemmell's home everything was homemade: scones, pancakes, pies and tarts.

Florence Hardwick's mother also did all the baking:
> It was an open fire, with an oven at the side. We did have a lot of baked potatoes, which would bake nicely in the oven. We had a lot of rabbits, hares and pigeons to eat, because my father had a gun license. Mum used to cook those in the oven, jugged hare and whatnot.

Monday, a busy day, would mostly be 'bubble and squeak' i.e. fried up leftovers from Sunday. Although working hard in the shop, Dora Norrington's mother always made sure they had 'a nice hot dinner'.

Of course Christmas was special, probably rather like that described by Les Sparrow:
> Christmas dinner usually consisted of roast chicken, Brussels sprouts, baked potatoes, roast parsnips, carrots and mostly the vegetables which had been grown in Dad's garden, as he was a keen gardener. Christmas pudding with custard and threepenny pieces inside. Mum used to say "now mind how you chew on those there are some little presents inside". We used to know it was money, sometimes you were lucky, and sometimes you were not, so you used to say "can I have a second slice Mum, please". We never had silver charms, we just had the threepenny pieces. I know we had to count them all and if there were any missing we had to watch when we went to the toilet. Doesn't bear thinking about, does it? But seldom did they lose a threepenny piece.

"Christmas was the one day we had chicken, as a treat", said D.Hurrell. "You didn't have chicken every day of the week like you can now. We had a Rhode Island Red chicken, which we fattened up in the garden. My brother won a cockerel in a raffle one year. My father made a little pen in the garden and fattened it up. On Christmas morning my mother kept saying, "I shan't eat it". My father did the necessary and it was on the table for lunch! "

On Gardiner's Farm a whole sheep would be roasted at Christmas.

In Dora Norrington's family, birthdays were special too:
> When birthdays came round my aunt always made my grandmother a birthday cake. We were all invited to Cannon House in Baddow Road, where granddad and grandma lived. Instead of having that cake she would bring out one that she had received the year before. It would be mouldy because it had just been stored in a cupboard. My aunt said, "why did you keep it?" Grandma thought it had been a pity to cut it!

Clothes

Given the lack of heating in the home, people dressed warmly, perhaps in 'combinations' (which Sadie Gemmell hated) or the dreaded 'liberty bodice'. Dora described what she wore as a child:

> We had bloomers, thick stockings, a liberty bodice, three petticoats and a very short frock. In the summertime we had the same but we had knickers with a frill on. The frill nearly always showed below the petticoats. We had to be covered up. When we played in the fields we used to take our shoes and stockings off, as we were so hot. We had special clothes for Sundays. If we went to a party it was a great treat to wear our Sunday dress and shoes. My mother made the clothes. In Chelmsford, where Woolworth's is now, there was a public house and next to that was a little cloth shop. I used to love to go to Mr Potter's. You went up four steps and into a very, very narrow and long shop. Mother used to buy yards of material and make our frocks and petticoats and she trimmed them with lace, which she was very good at making. We were very proud of them.
>
> You had to have a hat. Straw hat in the summer and either a woolly hat or a tam-o'shanter in the winter. We also had to wear a scarf. My mother decorated the hats. The main thing we had was a spray of flowers round the hat. We had two pieces of wide ribbon, as streamers, down the back. We were so proud, as it wasn't everybody who had them.

Dora's grandmother was amply dressed. She wore enormous skirts, numerous petticoats and long bloomers that came half way down her legs. She had a Paisley shawl, which was very pretty. When she went out she wore little tiny bonnets with flowers on the front, tied underneath the chin.

Upbringing, special occasions & entertainment

H.Ely, born 1885, writing about her life summed up the hardships many people faced:

> My mother told me that her father used to earn about 12s-0d a week (or 60p in new money), and they only had meat once a week, perhaps a bit of fat pork on Sundays. Grandmother was very good at making clothes for the children, but where did the material come from I wonder? Also the children and Grandmother had to go gleaning, then the corn was taken to the mill to be ground into flour, and Grandmother made bread from it.

Born some 30 years later Les Sparrow still felt life wasn't easy:

> Mother didn't have a lot of time for hobbies really with the family; nobody did in those days, with the family's washing and Dad's job. I wouldn't say it was a messy one, but there was plenty of washing from him every day. Yes, it was a very hard life.

And yet despite this, many former residents lived to a ripe old age: Dora Norrington's uncle lived to over a hundred. Jesse Pryke's mother Dorothea was ninety three when she died, John Jackson's uncle Will is ninety three and many of those interviewed were in their eighties and nineties.

Children were brought up strictly. Clive Barker explained:

> "We had a pretty strict upbringing, but I don't think it did us any harm. For example, during the war we would be at my grandparent's house in Beehive Lane for Sunday lunch and we could never start eating until grace had been said."

Les Sparrow told a similar story:

One of the things that they always drummed into us was that no matter what happens you are always to tell the truth. However unpleasant, if you told the truth the punishment was less than it would have been if you had not told the truth. You were to be respectful to your elders, and not to use Christian names. If Uncle Fred came in and you said, "hello Fred", you would have had a clip round the ear, it had to be "hello, Mr. and Mrs. Whatever-their-name-was". We were always instructed to treat others as we would like to be treated. I remember sometimes going home to tell my mother something and she would say, "that wasn't a nice thing to do, would you like that done to you?"

"Well no I suppose I wouldn't".

"Well then don't *you* do it".

They disapproved of bullying of any sort, which was really frowned on, as was swearing and use of bad manners, and good table manners were most important in those days. Punishment varied with the misdemeanour; it was mainly being confined to the house and not being allowed out to play, or in my case helping Dad in the garden before being allowed out to play. But very seldom was there any physical violence, well not in our house anyhow. There was a threat of it always. Dad had his big leather strap behind the kitchen door, on which he used to strop his cut throat razor and if he made a move towards that, it was enough - I was quiet and minded my P's and Q's.

Colleen Yaxley's grandfather had a similar code:

I can remember wanting a bike very badly in the 1940s. Granddad said, "you shouldn't get a bike, as they are all black at the moment. They are not good bikes, they're wartime bikes". He did let me have one though. He lent me the money, but I had to pay back every single penny. They were quite strict. This was the old fashioned way. They had always been poor. People were more diligent then.

Dora Norrington couldn't remember receiving any regular pocket money, and birthday and Christmas presents seem to have been much simpler then.

Les Sparrow told us:

We seldom had a birthday party on our birthday. I was born in July so I was lucky as I could have an outdoor picnic. At weekends we had friends round, tea in the garden. We had small presents for birthdays, such as socks or pullovers. Aunts and uncles especially gave clothing - I did not think much of it as a present, but Mum did because it saved her buying it. But my friends were told not to bring a present, which was frowned on because it meant the reverse if you went to their house. I think it was pretty general for the ordinary families.

Peggy Bradley was luckier!

I had quite a lot of birthday parties at Hampton's (the large house in Beehive Lane near the Marconi Social Club, where her father worked). Quite a few friends used to come. There was a lovely hollow oak tree we used to climb up. We used to pick Victoria plums and eat them up in the oak.

It was a similar story at Christmas where presents were quite small. In fact Sadie Gemmell never had anything special at Christmas or New Year until she was grown up. She was given annuals like 'Chatterbox', 'Children's Own' and a paint box.

T. Steggles recalled having few presents, but what he did receive, such as a steam engine one year, was treasured.

In Les Sparrow's case the presents consisted of boys' annuals and books:
> I like books. My uncle Alf always bought me some nice books. The biggest toy I ever had was a combined Christmas and birthday present of a Hornby Clockwork train set. That was a really big present as far as I was concerned, which we added to over the years with little items. We had stockings, ordinary stockings which used to be hung up and they would be filled with oranges, nuts and liquorice allsorts, jelly babies, sherbet dabs and sweets.

> Christmas was usually a family time. On Christmas Eve Mum always lit a fire up in her bedroom, the front bedroom (the best bedroom) and we used to hang stockings and pillowcases up. Presents were only opened in the presence of your parents, when we all went into their bedroom and sat on the bed in front of the fire and opened the presents from Father Christmas. We always opened the presents before breakfast, and I don't think Mum and Dad got much sleep in the early days because by 4 o'clock we were awake. We used to put decorations up, which were all homemade paper chains. We would buy the packet of coloured paper and for a week beforehand we stuck them all together. Mum made the flour paste using flour and water, and we had them festooned all over the house, up the stairs, we really went to town. We did have balloons in those days and we also had three fold-round paper bells and they were kept year after year; it must have been ten years we had those three.

> In between Christmas and New Year we had a family gathering. It was held in the Old Black Bull in Chelmsford, in the upstairs room that went right over the whole pub. Generally there were fifty to sixty people there on this particular day and a big long table was laden from end to end. Celery, meats, you name it, it was there. It must have cost a fortune and the party started just after teatime around about 7 o'clock. It was a buffet and everyone sat around, there were enough chairs to go round the whole room. The evening began with games, the usual games like 'postman's knock', 'pin the tail on the donkey', and when it finished, which was about midnight, some of the children might have been put in various rooms to go to sleep, but I never went to sleep. Uncle Jim had laid on a taxi for every family and they used to queue outside the Black Bull, there would be a dozen taxis sometimes. I don't know where he got them all from because there were not that many taxis in those days, and it must have cost a fortune, but that was his Christmas present and it was a nice evening.

At Christmas the family piano came into its own. John Jackson remembered that all his aunts and uncles could play the piano.
> At Christmas they would each play a piece, one after the other, perhaps four or five of them. Now you very seldom find anyone who plays. It's such a pity that radio & TV has taken over.

In Dora Norrington's family the children were made to sing and play instruments.

In many homes such as Colleen Yaxley's, the piano provided entertainment throughout the year. There was a piano in the living room and an organ in the parlour, which grandma played every day. At weekends in Les Sparrow's home, they would get around the piano and have a good old singsong, especially a tune his mother knew from listening to the wireless. It was common to have piano lessons, for example with the well-known Mr.

Burton, who was an organist who lived up Beehive Lane. Les's mother herself gave lessons and Les remembered sitting through endless scales whilst trying to do his homework!

With the advent of the wireless people's choice of entertainment increased. Mary Parson's grandfather was one of the first to have a wireless. It had a large horn with the maker's name 'Brown'. This was the same name as her grandfather, so Mary thought he'd made it himself!

Florence Hardwick's family had a wireless quite early, because her older brother built a crystal set. They listened to it with earphones. Les Sparrow's household was equally lucky:

> We had a crystal set radio, which we had to fiddle with, tuning the 'cat's whisker' to get a sound. My favourite programme was Uncle Mac on Children's Hour, who always said "Good night children everywhere".

Several years later Den Harvey remembers one of the first people in the village to get TV was Mr. Russell. He confessed:

> Old Laurie Russell, the landlord of my mum's place, was the only one to have a television and we used to watch it on Saturday nights. He used to be the fire engine driver during the war. (It was voluntary then). The siren would go and off Laurie went in his fire engine. I remember him giving me some stick, because at the place we called the dump at the top off Pump Hill, we once set fire to some bracken. He wouldn't let me go round there to watch TV after I had set fire to the bracken.

Natural History

Several residents mentioned the 'fauna and flora' of the area, and we are indeed fortunate living in close proximity to lovely countryside. Here are a few observations:

Peggy Bradley:

> My father owned two of the cottages on Pump Hill. He thought this huge plane tree was doing damage to the cottages, so he decided in the 1940s to have it cut down. Luckily someone told him that there was a preservation order on it so it is still standing today.

Colleen Yaxley:

> We had two apple trees, eaters, and two gooseberry bushes in our garden. My grandmother made jam and we had gooseberry pies but they weren't the lovely big fat, red gooseberries. These were small green ones, as they were never pruned.
> I can remember Jackson's in New Road growing tomatoes during the war. They also had a peach tree that hung right over the fence and when the fruit was ripe they were very tempting. I used to buy them for six old pence each.
> The Causeway was flanked on one side by a high brick wall that bordered the Vineyards. The swallows flew all round there and the bats swooped at night. I can remember walking through all the leaves that fell that side of the road. You could never see the Vineyards house then.

Janet Chilvers:

> We reared chickens and rabbits to supplement our food, and we grew lots of fruit and vegetables on the allotment in Maldon Road when we lived in the pre fabs in Maltings.

Den Harvey (Manager of the Millennium Centre):

> There are lots of foxes around here now. I see them here quite regularly, late at night, when I'm locking up. Six months ago, I was locking up and checking the windows, and there was a mother and two cubs rolling around just outside. I stood in the dark quietly and watched them for about ten minutes.

Robert Norrington:

Cats frighten the birds in my garden in Winchelsea Drive and there are squirrels about. Foxes still use the garden, and there are many in the area. Recently at 6.45 a.m. my neighbour saw one jumping my 6 ft fence, probably a dog fox. I've got sweetcorn and broad beans in the garden, which gets eaten. I think they come from the gravel pit next door or the allotments the other side of Baddow Road. Sometimes in the evening I put out a bone left over from a joint of lamb. By next morning it will have gone.

Christine Vernon (née Collins):

I was familiar with Rothmans when I was young. They had nectarine and mulberry trees in their garden.

Una Matthews (née Hockley):

The gravel pit ceased working sometime in the 1930's, causing some local unemployment. After that it became a fairly wild place. I think there were two deep ponds where frog-spawn, newts and small fish could be found. Children certainly roamed there, but it was thought by some parents to be dangerous.

Chris Woollard:

There were sand martins at Jackson's pit.

Conclusion

Compared with these accounts, our lives today seem much more relaxed and easy-going. Certainly the woman's lot has improved beyond recognition, though you may regret the disappearance of some aspects of family life recorded above.

Photo 4-1   The Wedding of John Boreham and Edith Freeman, née Jackson, in 1905, taken at the rear of Albert Villa in Baddow Road

1 - Bobby Jackson   2 - Charlie Freeman
3 - Harry Jackson   4 - Sarah Boreham
5 - Alfred Boreham   6 - Alice Boreham
7 - Harry Boreham   8 - Bella Boreham
9 - Unknown   10 - Solomon Jackson
11 - Kate Blanes   12 - Bertram Boreham
13 - Edie Boreham   14.- Harry Clarke
15 - John Boreham   16 - Edith Boreham
(née Freeman, née Jackson)
17 - Grandfather Solomon Samuel Jackson
18 - Ella Boreham 19 - Robert Jackson
20 - Herbert Jackson 21 - Edie Jackson
22 - Winnie Jackson 23 - Amy Boreham
24 - Gertrude Boreham

25 - Grandma Boreham   26 - Maud Liddiard   27 - Grandma Alice Jackson   28 - May Jackson   29 - Billy Jackson
30 - Nell Freeman   31 - Esme Boreham   32 - Edith Freeman   33 - May Boreham

Photo 4-2
Norrington Family

Photo 4-3
Well House Farm

Photo 4-4
Bathtime

Photo 4-5   Front Room

Photo 4-6
Mangle &
Washtub

Photo 4-7   A Typical Range

Chapter 5 - School Life

Introduction

There has been a school in Great Baddow since 1392, when Margaret, wife of Thomas Coggeshall, endowed the Chantry School. This building sits behind St Mary's and is now used as the church office, though it may have still been used as a school in the late 1800s or early 1900s. (Photo 5-1 & 5-2).

Derek Hurrell says:

> My grandfather, Fred always used to say that he went to school in the sexton's house, right at the end of the Chase, next to the church.

In 1731 Jasper Jeffery also endowed a school in the village, in a property built in 1600, situated in Maldon Road just above the Parish Hall. The schoolmaster was paid 50 shillings per annum and taught 25 local poor boys. The school premises were sold in 1911, but even in recent times children could win a Jasper Jeffery's scholarship to KEGS (King Edward VI Grammar School) or obtain help with their studies at other establishments. For example, in 1968 Sandon School asked for financial assistance for their Lapland expedition. (Photo 5-3).

Private Schools

Mention is made of several private schools, one in Chelmerton Avenue in the 1930s, another (a kindergarten) at 401 Baddow Road in the 1940s, but perhaps the best known one was that run by Lulu Turnage, daughter of the one-time head master of the village school. It was in the house now used by Copsey's dentist practice on Maldon Road. Lulu was said to be an exceptionally good teacher with pupils aged 5 to 15. Fees were about 75p (or 15 shillings in old money) per term. Dora Norrington's mother went to this school, being taught by Mr & Mrs Turnage, and Dora followed her. She was taught shorthand and typing by Lulu.

Sadie Gemmell (née Hodge) described how school took place in one room, the principal room at the back. The front room had a piano where they had piano lessons. There was no sport. There were no desks, just tables. They were taught religion and passages from the Bible. (Photo 5-4 shows the entire school at Hill House, which is believed to have become Baron's Store, now Copsey's dentist practice).

Reg Spalding said:

> Each day we had to repeat the following: The books of the Bible, the counties' capitals, rivers of England and Wales, Kings and Queens since 1066 and the Times Tables from 1 to12.
>
> When I went in 1905 to KEGS (King Edward VI Grammar School) the Headmaster said, "if you come from Miss Turnage's School you'll do!"

The Village School

However, the school which most of the interviewees attended was the Village or Church School, also situated behind St.Mary's Church. The school was built in 1837, supported by subscription and income from Mrs Henrietta Pugh's gift. New buildings were put up in 1877 and further enlarged in 1897. (Photo 5-5).

As in many villages throughout the country, Great Baddow School was a Church of England School for children aged 5 to 14. This meant that it was largely funded by the Church rather than the State, and religious tuition was high on the agenda. Leavers could seek employment or perhaps an apprenticeship with a local firm. At the age of 10, the pupils could sit for exams to KEGS, Chelmsford High School for girls or for the Chelmsford Technical School.

The village school is variously referred to by interviewees as Gt.Baddow School, the Council School, the National School, the British School or the Church School. Several generations of families went there. Derek Hurrell's father, uncle and brother went there for instance, and Una Matthew's father, Aubrey Hockley was there in the early 1900s; she followed him in the 1930s.

In 1967 the school was closed. Since then, due to the growth of the village we now need 4 primary schools for children aged 5 to 11: Meadgate Infants and Junior (opened 1965), Baddow Hall County Infant and Junior School (opened 1968), Beehive Lane County Primary School and Rothman's County Primary School (opened 1955). This was renamed Larkrise in 1992, reportedly after a visit by the Duke of Edinburgh, who asked why the school was named after a cigarette company. (Rothman's is of course an old local name, nothing to do with cigarettes).

Nowadays children aged 11 can transfer to the selective schools (Chelmsford High School for Girls, KEGS for boys), though most go to local comprehensives: Sandon School, Baddow High School or Moulsham High School.

The Journey to School

In the days of the one village school, however, virtually all children went to that singular educational establishment and local inhabitants interviewed share remarkably similar experiences. Everyone walked to school, as Rosemary Hill remembered, usually with friends. There were no traffic jams at the school gates then due to parents' cars, and many can describe the short cuts they took. Colleen Yaxley explained there was no anxiety about walking, though she did recall,

> From our upstairs window at the back of the house we could see all the old cottages in the Chase. At the bottom of the Chase was a thatched cottage, which we were frightened to pass, as it always seemed creepy and dark.

Some children went home for lunch, but many took sandwiches. Les Sparrow says,

> I tried hard to let my mother allow me to stay at school, especially in wintertime. There was a nice warm fire and most of the children who stayed at dinner-time were from the outskirts of the village, as far as the Army and Navy roundabout, and they generally used to have 'bread and marge' or 'bread and dripping' toasted in front of the fire, and it used to smell lovely. I used to ask Mum if I could stop at school for lunch and she used to say: "They'll think you haven't got anything to eat at home. You come home for your meals". So I had to go home, but I did relish the days when I could stay at school. I did manage it once or twice.

Tom Steggles told us that the headmaster made hot drinks with a big kettle and Tom took cocoa for this. Una Matthews has vivid memories of the roaring open fire, in the middle senior classroom, surrounded by a strong fireguard with square corners. "In cold weather, our ⅓ pt milk bottles would be placed, resting on the guard, to warm. Some of them would get very hot, and boil over, which was a diversion!"

Iris Easter recalls, "we were able to obtain cod liver oil and malt, via the infant's school, and possibly orange juice. I preferred the cod liver oil. A box of Cadburys milk chocolate, finger shaped bars, appeared occasionally. I think they were a penny or halfpenny".

Teachers and Other Staff

Perhaps understandably the clearest memories are of the teachers, and the same names occur over and over. Mr Amoss, the headmaster of the Boys' School, was an important local figure, who was also the umpire for the Gt.Baddow Cricket Team. There is even a road in the village named after him. Iris Easter describes him as "a very gentlemanly figure. He was a Norfolk man, I believe. He used to wear ginger-coloured suits, maybe a Harris Tweed ".

Mr Amoss succeeded James Makepiece Turnage, who died in about 1903, and he remained at the school until the end of World War Two.

Tom Steggles says that he was a strict disciplinarian, but well respected. Even when pupils grew up they still addressed him as "sir". Many tell tales of the canings they received, but Les Sparrow added, "to give the headmaster his due, he never held it against you. Once that day was finished you started off with a clean sheet the next day. For all the caning we got on well together".

Den Harvey's father may not have agreed. Den recalled,
> Mr Amoss the headmaster of the Village School lived in New Road, opposite where Mr Jackson lived at the plant nursery. Around 1960 when I was a plumber I was asked to do some work in old Amoss's house. My dad said to me, "go up into the loft and see if you can find that bloody old cane".
> Perhaps he wanted me to put it out of action. It was used quite a bit, as Mr. Amoss used to dish it out quite ruthlessly, so I am told. You could do that in those days.

Derek Hurrell added a rider to this account:
> Old Les Jackson, who used to run the nurseries, knew my father very well. He lived almost opposite Mr Amoss in New Road. When I visited him I found he had got Mr. Amoss's 'tickling stick', the stick he used to deal with unruly boys. I don't know how he found it.

Of the remaining teachers, the names which constantly recur are those of the infant teachers: Miss Ellis (head of the infants and a Sunday School teacher), Miss Stark (also a Sunday School teacher) and Miss Lambert. Iris Easter says that Miss Ellis was a wonderful, motherly lady, whilst Miss Lambert was a very quiet, sweet lady. I'm sure all the infants loved them both.

Les Sparrow told us that when the teachers came into the room for assembly they all had to stand up and say: "Good morning Miss Ellis, good morning Miss Stark, good morning Miss Lam**bert**".

Many former pupils were still able to mimic the way this greeting was chanted every morning!

Iris also remembers "Mr 'Tin-tack' the school caretaker - quite a small man but he had a big barrow. The story goes that he built the barrow in his shed. He couldn't get it out because it was too big".

The visits of Miss Hart, a school governor were recalled vividly. Iris says, "I can see her now, wearing her brown fur coat" and Una Matthews added, "she was very attractive, and fascinated me in her lovely clothes, which were probably Edwardian". Miss Hart was the daughter of a former village doctor.

It is interesting that the schoolteachers mostly lived within the village. Mr Amoss lived in New Road, whilst the head of the Infants, Emily Ellis lived at 101 Beehive Lane with her sisters Mary and Beth. Their colleague Miss Stark also lived quite near the school at 27 Maldon Road, the old house facing down the Causeway next to Copsey's (now the dentist's surgery).

Facilities

People have very detailed memories of the school facilities. Peggy Bradley described the horrid outside toilets, and many recall how cold the classrooms were, heated mainly by a stove called a 'tortoise stove' according to Peggy.

Alan Willis said, "I remember one winter was very cold and one boy who sat at the back of the classroom by an open window closed it. A few minutes later Mr Amoss said: "who shut that window?" and opened it again. He then sat on the fireguard near to a roaring open fire".

Being close to the stove was a privileged position, for Colleen Yaxley told us, "the children who were good at reading were allowed to sit around the fire in small round-backed chairs" (perhaps those at the back were shivering too much to hold their books still enough to read).

Bert Collis was able to join this élite group:

> My father was a lone village policeman. He was on night duty almost every night, on patrol for two or three hours. This meant he was almost always at home in the mornings, so before I started school he had taught me to read. The reading book was the Daily Express.
> Because of this I joined the readers' class group in the infants class. In those days the school was heated by coal fires, which had a metal fireguard round them. Those of us who could read had very small armchairs in a group round the fire where we sat and read Enid Blyton's Happy Stories books. Some of them I can remember. The school was divided into the infants' section and the senior section with separate boys and girls. The infants' classrooms were partitioned with curtains and opened up for morning prayers.

Derek Hurrell said,

> The teachers had to shout to be heard. There were wooden desks in those days, with a form with two desk-fronts, but there were no pens or inkwells in the Infants. We had slate pencils and ordinary pencils.

Iris Easter describes her cookery classes.

> Our cookery class was a walk away to Sandon Village Hall. I am sure we cooked in paraffin ovens. We used to go through the Bringey way.
> During the Second World War evacuees from Tottenham swelled the school numbers, so that there were three to a desk.

Colleen Yaxley was envious of the black gymslips and thick black stockings worn by the London girls.

One of the evacuees, John Kemp, can remember that even after the war the school was too small.

> John: When we first arrived in Great Baddow the school was already full. I think there must have been a hundred evacuees and we were distributed around. I went to school at Foxon's, next to the old brewery, in the front room. Then I went to the Parish Hall and

to what is now the Bell Centre. As the other evacuees drifted back to London I got into the main school.

Den Harvey told us:

The Bell Centre was the overflow for St Mary's school, even after the war, when there were boom babies born in the late 1940's. We did the attendance register in St Mary's and then went to Bell Street for our classes.

Janet Chilvers recalls:

In the Junior School we were split up. There was a class at the Parish Hall, I went to the British Legion hall and also out to Sandon youth club. This was before the big Sandon School was built. I often think about walking through quiet lanes like the Bringey, with friends, on dark and cold winter days. How would parents react now?

Several school photos have been included. Number 5-6 and 5-12 are dated 1937-38, numbers 5-7 to 5-9 are from the 1950s.

The Curriculum

Les Sparrow remembers that they were happy days.

Nobody left school without 3 Rs, they could all read; they could all write, though some could write better than others and they could all do sums. This was all learnt mainly parrot fashion, as there were not enough books to go round. We had to share books.

Bert Collis spoke about his maths teaching:

I can remember at West Thurrock, my previous school, at five we had done addition, subtraction and multiplication but we hadn't tackled division, whereas the middle class at Great Baddow had done division. When we were given division sums I carefully copied from the boy next to me and worked out how to do it. I was self-taught. I eventually passed through all the classes there into the junior school. I thought I was quite clever until one day Mr. Jones, who took the first of the junior classes, put a Union Jack flag on the wall. We had to look at it and draw it. Only one boy got it correct with the different widths of the white. I didn't. It was a salutary lesson to me that I wasn't as clever as I thought.

"There was country dancing with an old wind-up gramophone in the playground. We did Christmas shows. We learnt songs and hymns," said Colleen Yaxley.

For sport, classes would go to Baddow Recreation Ground. H.Ely (born in 1885) wrote an essay about her schooling, which by today's standards seems very basic, concentrating on the 3 Rs, but she considered that she had a good education.

We learnt arithmetic, grammar (parsing & analysis), poetry and music. We had school worship every morning and I still remember the words of many of the hymns we used to sing. Also passages of the Bible we had to learn. The girls of course had needlework and knitting, but the boys learnt drawing and algebra. We used to write on slates chiefly, at first. We also had copybooks, which I am afraid did not look much like the original, when we got to the last line.

Classes then were called Standards. For instance when children came up from the infants they went into standard 1 and so on, until standard 7, which was the highest. Standard 5, 6 & 7 were taken by the headmistress, with the exception of (some of) standard 7 who did more advanced sums. We had no organised games. We used to have drill I remember; I expect they would be called 'extension motions' now. We had a good pianist, we always had music for drill, and we learnt many nice songs, in 2 parts. 'Tonic Sol Fa' was taught from a modulator. We did not learn much Geography. We started to, but somehow it fizzled out. We also took History, but I only read one of Shakespeare's plays: "The Merchant of Venice".

I loved school and never had a sum I could not do, but when I saw my grandson doing a sum, I did not understand the methods at all. We also had dictation and composition. In fact I liked all subjects except Needlework. We generally had a week's holiday at Easter and Whitsun and Christmas and in the summer we had 5 weeks' holiday. We had books on Domestic Economy, History and reading books. The teachers used blackboards, and I remember we were told to **look** at the board, and see how words were spelt and also how sums were done. We learnt all the various tables which one can find on the backs of some exercise books, all the tables from twice 2 until 12 x 12. Also £-s-d, weights and measures. I still remember them, and it is an advantage in shopping if one can reckon up easily, although these days most large shops have machines which total up the cost of one's goods.

Discipline

Rules were strict and as we have seen discipline was very firm, with frequent use of the cane, even for girls at times. Rosemary Hill never forgot how Miss Clayton, headmistress of senior girls, administered cane to one girl (from a home for orphans or difficult children on Beehive Lane) on her hand for some misdemeanour, in full view of everyone (about 1931-34). It must have been a rare event as it made a big impression on her.

Having heard of his many exploits, we did wonder whether Les Sparrow has the record for being the naughtiest child of all! He said:

I was not the best-behaved pupil in the school, and had my fair share of the cane, as I used to get up to pranks. Mr. Amoss was the headmaster, and when I came out of the army I bumped into him along Bell Street. His first words were "Ah, Leslie Sparrow, how nice to see you. You will be pleased to know you still hold the record for most school canings". This was the first thing he said, not "How are you?"

He went on:

Rules were strict; we were not supposed to eat sweets in class, but we did of course. In The Chase there was a row of terrace houses on the left and right, then a pair of semi-detached houses and in one of them in her front room a Mrs Francis kept a sweet shop, very handy on your way to school. If you were a millionaire with a ha'penny (1/2d) to spend you could buy 10 aniseed balls or a sherbet dab or 'liquorice bootlaces'. If you spent a penny you could even have a paper bag, instead of having the sweets tipped into your pocket. They used cone paper bags. One thing I particularly remember were gob stoppers, 2 for a penny. They were big sugar coated balls, and the more you sucked them the more they changed colour. If you sucked them long enough, which took a matter of days, you came to an aniseed ball in the middle. We were not allowed to suck them in class, but of course we did, and if Mr Amoss the headmaster caught you he would confiscate anything you had which you shouldn't have, and he would put them in his desk. On Friday afternoon before going home time he would dish out the contents of this desk. He would say: "Right. All those who had things confiscated, come and stand in front of my desk". He would hold up a gob stopper, saying: "Who owns this pink one?" We would argue, saying "That's mine, mine was pink, yours was blue".

Whether we got the same one it didn't matter too much; we would swill them under the tap. I remember too in the wintertime, if Mr Amoss found someone with a runny nose he would ask: "Haven't you got a handkerchief, boy?" He might then call a hankie inspection. If you were caught or nearly caught eating a gob stopper you might hide it in your pocket where it would stick to the hanky. You had to be careful when he examined the hanky to conceal the sweet. Usually he never saw it.

We had coal fires in the classroom. There was a central heating system of sorts, and there were cast iron radiators but I think they cost too much to run, so we had open fires. If you were a good boy you could become ink monitor for a week. In the wintertime you arrived ¼ hour early, which was very nice when the school was nice and warm, to top up the inkwells. They were filled up from a stone jar with red ink or blue ink. For all the caning I wasn't all that bad, it was just for pranks mainly and I was sometimes chosen as ink monitor.

Florence Hardwick expressed most people's attitude to canings. "Whatever you did you took the consequences. There was no question of going up to the school and protesting".

Parents mostly supported the school regarding corporal punishment. Les Sparrow elaborated: Parents met on Monday evenings with the headmaster in the Meeting Room on Bell Street (where they played billiards or whist). Anything you might have hidden from your parents came out in a full verbatim report from the headmaster of everything that had happened during the week, and you were likely to get another clip around the ear if you had hidden anything.

There were exceptions! Les Sparrow told us that prior to her marriage his mother, then Miss Aldred, was a teacher. She said that once they got an irate parent who came to school to say that her child was a little angel who never did any harm. She got chased around the school by the irate parent, brandishing an umbrella. That was all sorted out eventually, with the headmistress's intervention.

The headmaster intervened on another occasion, as Bert Collis remembers:
Mr. P took the middle class of the junior boys. He was pretty free with his hands in chastising people. I've seen him hit a boy so hard that the boy flew across the room. One morning, in the middle of the lesson, Mr. Amoss the headmaster came in with a stranger, a middle-aged man in a good dark grey suit. They spoke to Mr. P and then beckoned to me. I went out with them to the cloakrooms. I had no idea what was going on. This man was a schools inspector, as it turned out. He said to me, "you are in Mr. P's class. Has Mr. P ever hit you?"
I was a policeman's son, so Mr. P had never hit me. I said, "no, he's never touched me".
He said, "would you recognise your mother's handwriting?"
I said I knew it very well.
"What is your mother's Christian name?"
"Isabel Louisa".
"Her name doesn't begin with G?" He showed me a letter, written by a Mrs.G.Collis, purporting to be from my mother, complaining that Mr. P had hit her child. Someone had obviously wanted to complain about Mr. P, but didn't want to do it in their own name. They had picked the wrong one.

Leaving School

Many of the people interviewed spent their entire school career at the village school. Mrs Ely wrote:

> I left school at the age of 14 + 5 months, but some left earlier. It was not necessary to stay on, if anyone wanted to leave at 12 years of age. I always wanted to be a schoolteacher, but we didn't even have a High School in those days, (1899) so there were no chances for anyone to do what he or she wanted to.

Alan Willis left at a similar age, 14.

> The war started in August or September 1939, and I left school at Christmas. I started work in January 1940.

Derek Hurrell left school after the war in 1948, when the schoolmasters like Mr Cook had started to come back from their wartime service. Derek felt he should have left earlier. He explained:

> The worst period I had during my last year or two at the school, was the fact that the school year was changed. It had been January to January. They changed it to September to September as it is today. At the very last minute I had to stay on another year because my birthday was in December. I remember doing the same syllabus that I had done for the previous two years with Mr Cook. We used to have to write compositions on 'A Day In The Life Of A Coal Miner' and things like that. Mr Cook, whenever he had new students at the school who came from elsewhere, wherever they had come from always said, 'I know that place very well'. He knew everywhere!

There were also youngsters who left Gt.Baddow village school at 11, having passed the entrance exam for the grammar school. Les Sparrow recalled:

> I managed to get a Jasper Jeffery's place to the Grammar School in 1930. There were two awards to get to the grammar school apart from fee paying. There was the County Scholarship that was funded by the ECC and there was the Jasper Jeffery scholarship. He had left a sum of money for the education of ordinary non fee-paying children. Covering the whole of the Chelmsford district there were six scholarships a year awarded. Most children at the grammar school were fee paying and there were a lot of boarders. We had a school uniform, which was blue blazers, cap with coloured star on the top to indicate Strutt, Holland or Mildmay house. I had to leave at the end of the statutory term, which was 3 years, because my parents couldn't afford to keep me on to take the school-leaving exams, so I came away without any qualifications.

Reg Spalding also went from the village school to King Edward VI Grammar School (KEGS) around 1905. He said we had to walk to KEGS (from Meadgate farm).

> One boy used to come from Sandford Mill, another from the other side of Gt. Baddow. We all used to meet and arrive at school at 8:50 am. At that school we had some very good masters, who were dedicated men devoted to their jobs. They endeavoured to make you love learning. At that time there were around 160 boys. Most were paying fees of £3-12s-0d (= £3·60) per term. Some were boarders and some were scholarship boys. The latter were looked down on; the class distinction of birth was greatly adhered to then, but they were practically all very nice lads and I have fond memories of them and their kindness.
>
> Luckily learning was fairly easy, and having had such good grounding and having the advantage of such good teachers I was fairly well advanced by the time I was 15½.

Farming at that time was not very good and after seeing the worry that my parents had had financially I determined to try to get into the Civil Service as Inspector of Taxes. I had an entrance exam plus an interview, and subject to me passing what was then the equivalent of the GCE (O level) I should have entered in September 1910. I always wanted to read and never wished to be a farmer, and I thought that the money I would have earned would help the family. However, it was not to be. I had to leave school at 16 when my father died 2 days before my 16th birthday.

John Jackson's school career was also cut short, when WW2 broke out, and he was allowed to leave before he was 16 to help in his father's business.

Bert Collis's triumph came after he left school. He told us:
> I particularly remember my final report. I was a fairly anonymous child, I didn't do much wrong and I didn't do much right. In my final report from the Grammar School, the headmaster wrote rather ambiguously "It seems he may do rather better than at one time thought possible". It was with great pleasure this last year that I got the opportunity to engrave designs on the glass doors to the new music school. Fifty years too late I've left my mark on the school.

The career paths of just two other interviewees gave us some idea of increasing educational opportunities. After achieving A-levels at KEGS, John Parkinson went on to University, as did Philip Taylor of Lathcoats Farm a few years later. John trained to be a pharmacist and Philip read horticulture at Nottingham.

The Teacher's Perspective

There are other residents in the village - teachers, heads and governors - who can give us their reminiscences from the "other side of the desk". Les Sparrow's mother was a teacher at Gt.Baddow School and nearly got into trouble with the head herself.

Les: "She was interested in Botany, and when she was teaching at Baddow School, being on a farm, she had all sorts of opportunities for acquiring wildlife, insects, newts and all this sort of thing and, in particular, grass snakes. There were loads of grass snakes in the old manure heaps. They used to hole up there in the Winter time for the heat, and when the farm workers were taking one of these manure heaps to pieces to spread on the land they came across some snake eggs and Mum said: "I'll take them to school". At school they had a vivarium, and she put these snake's eggs in there and put the lid on. There would have been 30 or 40 of these eggs and after they had been in there 3 or 4 days, when she went to school the head mistress was waiting for her and said: "Miss Aldred, what have you got in that classroom of yours? It's alive with snakes!" The snakes had hatched out, they'd got out of the vivarium, and they were all over the floor. They were only little things, but they were everywhere". (Photo 5-10)

Eileen Hance ran a playgroup in her home for 18 years and has a fund of amusing stories.
> I remember when they were building the houses in Canford Close at the bottom of the garden I asked the builder, "do you mind if I bring my children to see what you are doing?" I thought it would be interesting for them to see him bricklaying etc. He said "Not at all", but he was surprised when I took 20 children. I did reassure him they were not all mine, she laughed.

She went on to tell us a lovely story:
> I always took them into the garden in the early morning in the autumn to see all the cobwebs. One little boy said, "I've got those all over my bedroom!" I did not tell his mother!

We used to have little sessions with them after a weekend or after a holiday when I asked them, "what did you do?" The answers I got were absolutely amazing; I could write a book, but I won't.

After a varied early career with children, Florence Hardwick became a teacher and then head of London Road Nursery School from 1949 to 1972. She recalled:

We were very short of money of course. It was in the time when toys were in short supply and we didn't have educational supplies. We used to buy books and paste one picture on a piece of plywood. We went to Colchester to do this, St Helen's school. We made jigsaws out of it. We used another book as a source of pictures for the children to copy. We made furniture for the Wendy house too, in our spare time.

It was clearly a very successful school, for at one time there was a waiting list of some 600.

Jeanette Williams spent a similar length of time at St.Mary's Nursery School as 'supervisor of the babies'. The Church had purchased the old village school and the Play School started in 1968 to help to pay the mortgage. (Photo 5-11)

James Hodgson, founding headmaster of Meadgate School (now retired) spoke passionately about his ideas on education. He explained:

You can teach anything given time, care, money, and an approach which is appropriate.

This will produce the interest and response that equates to good educational practice.

He summed up his philosophy thus: "Greater love hath no man than that he should pass on the skills he possesses in ways that are courteous, loving, charitable, kind and unstinting".

A similar phrase could be used to describe Eileen Hance's work in the community after she gave up the playgroup. She has been chair of the governors at Meadgate School and a governor at Beehive Lane and Thriftwood. She described the latter as a wonderful purpose built school, for those with moderate learning difficulties.

Pupils come from Burnham & Maldon & all around. It isn't residential. The young people are taught how to be good citizens; they have work experience in Tesco's for instance, always within their limits. Whatever they can do, we get them to do to the best of their ability. When they are in main stream they are inclined to think, "I can't do that". Class size is no more than 10; they get wonderful opportunities. They are taught how to use computers, how to live with other people. If only we could take all those who would like to attend.

Children's view of School today

The next section has been based on interviews in 2002 with a selection of 8 to 11 year old pupils at Larkrise, Meadgate and Baddow Hall Junior Schools. The interviewees are largely anonymous, only their first names being referred to. The head teachers gave permission for the interviews, and the children were selected by their form teacher. The reader is asked to contrast the teaching environment, the equipment, the leisure activities and the attitudes of modern children with the remembered experiences of fifty or sixty years ago by older Gt.Baddow residents. Some of the differences are dramatic, but many of the attitudes, and the young characters that expressed them, are very similar to those of fifty and more years ago.

Larkrise Junior School

The children were asked first about their earliest memories. These centred on either play school or accidents at home, and fighting featured quite a lot. Very little was remembered before the age of 4, even with children now only 8 years old.

Memories of Playgroup include drawing and painting, playing games and doing PE.

The children were asked about the subjects they were studying at the junior school, what their favourite and their least favourite subjects were. As might be expected, there were wide differences in favourites; however, Religious Education was regularly mentioned as least favourite. The old Church School gave priority to this subject, though the subject appears to be differently taught these days. The concentration on Christianity has been replaced by a wider view of comparative religions and looking at a variety of faiths.

As well as RE, the curriculum these days covers old faithfuls such as Maths, Art, Science, PE and History.
Less familiar subjects mentioned include Athletics, Literacy (English Language), Technology and Drama. Sometimes Maths was referred to as Numeracy. The children also mentioned IT or ICT (Information Technology and Computing) and Design.

Eight-year old Zara was asked, "What do you think is the point of literacy?"
She said: "To help your spelling and how to pronounce words properly, and see if there is a verb, which is a connecting word. In other words, how to put sentences together". I was quite impressed.

The second group at Larkrise were 4 ten to eleven year old pupils Martin, Jade, Olivia and Max.

Max said he found sums and tables and division boring, and he found literacy boring because of the writing. However, he was well aware of the purpose of the Maths and English teaching. He did not like writing and said he would rather type into the computer because he enjoys using the computer.

Martin said, "I enjoy Art, Technology, some Science; also I quite like Literacy and Maths". However, for his least favourite subject: "It's got to be History, and I don't like Science that much," When asked what bits of science he did not like he replied: "I don't like having to do loads and loads of writing off the board, because every time, you start writing, but you can't get it done in time. You don't know what the next word or sentence is, because the teacher keeps rubbing it off the board".

[Ed: I recall saying much the same in 1947 when I was ten! In those days I dreamt of photocopiers to provide the method or instructions for carrying out the experiment, so that I could concentrate on the science, understanding the objective of the experiment, drawing conclusions and writing a good report. Even in 2002 the concentration is apparently still on the writing].

In Science, Martin liked testing things, like separating water, salt and sand. *He* did not like writing up the results.

Jade's favourite subjects are Art, P.E. and Technology.
To the question: What do you study in technology? She said:
"I like making model cars, but you've got to make them move. They are made from wood and cardboard boxes. I like Technology because it's fun".

Do any of our older 'students' remember 'fun' being on the curriculum?

Olivia said she liked Science and Drama and English.
She was asked what she liked about drama, whether she was OK at learning lines and what sort of parts had she played?
Olivia said: "I'm OK with learning lines. I went to this thing called 'Stagecoach' and we had one hour of acting, one hour of dancing, one hour of singing. We performed parts of plays, acting different people. We practised two people having a conversation".
This is certainly a new way of teaching the art of communication, and most of the children interviewed were confident and well able to communicate their views to the interviewer.

Max was asked about literacy.
Max said: "I don't like writing stories; I never get the stories finished. I must try and write much shorter stories, because my stories are quite long".
When asked whether he was looking forward to secondary school he was very positive about the next school not being so free and easy, being stricter, replying, "I don't mind. You can get on with your work without people running around".

This group was asked about their ideas for a career, and came up with a few interesting new ideas.
Martin said: "I would like to work in a zoo, be a vet, be a footballer or try and make a career out of art".
Jade's response was: "I want to be an artist because I think that I am really good at drawing".
Olivia said, "I want to go to university first and study drama".
Max said, "I might go to university and then I might be an archaeologist or a 'bloke that goes round' [Ed: a surveyor, perhaps?], or designer of computer stuff".
Thankfully the opportunities exist nowadays for them to fulfil their aspirations.

Baddow Hall Junior School

Robert, who is nine, Stephen, Rebecca and Rosie who are ten spoke to our interviewer.

Rebecca said:
"My favourite lessons are Poetry Writing, History and PE. I write lots of poems. I like describing things and using rhymes. I like doing gymnastics. I like learning about history and about all the things that people have done. I find that really interesting".

Rosie was asked the same question. She said:
"I like Art and Music. I play a lot of instruments and I find it fun learning to play. I play the tenor and descant recorders, the piano and the clarinet. When I first started, I kept doing it wrong".
My keyboard teacher said, "will you ever do it right?"
This kind of comment sounds familiar, though I doubt her teacher raps her knuckles with a ruler, as happened to one of our older contributors when he made a mistake.

I received some illuminating responses when I asked what they wanted to do when they leave school (meaning at 16 plus). One boy said:
"My dad probably wants me to be a banker, like he is, but I don't fancy that. There's too much money involved. Money this and money that. You come home grumpy because you lost the deal".

Stephen had thought about a career:
"I would quite like to be a footballer or a game console designer. I might like to be an accountant, because that's what my dad is, and I'm pretty good at maths".

Rebecca:
"I would like to be a professional show jumper. If I have to stop horse riding I might be a beautician because I like playing with make-up". These careers are certainly more in keeping with the 21st century than the middle of the 20th.

I don't remember many of these careers being on offer in the 1950s, do you?

Meadgate Junior School

This is a recording made by pupils in Mrs Leatherdale's class at Meadgate Junior school on 11th July 2002. The interviews are by children of children and are believed to include the voices of Joseph, Daniel, Cassi, Leanne, Sam, Alex, Gemma and Kayleigh. Consequently the questions and answers are different to the Larkrise and Baddow Hall contributions.

What is the furniture like in 2002?
We have rectangular tables with metal legs and a wooden top with wipe-clean surfaces. So we can get all the stuff off. We have small plastic seats of different colours.
Different age groups have different size tables and chairs for their ages.

We started using white boards about three years ago and now every class is using one. The teachers write on them with dry-write pens. Before we used to have black boards with chalk. With blackboards and chalk when you rub it out it makes a horrible sound and I don't like it.
I prefer whiteboards to blackboards because blackboards were bad for my asthma, and whiteboards don't make as much mess.

When the teacher was rubbing off the blackboard people kept getting dust all over their clothes. You needed loads of polo shirts in one week.

We have two wooden cupboards for our storage with plenty of shelves, an art table with storage boxes underneath. There is a walk-in cupboard for the teacher.

Where do the children keep their personal things?
Every child has their own plastic drawers with their names on. Outside the classrooms they have a cloakroom to hang their coats and bags and belongings.

What technology do you use in your classroom?
We have a CD player that we use for our music lessons. We have a computer in our room, which is linked up to the (school) computer network. We use the computer for writing stories. We go on to the Internet for finding information. We use it for drawing graphs and analysing

science experiments. We play games and we use virtual realities for science experiments. We use the tape recorder for mental arithmetic tests but we don't use it for music as the CD player has taken it over. We use an overhead projector to illustrate pictures and to enlarge studied work. In the hall we use one to project hymns and stuff.

What can you see from the classroom windows?
We can see our wild life area, which has a very big pond in it. We can see lots and lots of trees and greenery. We can see the playground and our indoor swimming pool. We can also see our hall where we have assembly, PE and we also eat our lunch there. We can see our circular patterned patio, on which we are going to have new picnic benches.
We have 'Matthew's garden' in memory of the people who died of leukaemia. It is a quiet area where you can sit still and think. Sometimes we can eat our sandwiches there.

What games do you play at playtime?
We play all sorts of games including 'It', 'Tally Ho', skipping and football. We also play 'It build ups', 'squashed tomatoes', 'maggots' and other games.
Sometimes the little ones use leaves and play with them like running in the woods and stuff like that. They play rhyme games like sing songs and dance.
We also have a very large field, which we play on in the summer. We have some basket ball hoops, which are attached to the swimming pool wall, so that we can play netball and basketball.
The dinner ladies sometimes bring out a box of toys that we can play with but not when it's wet.
We are very lucky because we have lots of trees so that at snack time and lunchtime we can have a lot of shade. Our playground backs on to the busy Southend Road. It is noisy in the winter but in the summer the trees block out the noise.

What subjects do you study at school?
Usually in the mornings we study Literacy and Numeracy.
This year we have been studying the Vikings in History. In RE we have been studying Judaism and Christianity. Sometimes we do Art using pencils and pastels and paintings. We also study Geography. In music we play with instruments and we sing songs all together. In PE we do things such as games, gymnastics, dance and swimming.
We also do Design and Technology. Each class studies Science, which includes doing experiments. We do ICT and find out information on the computer.
We do Drama and Productions. This year years 5 and 6 did 'Mini Beast Madness'.

Other things about our school.
Our school (day) starts at a quarter to nine and finishes at twenty past three for the children. There are nine spacious, brightly coloured classrooms. There is a computer in each classroom. There is a range of food in the kitchen for only £1·30. We have toilets and water fountains.
We have a library so people can find out things. We have cupboards around the school so we can keep things in. We have toilets, changing rooms and showers in the swimming pool.

Each classroom has a heater to keep us warm. Every single classroom in the school has a clock.
The Reception classes have special lessons as well. They also have their own little playground which has a Wendy house, a scooter, bike, tyres and lots of other things.

Our school has a nursery for little children. We also have a secretary that works very hard to phone our parents if we ever forget things. Two years ago we set up our first school council. Children were elected from each class to help with the development for the school.

In Year 2 and year 6 children have to take very important tests called SATs. People all over the country have to take them as well.

The children finished by saying in unison: -
"We wonder what school will be like in THE FUTURE".

Conclusion

The responses of our contributors shows school life which varies from a Victorian approach to the more relaxed but wider approach practised in 2002. Education has tended to fit in with the lifestyles of the age. When opportunities were restricted, education was much narrower, and now we see ambitions and aspirations that were unthinkable a few years ago. Thank goodness there are young people in our schools who want to work and learn and to take advantage of these opportunities. This came across very strongly with the majority of the children. They know why they are at school and the whole point of education. Moreover most of the time they enjoy the learning process.

Photo 5-1
Chantry School

Photo 5-2
Chantry Plaque

THIS 15TH CENTURY BUILDING WAS PROBABLY THE VILLAGE CHANTRY SCHOOL

Photo 5-4
Private
School
Group
Back row:
Sam Lowe, Doris Thame, Edith West, Molly Porter
Front row: Sadie Gemmill (nee Hodge), Robert Hodge,
unknown girl

Photo 5-3   Jasper Jeffery's

Photo 5-5
GB Village School

Photo 5-6 GB School 1937-8

Back Row: Bill Maslin, John Pitts, Paul Turner, Peter Manning, Graham Kemp, Bill Kemp, Geoffrey Richell.

Second Row: Audrey Lamdon, Beryl Kemp, Brian Lorking, Peter Davis, Norman French, Patrick Hutton, David Soley, Dorothy Chilmaid, Kathleen Tucker, Sylvia Kemp.

Third Row: Iris Collis, Christine Calver, Doreen Alchin, Barbara Dawson, Stella Rayner.

Front Row: Doreen Hunt, Yvonne Spooner, ? King, Daphne Coward*, Doreen Ford, Doreen Coward*, Joy May, Evelyn Norton. (* twins)

Photo 5-7 GB School 1950s Class 1

Back Row: Tony Pennack, Pat Hiscox, Micky Wilson, Judy Scales, boy?, girl?, David Everett, girl?, Richard Hance

Second Row: Colin Wigmore, Nancy Fairhurst, Susan Collins, Michael Mills, Sylvia Mulley, Ian Ketley,

Gillian Snelling, Keith Cooper, Ann Needs, Frank Pamplin, Pauline Harvey, Peter Lovegrove.

Third Row: John Orrin, Janet Brame, Mrs Trevillion (Form teacher), boy?, Graham Pearson

Front Row: Micky Dowsett, Rowland Steele, Brian Stunt

Photo 5-8 GB School 1950s Class 2

Back Row: Jean Money, Joanna Sjollema, David Churcher, Ann Durgan, Alan Dowd, X?, Ivan Garwood, Pat Mills, Peter Joslin, Brenda Brooks, Nigel Boreham, Joyce Banham, Keith Wigmore, Diane Gray, Jimmy Bell, Helen Edwards, Roger Norrington.

Second Row: Mr.Cook (Form Teacher), Olive Greenwood, Pat Bundock, Rosemary Clapperton, Terry Pigrem, Maureen Brewster, Jonathon Nutbeem, Jennifer Phelps, Brian Riches, Marion Hull, Christopher Halls, Doreen Cox, Douglas Impey, Lorraine Ellis.

Third Row: Bobby Halls, Audrey Wilks, Richard Fairley, Lorraine Wooffitt, Douglas Christy, Ann Burton, Keith Cooper, Jackie Bartlett, David Penney, Pauline Gray, James Millham.

Front Row: Colin Sheffield, Gordon Webster, Clive Angel, Gordon Bailey, Edward Hiscox.

Photo 5-9 GB School 1951 Class 3

Back Row: Mr.Peter Cook, Frank Pamplin, Alan Farrant, Colin Shefield, Clive Angel, Ronald Steele, Peter Joslin, David Penney, Jimmy Bell, Pat Bundock.

Front Row: Jimmy Little, James Millham, Robert Kemp, Nancy Fairhurst, Pauline Gray, Helen Edwards, Joanna Sjollema, Angela Pennack, Bobby Halls, Alan Dowd, Jimmy Hiscox.

Photo 5-10
Grass Snakes in the
Classroom

Photo 5-11
Williams Pupils
1988

Photo 5-12   Gt. Baddow Girls School 1938

Chapter 6 - Farming

Introduction

Do you think of Great Baddow as a farming village? Possibly not, but within the memory of many of our older residents, there were dozens of farms in and around the village. They gradually disappeared over the years, making way for new roads and housing. Many of the old farms now only survive as road names, but at least two are still working farms. Reg Bush reminds us:

> Most of the villagers in Sandon and no doubt many from Gt.Baddow were employed on the local farms, and were housed in low cost cottages, often sharing a wash-house, with an earth toilet at the bottom of the garden. Generally Gt. Baddow residents were better off than their Sandon neighbours as far as domestic amenities were concerned. My parents kept two ponies, some poultry and a pig, and grew their own vegetables. Turnips and mangel-wurzels were popular then, and no one bought vegetables in those days. They bartered goods, and swapped excesses in one thing and shortages in another. Most of the villagers worked a seven-day week, especially those who tended animals.

Beef cattle from farms in the area were driven to market on Friday mornings and back to Copsey's in the evening. Mr Copsey had a field behind his premises where the animals grazed until 'needed'.

Local Farms

Old Well House Farm

Life in Old Well House Farm in the High Street was described for us by Les Sparrow in the chapter on Family Life. In addition we learn:

> In the farmyard there was a pond that was spring fed, plus barns, stables and farm buildings at the top of the yard.
>
> It was mainly an arable farm. We had two horses, a house cow and loads of chickens of course. It wasn't what you would call a cattle farm by any means. Most of our grandfather's land, apart from the fields near the house, he used to hire, as some of the farmers still do today. It was a two-man farm. My grandparents got in extra labour at harvest time, but it was hard work, mainly just the two of them.

Meadgate Farm, Spring Pond Close

This farm is owned by Betty Spalding, the widow of farmer Reg Spalding. Betty's account plus Reg's journal provided the detail:

> The farmhouse here was built in the late 1700s, about 1780. The Chapman & André map of 1777 does not show it, so it must have been built soon after that. It has been twisted around, because the front door should not be where it is, it should face the way the house faces (i.e. south towards Baddow Road). Grandfather Spalding put his grapevine in the big conservatory on the south side. So we have this awkward squidgy front door (on the West Side).
>
> The front and back doors have been altered, and where we have the bathroom was the 'Garden Hutch', the room the hired man would have lived in. There was no access to this room from the inside of the house, it had a door on the outside. On the outside we've got the brew house still. All Essex farmhouses had a brew house. Beyond the brew house we've got a ramshackle building which was a slaughterhouse. In more recent times it was used to incubate chickens. It was mainly a dairy herd of about twenty five

cows in 1900, though some was arable and general farming. They did three milk rounds around Gt.Baddow. The Spalding family's association with the farm began when Grandfather Fred Spalding retired from his photographic business in Chelmsford and took over Meadgate farm in 1887 (after a brief unsuccessful spell farming Lathcoat's in Beehive Lane). Fred was succeeded by his son Henry in 1895 and then by his grandson Reg in 1910, aged sixteen, due to the untimely death of Henry. The farm covered 42 acres, 5 of which were on Baddow Meads. The farm spread from near the Army & Navy[1], down to the river, to the backs of houses on Baddow Road. The way into the farm has been claimed as a public footpath from Baddow Road into Lathcoates Crescent, but it never was a public footpath. It was the drive down to the farm.

In the 1950s the building of the Meadgate Estate, and in the 60s the construction of the Baddow bypass led to the compulsory purchase of much of the farm land at £100 per acre. This was the lowest rate the developers had to pay for agricultural land, according to Betty Spalding.

Up here by the farmhouse the garden and orchards were lost. Reg missed the owls most of all. After I came here I was digging out the levels to get back to where the paths had been. The Meadgate builders increased the levels of the ground. We have a little cellar that always had water in it after the building of the estate, whereas previously the water had drained away. They altered the natural drainage of the land. I had the floor raised and it is dry now, but you have to be a bit of a dwarf to go in there.

Reg Spalding kept a diary for most of his life, right up until he died in 1982. Much of the subsequent detail in this chapter is drawn from this fascinating record. This farm is still run by the Spaldings, and their herd of some 25 beef cattle can be seen grazing on the Meads. The farmhouse stands isolated amongst Meadgate's housing estate. (Photo 6-1).

Gardiner's Farm, Beehive Lane

This used to stand opposite the Chelmsford Star Co-operative store, but was damaged by fire in the mid 1900s, to be replaced with a home for people with Down's Syndrome. It was farmed by Fred Carter, whose family owned and ran several farms in the area. Fred's wife Ada had three daughters at home plus a maid of all work. The girls made butter for the Essex Show and repeatedly won first prize every year. Above all the farm was known for its Friesian cows, and Arthur Carter, the son of Fred, was an authority on these animals. He knew all their names and histories. Den Harvey's grandfather was a tenant farmer for F.J.Carter and he used to show cattle for Carters at all the cattle shows in this county. The big one around here was the West Hanningfield show. It used to be held opposite the Ship pub at Stock. He also went to the Essex show, at Great Leighs, and to various other shows, in neighbouring counties, Buckinghamshire, Bedfordshire and Kent.

Den: My grandfather & I went away to cattle shows, when I was seven or eight years old, taking time off school, to Princess Risborough cattle show in Kent and the Royal Bucks show in Buckinghamshire. If the weekend show was Saturday and Sunday we went on Friday. My grandfather and I slept in the back of the cattle wagon. An old boy used to come with us, Sid Macer from Billericay. We used to put down a bed of straw, tarpaulins and horse blankets. We wouldn't be allowed time out of school now.

Peter Newman has similar memories, saying:
I knew Ernie Harvey, showman at Carter's Farm, who showed cattle at shows on behalf of Mr Carter. Ernie lived in a lobby over the lorry cab. I used to go around the farms, where Mr. Harvey worked, preparing animals for shows which took me as far as

1 This was the old Army & Navy pub, which was where Hadler's motorcycle shop is.

Rutland, Kent, Surrey, Essex and Bucks. When we went to shows in the cattle lorry (owned by a Mr.Sid Macer from Billericay) I used to sleep in the lorry over the cab. This happened only if the shows were quite a long way away; then we travelled the day before the show so the cattle could have a night's rest before the actual show day. I found this quite exciting.

Gardiner's Farm was very much part of the lives of those who grew up nearby. Una Matthews said, "I can still remember the sound of the threshing machine at the farm".

The houses in Winchelsea Drive were built on fields formerly part of Gardiner's farm around 1937. Subsequently the Marconi Social Club with its extensive playing fields was also built on Gardiner's land. Rumours abound that this building will be replaced by housing development when the lease expires.

Manor Farm, Maldon Road then Sandford Road.

The original Manor Farmhouse was behind the Village Hall in the centre of Gt.Baddow village on Maldon Road, where a small parade of shops now stands. It had been owned by the well-respected Tabor family for many years. It was part of a larger land holding in Gt.Baddow. (Photo 6-2 shows old Manor Farm).

The old farmhouse was pulled down about 1955-6 and two new farm cottages were built in 1975 and 1977 near the corner of Maldon Road and Longmead Avenue. These are still part of Manor Farm today.

Numbers 1 to 6 Ebenezer Cottages, in Baddow Road opposite the Blue Lion, built around 1850 were also part of Manor Farm at one time, though they were sold about 1962. This was when the new farmhouse in Sandford Road was built. Manor Farm had been farmed by Alfred Carter, then by his two sons for about seventy or eighty years, when Richard Carter the current owner began renting it in 1958. Richard:

> When I took over Manor Farm the cows had all been sold, and it was purely an arable farm. The year I took it over the potatoes had been flooded, and some of the corn was un-harvested. Baddow Meads had already been ploughed up, but it was in a very poor state, following the dramatic flood of 1958.
>
> The Carter family eventually bought the farm in 1972. Like Meadgate Farm, Manor Farm was affected by the building of the bypass in the 1960s. When the road came through, all the old farm buildings, including the dairies, the tractor sheds and the Dutch barn were pulled down. The development took place both there, and on any of the Manor farmland that was south of the Baddow by-pass. Any land north of the by-pass I continue to farm today.
>
> Manor Farm is situated along the edge of the Chelmer and the Blackwater canal. I can remember barges going up and down to Brown's timber yard, in Chelmsford, loaded up with timber. I can remember the barges going through the locks on the way.

Richard Carter told us the Carters still farm Manor Farm and most people will be familiar with their farm shop on Maldon Road, where a range of products, plants and garden furniture is sold. Janet Chilvers remembers working there many years ago, when they were only allowed to sell their own produce from what was a simple hut. She described the coach loads from the East End who came strawberry picking after a day in Maldon, when the best fruit had already gone!

Richard reminisced about a few Gt.Baddow characters:

> When I started I continued to employ David Ambrose, who was a member of the Ambrose family, an old Baddow family who had lived here many years. His father lived in Ebenezer Terrace, and was a very old man when I first knew him, with a big white beard looking rather like Father Christmas. David worked for me until he retired. His son, Henry, had also worked for the family for many years before that.
>
> One of our neighbours at the old Manor farm was Reg Spalding, and he was a character in his own right. He attended my grandfather's funeral on his tractor, because his car wasn't available.
>
> One of the old maids I knew was Mary Frost, who worked for me for many years, off and on. She sorted or picked potatoes up out of the fields. Latterly she lived in a caravan just down from the farmhouse here in Sandford Road. She was a very hard working lady of Irish descent and a bit of a character. She used to go shopping regularly with an old pram, and put anything she wanted into it and push it around the village. Mary Frost had various men friends that used to come and work for us. They either lived in the old blockhouse, which is behind the farm buildings here, or slept rough in the fields, or in a shed and did casual work for us.

Ruth Brooker added a little more about Mary Frost:

> She was probably only in her forties, but I don't know for sure. She used to dye her hair an auburn colour. In those days people didn't dye their hair much, just put a little lipstick on. She pushed an old bike with all sorts of things on the back of it. Loads of shopping and things like that. She used to wear a big old mac, tied round with a piece of string, old trousers. She was quite a character in Baddow, and she was nice to speak to. She cycled all the way from Sandford Road to get her papers and things like that from the shop where I worked.

Before the Carters' involvement James Duffield had farmed Manor Farm. Then it was farmed by Frank Freeman, a rich dealer, who had started from nothing. Frank Freeman also farmed Potash Farm in Sandon. There were about fourteen men working here at Manor Farm. The head horseman was Mr Hills, who lived in The Chase. Mr Freeman was a big dealer and always had a lot of bullocks and sheep. Frank Spooner was the foreman; he was known as 'Duck Spooner' as he reared so many Aylesbury ducks. The farm was owned by Mr. James Tabor of The Lawn, Rochford. When the farm was let the tenant had to employ and lodge an old retainer called Dawdy (George) Everett who looked after the bullocks. He couldn't read or write but he used the old tally stick on which he made cuts for each five animals thus ⊔╫ as they passed him, and he never made a mistake.

Lathcoats Farm, Beehive Lane.

Philip Taylor talked of his family's association with the farm:

> My grandfather, Lawrence Taylor, came to the farm in the early 1900s. (Photo 6-3). I have very few memories of him, as he died when I was five. Some of the ladies who still work on the farm knew him very well. Apparently he was a bit stricter than I am! I think when he came here it was much more of a mixed farm, with livestock. He kept that going and bred pigs. (Photo 6-4 shows Essex Saddlebacks). He gradually planted up the orchards over the years.
>
> When my father took over he bought land in Rignalls Lane and at East Hanningfield. Where we are now around Lathcoats Farm it's pretty much the same. Although there is a small piece that was compulsory purchased from us when they built Tile Kiln estate.

My father stayed on the farm during the war. We have some very interesting photographs that were taken by the government at the time, as a way of showing people that the country wasn't starving. (Photo 6-5 shows an apple spraying machine and 6-6 shows a slight apple overload).

The farm is now run by Philip's brother, who grows the fruit, and Philip who sells it. He describes the farm as a "nice little island" in its relatively urban setting. The car park for PYO (pick your own) is in a 70 or 80 year old orchard with big old Bramley trees. They sell some 40 varieties of apple, including the Essex apple D'Arcy Spice; they "rent out" apple trees and hold occasional farmers' markets. Philip recalled that between the war and the 1960s British fruit growing had a bit of a golden era. There used to be loads of fruit farms in the area - Galleywood, Gt.Baddow, Danbury - but the first problems arose in the 1970's with competition from French Golden Delicious. The rise in supermarkets was the next problem and now it looks as if China is to enter the market with cheap exports of apples. The recently refurbished farm shop sells a wide range of local produce - meat, cakes, pickles, fruit and vegetables. It attracts increasing numbers of customers who wish to encourage local shops and who worry about the supermarkets' monopoly.

Abercorn Nurseries, Beehive Lane.

Although not strictly a farm, the nursery is another important producer for the village. Begun on a three acre open field by Donald and Ethel Bliss in the 1960s, the nursery is now run by their grandson David Norman. They employ the equivalent, in man-hours, to twelve to fourteen full-time staff and there is now a manager in charge:

David: "In the early days I remember coming home and finding the house covered with cuttings of geraniums and fuschias, in the conservatory, the kitchen, anywhere there was spare space. They sold seedlings of bedding plants direct to the public. They used a sterilising furnace and made up their own mix of compost, which was used for containerised shrubs, and sold to customers.

Now the nursery has modern aluminium and steel greenhouses, a revamped retail area and plants growing under a multi-span canopy".

Other Farms

Many other farms are mentioned in people's reminiscences:

Whitehouse Farm at the bottom of Baddow Road was farmed by Elijah Sorrell.

Up Beehive Lane was Sawkins Farm, farmed by Natty Poole.

Further up was Galley Farm, farmed by Billy Wiffen. Lathwates (presumably Lathcoat's) also up Beehive Lane was farmed by Harry Hasler prior to the Taylors.

Seabright's estate belonged to Baddow House and included Gt. and Lt. Seabrights farms, also Duffields, Brook, Whistocks and Hollywood. The first two are farmed by the Carter Brothers; the next two by Messrs Duffield and Moors, and Mutton Hall or Hollywood up Galleywood Rd by Messrs C & R Finch.

Great & Little Seabrights was farmed by Henry Carter, (called Billy Goat from his beard). (Photo 6-7 shows Great Seabrights and photo 6-8 shows the barn now converted into a restaurant).

Brook Farm was farmed by Messrs Duffet and Moore from Yorkshire.

Duffield and Day's Farm farmed by Mr.Cornell.

Great Mascalls was farmed by C & R Finch.

Little Mascalls was farmed by Samuel Stacey.

Great Sir Hughes was farmed by William Prior Johnson. (Photo 6-9 shows the new and photo 6-10 the old building).

Little Sir Hughes by Charles Ratcliff. (Photo 6-11).
Baddow Hall Farm by Smiths from Sandford Mill.

It is understood that later on Great & Little Mascalls in West Hanningfield Road, Duffields Farm along Vicarage Lane, Gt. & Little Seabrights, and Hollywood Farm in Galleywood Road were all owned by old Mr Carter.

Former farmhouses and old barns can still be seen dotted around, if you know where to look. The current Russell's restaurant is within a 14/15th century grade 2 listed Essex barn. The restaurant has been renovated but retains many of the architectural features of the old barn. During the mid 20th century the thatched roof was replaced by a corrugated iron covering (possibly to avoid potential fire damage during the war) and was used to store plumbers items, building material, timber etc for Mr Russell and his successors.

Reg Spalding wrote about this barn in his notebook. He says by the left side is an entrance to the village Tithe Barn. An old man, John Gunn, whose grandfather or great grandfather used to be the Tithing Man, lives in it. On one side of the entrance are bundles of tithing sticks. When a farmer had cut his corn or hay he (the farmer) had to stand his corn up in 'traves'[2] and his hay in 'cocks' and he could not cart any away until the Tithing man had come to the field with his sticks. He could start anywhere in the field to put a stick into a trave or cock, but once he had started he had to keep on and select every tenth one (for the church). This was to prevent the farmer making the tenth one smaller each time. The corn or hay selected by this method was stored in the Tithing Barn. Some bundles of tithing were still in the barn when Reg wrote the entry. This practice was stopped by the Tithe Act of 1835. To save trouble many of the parsons used to try and guess the size of the crop and bargain with the farmers.

Also in Bell Street is Mary Brittern Cottage. Former owners believe this was a farmhouse, probably in the 18th century.

Work on the Farm

Having grown up near farms, or been employed on them, many of our interviewees had clear memories of activities on the farm. Reg Spalding, born in 1894, writes in his farming diary about many of these tasks:

Land Draining

Land draining was a very skilled job. A trench about one foot wide and from 24 to 30 inches deep was dug. Along the bottom of the trench 2 inch or 3 inch porous pipes were laid end to end. Before pipes were made they used what was known as the Book and Tile drain. The book part looked like this:

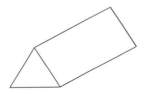

---

2 Trave is an obsolete word, and the Shorter Oxford Dictionary defines it as an enclosure of bars in which a restive horse was held while it was shod. The sense of the paragraph above suggests corn in bales or sheaves, but obviously the amounts were variable, allowing for some cheating by farmers.

The tile was an ordinary flat roofing tile. They were laid along the bottom of the trench and the book tile was laid on top of them thus:
The drains were always laid across the slope, not with it.

High side of field

These drains were usually 2 rods (33 feet) apart

Low side of field

Ditch

At the lowest end 4 inch pipes about 3 feet away from the ditch and parallel to it were laid, and at intervals it was led into the ditch. One theory was that the deeper the drains the further they could be apart.

Old Mr Petchey gave me a home made level but it became worm eaten and fell to pieces. It was a flat board about 1 foot long and 8 inches broad. About one and a half inches from each end a hole was bored. Then pieces of nut wood thus Y Y of equal length were put in. Along these a big straight piece of hollow cow mumble[3] was tied. This was floated on a bowl of water and the hollow peeped through.
Another way to get levels was to tie a medicine bottle nearly filled with water flat along a gun barrel. If you were a bit richer you could buy a real spirit level.

Ploughing

When I was young a lot of ploughing was done by steam engines, one on each side of the field. Under each engine was a big reel around which was wound a long wire rope. Attached to these ropes was either a 7-furrow plough or a very heavy cultivator; these were pulled from one side of the field to the other, with one engine pulling with the other unwinding.
The operators started at about 4 a.m. in the summer and worked until dark. There was an engine driver on each engine and a man sitting on the plough to steer it.
The farmer found the coal and the water. A man was kept very busy filling both engines with water and then carting coal to them as they moved across the field. Best hard steam coal was used which cost 17s-6d per ton (= 87.5p) at the nearest railway station. It made a very hard day for all, but it made a very good job of the field, especially when using the cultivator. When the ground was hard one could hear the land bursting up in great clods. It was a very hard and rough job for the operators, some of whom lived miles away. They either used to walk to the job, or slept rough. The engine drivers had to get up extra early to get steam up. Now tractors do all this work.

---

3 The term 'mumble' is puzzling. The dictionary definition does not help. One assumption is that some inner part of a cow such as a tube could be used to simulate the glass tube in a spirit level. An alternative suggestion is that mumble was cow parsley, used by small boys as a peashooter. The hollow tube could conceivably be made to hold liquid and the bubble necessary for a makeshift spirit level.

Turning the Muck

The old farmers had the bullock yards cleaned out early in the summer. It was carted out onto big heaps, and they were consolidated by the loads being carted over with the help of a 'trace horse'. The farmer hid several things on the ground under the heap, such as marked ploughshares. In the autumn a man would contract to turn the whole heap for an agreed sum. The farmer would not pay out until all the hidden items had been returned to him.

Haymaking

At Meadgate we used to make a lot of hay, around 70 acres. By then we had increased our area quite a lot as many people gave up and we either bought or hired land, and by 1934 we had about 120 acres around Gt.Baddow + 20 more at West Hanningfield. I used to make hay for all the big houses in Baddow. Unfortunately hay prices collapsed beside the corn and potatoes. Hay which pre 1914 we used to sell in Chelmsford at about £4-10s-0d (£4-50) per ton went as low as 30s-0d (£1-50) delivered, and potatoes were 25s-0d (£1-25) per ton wholesale. This meant that I had to work very long hours, as it all had to be done by horses.

One of the best labour-saving machines was a Massey Harris hay loader. This was drawn over a row of hay made by a side delivery rake. To get a fluent flow, three good horses were used, and the man at the back of the wagon had a hard time. I used to love that position and if I had a good man (sometimes a land girl who often was even better) I could put on a very big load, nearly twice as much as could be pitched by hand unless they had been well-made haycocks. If all went well it only took one hour.

With the first rakes the horsemen had to walk behind and pull a handle each time to empty it. When rakes were invented with seats on them so that the men could ride, the foreman at the Manor Farm took them off for fear they made the men lazy!

The old people told me that before mowers were invented they used to start scything grass at 3 am. They cut till 8 am, then they went home and did other jobs. They came back at 7 pm and cut until 10 pm. They were paid 2s-6d (12.5p) per acre. In the daytime women with rakes turned the cut grass. The next day they turned it all again and then heaped it. Later on the men made it into cocks where it stood for a few days till it was ready to cart. The ladies wore cotton dresses and hoods.

Harvesting

Harvest time was of course the big event in the farmer's year, and a good chance to swell the meat rations. The horse-drawn reapers cut the cereal crop starting at the outside of the field and moving in ever decreasing circles. Youths waited in the centre of the field with their terriers to catch rabbits and mice.

Threshing

We get some idea of how labour intensive farm work was from his description of threshing, where we also read of the gradually improving machinery:

When I was a boy threshing was mainly done by traction engines, but some people still used the portable engines. Sometimes it could take 3 to 4 hours to pull the latter from farm to farm. When the machine had finished at a farm the farmer took the threshing drum to the next farm, then the portable engine.

With the traction engines the barn-work[4] was drawn and put into position at the stack and then the driver positioned his engine exactly in the right place so that the belt was exactly in line with the pulley on the barn-work. (Photo 6-12).

Then the men on the stack started pitching the sheaves to the feeder on the drum, who cut the strings and fed the sheaves gradually into the beaters.

A sacker stood at the back, and as the sacks filled he tied them up and loaded them onto a cart, which was backed up ready to receive them. Around 1900 all the corn was taken into the barns and put through a 'dressing machine', but later on the barn-works were improved and a very good sample came through which did not need dressing.

Two men with long straps stood at the back to take the straw to the stack. Later on they invented a trusser which tied the straw into trusses with binding twine, which was much better. The worst job was handling the short pieces of straw and chaff, which a lad used to fill into big bags; that was a very dirty and dusty job. It took at least twelve men to run a machine efficiently.

We used to get 1s-0d per quarter hundredweight for threshed oats, 1s-4d for barley and 1s-8d for wheat.

Les Sparrow, born some 25 years later, describes a similar scene:

Once a year they use to thresh the corn that was brought in to the stacks in the yard. You knew when it was about to happen because a huge stack of Welsh steam coal used to appear in the yard, brought into the yard by horse and cart. Three days later the threshing tackle with the traction engine was set up in the yard next to the stacks. On the morning of the threshing all the windows in the house were closed early to keep out the smoke and the dust and the husks. The threshing used to go on all morning; it was most enjoyable as a child. There were two people on top of the stack feeding in the sheaves into the thresher, with 'sack men' or 'bag men' as they called them at the bottom filling them up, tying them off, taking away the full sacks and tying a new one on. Everyone who was working in the stack-yard had their trousers tied just below the knee with cord to stop rats and mice 'interfering with the wedding tackle'. That event was most enjoyable.

The young Florence Hardwick remembered the fun, saying, "In the summer, when they cut the corn, we used to go into the fields and ride on the old binders, a machine that had flails that went round and round". (No Health and Safety rules in those days!).

Pea Picking

Janet Chilvers spoke about pea picking:

In my teens my dad and I went pea picking on the Boreham Road. We got paid very little. My dad made me get up at four or five in the morning because the peas were damp then and weighed heavier.

Dora Norrington and her friends got into trouble for picking peas, as she explained:

A crowd of us went up to Curry's fields once. We had a neighbour's baby. They said 'you stop with the baby while we go and get the peas'. They thought the pea pickers had been, and they could continue the work, but they hadn't, the peas had not been picked. All the kids were picking peas when Mr Curry came out. There was awful trouble over that. The parents were told. Mr Curry said, 'I thought that you would know better, they're not ready to be picked yet'. Thank goodness I was holding the pram the other side of the stile.

---

4 From the context "barn-work" must be the threshing machine itself, taking stalks of cereal in the top and spewing out grains of corn, oats or barley into 1 set of bags, and straw from the back. A pulley on one side picked up the motive power via a belt driven from the traction engine. It was a highly dangerous system.

Sale of Farm Produce

Sadie Gemmell explained:

> Samples of the corn were taken to the Chelmsford Corn Exchange. If the merchants liked the samples they would buy the grain. They said, "I'll buy your grain at such and such a price". If you said yes they would come and get it and take it away in lorries. Nothing was ever signed.
>
> The milk was sold to a dairy on a yearly agreement, for a set price. Some got more and some got less for it. If the milk rounds people liked your milk they paid more for it. Originally the milk was taken in churns to a depot in Chelmsford or to the railway station to London. Sometimes they had a ride on the milk lorry, or before that on a horse drawn cart.
>
> The ten gallon churns were wheeled onto the cart. The milk was cooled by taking it into the dairy and run over a water cooler. Lovely milk!

Reg Spalding: A little later on things started to improve in Agriculture. A bounty was put on wheat, at roughly the difference between the market price and what was estimated to be an economic price. Also a Milk Marketing Board was set up. This board did all negotiations as to price and collected the money so there were no bad debts.

Livestock

Everyone knows what a large part horses played in people's lives in the past. Reg Spalding recalled that farm horses were very intelligent and would answer to a call thus: "Who See" to the right and "Cobbey Wee" to the left. One could go all day hoeing without reins.

He continued:

> When I was young every lad on the land seemed to want to be a 'hoss man' i.e. a horseman. It was the happiest day of one's life when one took over a pair of horses. Horsemen thought more of their horses than anything else. All the harness was kept perfectly oiled and brasses polished, and when they had to go carting on the road they would start at 3 a.m. to groom their horses and clean everything up. The farmer used to ration hay and corn but the men would always try and steal a little extra for their particular pair.
>
> The story goes that a man applied for the job of a horseman. The farmer asked him if he would steal for his horses. He replied, "of course not". The farmer said, "well if you won't you're no good to me".
>
> There was always a row when the farmer sold the best horses to go for town work and replaced them with colts.
>
> There were some very good horsemen who could plough with unerring straightness and drill perfectly. One of the best that I can remember was a man named Hills who lived up The Chase in Great Baddow and worked on the Manor Farm.
>
> Horsemen used to wear peaked caps and leather collars covered with celluloid coloured with black and red stripes.

Les Sparrow has fond childhood memories of the horses at Well House Farm:

> We had two horses only, big shires or Suffolk Punches I suppose. They were called Blossom and Prince. I think that's what the names were on the horse brasses on the

door. The two horses were used for general farm work. Apart from the land with the house Granddad hired an orchard in what is now Sandon School playing fields, down towards Ladywell Grove. They had a big orchard there, about 3 to 4 acres.

Once a year the apples were picked from the orchard, and when it was time for harvesting the apples he hitched up the horses to the cart, put barrels onto the wagon, and if I was around he would take me with him if it was a fine day. I would be up on the platform on the front of the wagon and we would go up to the field. There they would un-hitch the horses out of the shafts and let them loose in the field. The barrels would be unloaded and filled with apples. Meanwhile, I would be playing and the horses had nothing better to do than eat fallen apples, which they shouldn't have done of course. Once the barrels full of apples had been loaded into the dray, I would be put back on top on the platform; Granddad would turn the cart around and back we would come through the village until we came to Baddow brewery to unload the apples to make into cider. I would be tied onto the platform, the reins would be tied on the rail, Granddad would slap the horses and away they would go, on their own back home, with nobody bar me (aged 4) in charge until we got to White Horse corner. There was always someone there to meet the horses and negotiate them round the corner and take them back onto the farm.

Having got them back onto the farm in the village they would be un-harnessed and allowed a drink in the pond. This pond had a big fence coming down from the house into the pond, and this fence stopped the horses and other cattle going into the house garden. Meanwhile they could have a drink in the other part, walking parallel to the fence.

I was always precluded from getting on the horses and told I wasn't allowed on the backs of the horses. Being a boy I disregarded this sound advice and one day I climbed from the fence onto the back of one of the horses and sat there, proud as Punch. This was fine until the horse bent his head to drink, at which time I slid off his neck into the pond. Luckily Philip saw what happened and apparently he dived, no he didn't dive, he waded into the pond and rescued me, otherwise I might not have been here today.

Bulls are remembered with less affection! Peggy Bradley says:

I can remember a bull being tethered out in the field where we used to try to make our way home from Baddow School. This was when my parents were caretaking at Hampton's on Beehive Lane. One day I couldn't be bothered to walk all the way back. This bull was tethered near a gate that I wanted to get over. I waited for its head to turn in the right direction, and never moved so quickly as I climbed over the gate.

Den Harvey's granddad had two bulls and he added that every one of Carter's farms had a bull. Jesse Pryke explained:

Old man Carter often walked his bull with a ring through its nose through the village, up Galleywood Road past my house and into a field on the right hand side near Hollywood Farm where Dorset Avenue now is. He used to stop at the houses and the children stroked it.

The Farms and Daily Life

No one could fail to realise they lived in a farming community when market day came round. This is what Les Sparrow has to say about it:

Fridays was always Market Day in the town and was known in the village as 'Pancake Day', because all the droves of cattle, as they were driven through the village, used to leave their mark (i.e. the 'pancakes'). Not a pretty sight at eleven o'clock in the morning, especially in the summertime. Most of the main roads had cattle coming through in the morning and you had to make certain your gates were shut. A bullock got into our farm because we had left a gate open, and it created a bit of havoc in the farm. I think one or two of the terrace houses on Baddow Road had their gardens damaged. Some of them didn't have gates so they had to be there to make sure the cattle did not get in. However fences got damaged. Cattle came from Danbury, the Hanningfields and Galleywood to Chelmsford all via Southend Road as we called it then, now the High Street. There were no fences at White Horse corner, so they used to have 3 or 4 drovers there guarding against the animals going up Galleywood Road, Vicarage Lane or Bell Street. It was a bit dicey there unless you had a good lead animal.

Dora Norrington found it all rather frightening:
They used to drive the herds of cows down the road. Often they couldn't control them. Many a time a cow came down the passage and looked in the kitchen window. They had an awful job to get the cows back up the passage. The cows frightened the life out of us. We shot indoors while the drovers got them to go the proper way. The cattle took over the High Street. We were in town one Friday morning and a great herd of cows came and three people were knocked off their bicycles. I can remember being pulled into one of the shops to get out of the way. The drovers weren't very good. They had great sticks to rap the cows on the back.

"I have this picture of all these cattle walking down the main road to Chelmsford market in the morning, then back to Copsey's abattoir in the evening" recalled Rosemary Hill. "When they built houses on Copsey's land where the abattoir had been I didn't fancy the idea of living there, knowing what had gone on there before".

Rosemary remembers a particular drover:
I can remember cattle being driven on the Southend Road, on their way to market. The drover was called 'Tiggy' and we children were frightened of him. His eyes were wild and I think he slept rough. My mother was chatting to him one day and he said he was sorry the children were afraid of him.

There were many benefits to living in a village surrounded by farms, not least the availability of fresh local produce, even during the war. Sadie Gemmell grew up on Great Mascalls farm in West Hanningfield Road. She kept poultry and sold eggs:
The eggs were hatched in an incubator or by broody hens. We picked fruit, which was sold to Fulchers, in Chelmsford. The eggs were sold privately or in Chelmsford market. On Fridays there was a big sale of poultry. Any that were too old to produce eggs her father took for auction.

In her Mother's house in Baddow Road, Dora Norrington (née Boreham) recalls that milk was delivered daily from a farm in Galleywood. The Boreham ladies (mother and daughter) delivered it in churns around the village using a barrow to transport it and quart, pint and gill measures to ladle it out to customers. (Photo 6-13 shows Dora's sister and mother on their rounds in 1913).

Reg Spalding's father had two milk rounds around Chelmsford and also sold butter, cheese, potatoes and cabbages. The milk wasn't always safe. Reg wrote:
When I was five, I was diagnosed with consumption of the lung (TB) caused through drinking (unpasteurised) milk from one cow who later died from the disease. At that time people would pick out the best looking cow and order her milk for their babies.

The Carters also had milk and bread rounds. Some people even grew grapes. In her greenhouse Betty Spalding still has a vine, a cutting of the vine at Hampton Court Palace, planted by Grandfather Fred Spalding.

From Baddow Road (East of the Star pub) you can still see the 10-ft brick support wall for the lean-to greenhouse where Robert Norrington's mother's family Harris Nurseries grew black Homburg grapes, but these were for the London markets! If your house is built on old orchard land you may still have a surviving fruit tree in the garden! Some of the houses in Baddow Road opposite the end of Chelmerton Avenue are built on what used to be a very large orchard belonging to Meadgate Farm.

The Harvest Supper

For many involved with farm work the climax of the year may well have been the harvest supper. Richard Carter has vivid memories of these events. He says:

> As a young boy I remember going to Gt.Baddow Village Hall. My grandfather always hosted a harvest supper, every year for everybody who worked for him. It filled the Village Hall. Various comic turns took place there. It is one of my earliest recollections of village life.

These are memories shared by Les Sparrow:

> I do remember being taken by my Granny when I was about 3 or 4 to one of the barns at the top of the yard. The barn was set out for what must have been the last harvest supper in Great Baddow. The farmers used to come with their families and farm workers. There were straw bales set out all around and 4 big barrels in the middle, presumably containing the local beverage. There were hurricane lamps ready to be lit. Then I was put to bed, so I didn't see any more.

The Good Old Days?

It is difficult not to regret the disappearance of so many of the old farms, but we should not romanticise the life. Most farm workers lived in tied cottages, although as Mrs H Ely tells us, this could be an advantage. "Tied cottages went to farm workers, with the job. My mother's father was a farm worker and there was always a cottage for him and his family to live in".

Florence Hardwick's father was a farm worker and the only way he could improve himself was to move. The houses were always tied to the farm. He was constantly on the move.
Derek Hurrell echoed this. "Farm workers in those days moved about a lot. They got work where they could".

Pay was poor. John Kemp recalls that he was on piecework when threshing for Carters "so the more you did the more you earned".
[Ed: Remember there were 240 old pence or 20 shillings to the pound. Also 12d =1s-0d, equivalent to 5p. Divide old pence by 2.4 to calculate new pence. Thus 15s-0d = 180d =75p. Remember a house could be bought for a few hundred pounds in 1910].

Reg Spalding recorded workers' wages in his journal.

> When father died in 1910 he had four men working on the farm. By a most peculiar coincidence the old horseman's name was Gaul (or Gall), the cowman's name was English and the old oddman's name was French. Their wages were as follows:
>
> The cowman received £1-1-0 per week working 4 am to 5 pm.
> The horseman got 17s-6d per week working 5 am to 5 pm plus three hours on Sunday.
> The dayman got 15s-0d per 6 day week.
> The oddman circa 12s-0d but he was an old man.

Overtime was paid at 3s-0d per hour but both the cowman and horseman must have put in many hours for nothing, as they loved their charges so much. For them it was a seven-day week and nobody had any holidays except Christmas Day. Boxing Day was always occupied in rabbiting, with everyone helping everyone else so that they could have a bit of sport. On Good Friday it was the custom to give the men the afternoon off as long as they attended the three hour service.

Florence Hardwick's father experienced just such conditions. He used to look after the horses. "It was very hard work because he used to start work at 6 o'clock in the morning, and worked until five. In those days, the only holiday he ever had, was Good Friday and Christmas Day".

As a boy in the 1920s Les Sparrow heard the day's work begin nice and early:

Very early in the winter long before daybreak there were people astir in the house, Granddad in particular, and Philip in the barn. We could hear long before daylight the chink of the harness as he fitted it onto the horses ready for the day's work, whatever it might be, and Granddad would be astir in the living room. I didn't see him; I was upstairs still in bed of course. They would be out in the fields very early, so that they were ready to start work at daybreak. They were long hours. If he were working close to home he would come home for some lunch, not a proper dinner, just a snack. If he were working farther afield Grandma would pack him some sandwiches, with cold tea. That would be the last we would see of him until sometimes 8 or 9 at night in the summer, perhaps fourish in the wintertime.

All the horses and carts had lights, oil lights, so that if they came back after dark they could be seen on the road. They weren't likely to get hit by a National Bus, because there weren't any about, but there were other horses and carts about, and they were really tired after a long hard day. How typical this must have been!

Farming Crises

Over the years farming locally has gone through various crises like that of the 1880s. The Spalding notes explain the background:

On retiring from the photographic business my grandfather Fred Spalding had initially tried farming at Lathcoat's Farm in Galleywood, but in the depression of the 1880s he lost all his money and he retired a broken man to Meadgate Farm, Gt. Baddow in 1887.

When I was born in 1884, more than half the farms in Essex were empty. The bad times had started in 1870. 1879 was wet from February to November. Crops were lost, cattle died in the fields, then imports of corn came in from Canada and America. The big landlords could not afford to cultivate the farms they could not let. They put advertisements in newspapers in Scotland offering their farms free of rent for several years. A lot of Scottish and Devonian farmers came to Essex and started with cows and sheep. Their wives and children did most of the work, working all the hours they could. Farming improved, but very slowly. Then the 1914-18 war started and farming became quite prosperous, but in 1921 everything became bad again.

Between 1900 and 1935 the land was mostly farmed (when not in the hands of the owners) by small farmers who gradually started keeping cows, mostly small herds of 20 cows plus one bull. Practically all motive power was by horses, although there were some very good steam ploughs and later on the 'Darby Digger'[5].

---

5 The Darby Digger was a light traction engine designed for ploughing fields, invented by agricultural manufacturers Darby of Wickford. It could cultivate one acre an hour to a maximum depth of 14 inches.

Baddow Meads

Baddow Meads has been essential over the centuries to act as a safety valve for the river Chelmer during the rainy season. The area has also been used for growing hay and for livestock. In his journal Reg Spalding painted a picture of bygone times when the Meads were divided into plots and were 'managed' by an overseer:

> The Baddow Meads were described in old deeds as undivided freehold lands situated on the bed of the old river. There were about 90 plots on the 120 acres. They were called shots or hopes and range from a quarter of an acre to 7 acres. They were managed by a committee of owners, presided over by Mr Henry Marriage of Ayletts, Broomfield. There were about 20 owners.
>
> When I was a boy (presumably 1900-10) the owners were as follows:
> > Messrs W & H Marriage going with Moulsham Mill,
> > James Tabor Rochford going with Manor Farm,
> > The Mildmay family, some belonging to Whitehouse Farm, Moulsham Lodge & Tile Kiln Farm, Galleywood,
> > One plot belonging to Blue House Farm, Widford, belonging to Hylands Estate,
> > Two plots belong to John Coplands,
> > Two plots belonging to Mr Slade of Liverpool,
> > Two plots belonging to Rev Colley,
> > One plot belonging to Mr Golding,
> > Two plots belonging to Baddow Park,
> > Seven plots belonging to St.Mary's church,
> > Four plots belonging to Coplands Gardiner's Farm,
> > Three plots belonging to Meadgate Farm,
> > Eight plots belonging to Dr Bodkin,
> > Three plots belonging to Chaplin's Farm, Galleywood,
> > Five plots belonging to Sawkin's Farm, Beehive Lane.

The strips were at right angles to the riverbank and marked by a post at the river end of the strip. Photo 6-14 shows a sketch of a typical ownership post constructed of metal or stone, about 36 x 4 x 2 inches, bearing with the name of the owner on them. The strips were not fenced off so the animals intermingled. Hence the need for branding, to identify the owner when the animals were split up.

The rules of the meadow committee were as follows:
> Mr Henry Marriage was chairman. Mr.Chaplin & a Mr Savill (of Alfred Savill & Sons) for Mr James Tabor were members.

A Bailiff was appointed 1900-5, a Mr Fred Aldred. He was the overseer, and was allowed to let 6 acres of the after feed to cover for riding round each day to see that the animals were safe and well. He also had 3 acres of feed to let to buy a new gate and lock. He had to brand each animal with a mixture of hot tar and pitch and then turn it out onto the meadow. He was also responsible to see that the owners took their animals off the land by 12 o'clock on Christmas Day. Any left were to be impounded in the Village pound. Eventually Mr Aldred was dismissed and my father was appointed, and when he died I took the job.

When my father died Mr Marriage sent for me:
> a.   To prove that I could ride.
> b.   To give me about two hour's talk on honesty.
> c.   Then he appointed me.

Meadgate Farm had the opening piece on the Meads, so we were allowed to start cutting on July 1st. The rest were allowed on the Meads on July 4th. Each plot was cut out and it was quite a skilled job to drive the horses on the mower to keep the sides straight.[6]

On the last Saturday in August even if everybody had not finished mowing the whole meadow became common to all owners. Each acre entitled the owner to turn out two head of neat stock or one horse.

Welshmen used to walk their cattle from Wales. They would arrive footsore and their cattle would have lost weight. They would hire feed and put their cattle out on the Meads until November Fair (Nov 11th) by which time the cattle would be fit and well. Since 1910 Mr Tabor, who owns the Manor Farm, and myself have bought all the plots between us and now we own about 60 acres each.

Conclusion

It is hard to picture the village as it must have been in the 1920s and 30s, with its farms and fields.
As late as 1969-70 the area above Larkrise School was an open field. (The name was chosen to recall the larks that used to sing there). Now we are seeing renewed pressure on open spaces around the village; even private gardens are being examined by hungry speculators, with the call for more and yet more houses.

Photo 6-1
Meadgate Farm

Photo 6-2   Old Manor Farm

Manor Farm

Water Exit

Photo 6-3
Lathcoat's Farm

Photo 6-4
Essex Saddlebacks

Photo 6-5
Spraying Machine

Photo 6-6
Apple Overload

Photo 6-7
Great Seabrights

Photo 6-8
Seabrights Barn

Photo 6-10
Old Gt. Sir Hughes Farm

Photo 6-9
Gt. Sir Hughes Farm

*Photo 6-11
Little Sir Hughes*

*Photo 6-12
Threshing
Machine*

*Photo 6-13
Mrs & Miss Boreham
Milk 1913*

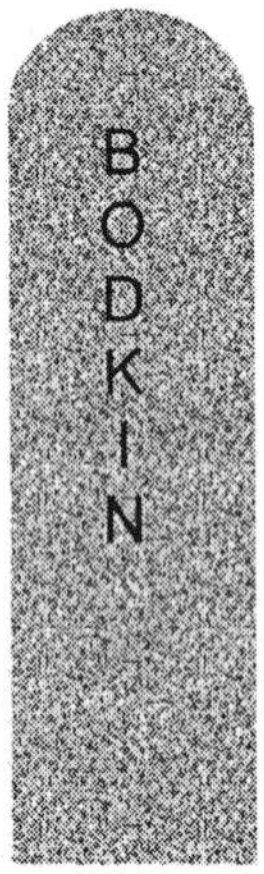

*Photo 6-14
Meads Post*

Chapter 7 - Working in Great Baddow.

Introduction

This chapter looks at the labour activities of village residents. We examine some of the jobs associated with agriculture that have disappeared, and the careers of men and women over sixty years.

Long Lost Jobs

Since Gt. Baddow ceased to be largely a farming community, jobs in agriculture and those connected to it have mostly disappeared. Of course some of these jobs were long gone! In the early 18th century there was a tannery in what is now Tony Pennack's shop in Maldon Road. There is no longer need for a local smithy, where once there were at least two: as we have seen one in Southend Rd, run by Reg Bush's grandfather, the second on the site of the Kingham flats, kept by Les Sparrow's grandfather and then his uncle Dick. (Photo 7-1 shows Reg Bush's father busy at his Sandon forge, doing much the same work as his father before him).

Reg: During the First World War the army had barracks where Maltings estate is now, with several hundred horses stabled near the brewery. My father had the job of dealing with the wildest horses and mules, and some of them were capable of kicking their way out of the average stable. Dad installed special harnesses and a winch for lifting the horse's back leg, so that he could shoe the animal without being kicked.

Les: I remember with affection as a child going in the smithy sometimes on a cold winter's day, when they were shoeing horses and helping to pump the bellows. The smell of the parings and the hooves and the warmth. Grandad always put on an impromptu 'fireworks' on the fifth of November. This was not with proper fireworks, but on the anvil there were various sized holes for punching nail holes through. He used to get saltpetre and something else, he never told us what, plus iron and copper filings. He sprinkled handfuls of these on the forge fire and they used to spark away. He put in the holes a mixture of these chemicals plus a striker pin and banged it with his sledgehammer to make the loudest bang in the village.

There once were a good many wells in the village, but with running water there is no further need for them. Alan Thomson can remember how they used to be sunk. He explained:
A 'barrel' consisting of a metal ring the thickness of a brick, and 5 ft in diameter was loaded into a 5ft-diameter hole in a suitable area of ground. Bricks were added onto the ring, then the hole was deepened and more layers of bricks added on top. The weight of the bricks lowered the barrel. No cement was added between the bricks, hence when complete, water could seep through the gaps into the well from the surrounding ground. I believe a boy was used to climb inside the well to deepen it. This involved digging under the bottom layer of bricks as well as in the centre of the well. I'm not sure whether the bricks were specially shaped to fit the circle, or standard oblong bricks.

There was also a means of lifting the soil out easily, and getting the boy out of the well when it was finished. I think it was also a work of art keeping the brickwork level and stopping it collapsing. The drawing below gives the general idea.

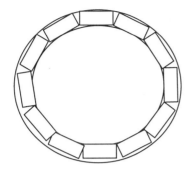
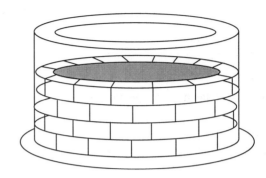

Plan View

Sinking a Well

Gone, too, are the village abattoirs, one behind Copsey's butchers producing beef for local consumption (now an Indian take-away, previously Rothmans Café). Another this side of the Army & Navy, where old horses were made into pet food.

A good many jobs have changed beyond recognition or disappeared with advances in technology, such as electric street lighting. At the end of the 1800's Mrs.H.Ely's father (Colleen Yaxley's grandfather) was the village lamp-lighter. This was when gas lamps were in the village, with incandescent mantles. The gas powered street lamps had to be lit when it got dark, and put out at 11 p.m. One method was to use a stick about ten feet long. The hook on the end was put into a ring on a pivoted arm near the top of the lamp; the ring at one end of the arm turned the light on and the ring at the other end turned the light off. Apparently some lamp-lighters propped their bikes against the lamp-post, climbed onto the saddle and hooked the on/off rings by hand or using a short stick.

Tom Collins the village carrier used to go to Chelmsford twice daily with his horse and cart, hired to take or collect goods, but the role of carrier disappeared long ago with the advent of the car.

Les Sparrow recalls the hard manual work used in maintaining the village:
Pre-war horse dustcarts used to come round, with sloping top and sides, and side shutters that used to open up. The bin men physically lifted every one of the hundreds of bins in the village to tip the contents into the dustcarts. They used to wear an old potato sack with the corner tucked in over their heads, so that none of the dust from the metal dustbins went down the back of the neck or where it shouldn't go. (Photo/sketch 7-2)

Drains were cleared. The road drainage people used to come round with a horse and cart. The workmen had a big long broom handle with a ladle on the end. They used to take the drain covers off and lower these long poles right down and scoop out all the silt at the bottom, which went into a special cart. In the bottom it had holes to allow the water to drain away. The drains were flushed out; they used to put a pail underneath to catch anything worth recycling.

This was done once a month I suppose. We children used to follow them around because sometimes they used to turn up a coin or two. The odd ha'penny might be down there, and if we saw it first we had it, but most of the time they saw it first.

For road repairs we had the steamroller. They used to rip the road up with the anchors (a hefty spike at the back). The County Council had a depot in Bell Street for steamrollers and any other appliances that were working in the village at the time. I had a paper round in those days, and I knew the engine driver. He would lay his fire the night before and I could go on my paper round a bit early and put a match to the fire, and he might give you a ha'penny at the end of the month for doing it. Then later we came along as the steam was getting up. They had road gangs then. If they were putting a sewer in or digging out a drain they would follow up the steamroller when it ripped up the tarmac. They would dig out these trenches by hand. If there were no steamroller they would break through the tarmac themselves. There would be three of them in a gang; one man held big pincers and a wedge. A man with a sledgehammer would be going dumph, dumph, dumph, and they would lift the concrete and give it a blow sideways. They were really good. If they had a road up they used to have a night watchman to safeguard the public and stop them falling into the trenches. In the Maldon Road he would have his watchman's hut just past Crescent Road, where the bus stop is. I can remember going up there especially in the winter, and there would be a coke brazier going. He had a special shovel, which he had polished, and he had his egg and bacon on this shovel. It used to smell lovely. He was responsible for filling the oil lamps, and putting them at intervals down the road.

Much hard work was associated with the Chelmer & Blackwater Canal, now largely used for pleasure craft. Reg Spalding described the canal:

The Chelmer and Blackwater Canal passed through Meadgate farm starting at Heybridge and ending at Chelmsford Wharf. It carried coal, wood and granite from Heybridge, and was started in 1795. Men and horses from Chelmsford, and men and horses from Heybridge operated it. Apparently the two groups of men hated each other. A recognised day's work was for two men to take an empty barge down to Heybridge, known as The Basin, and then pick up a full barge for Chelmsford. This they took up river as far as Paper Mill lock, where the horse was stabled and the men slept rough for the night. The Heybridge men used to sleep in a shed in the left side coming up and the Chelmsford men slept on the opposite side of the river. I have been told that when work was scarce eight men would pull the barge instead of the horse. (Photo 7-3).

When the barge arrived at the wharf, then known as Coate's Wharf, the coal was shovelled into a basket holding 1 cwt (1 hundredweight or 112 pounds) which was pulled up with a crane and a man carried it to the gas works on his shoulders. Coal used to be discharged at Marriage's Moulsham Mill on the Baddow Road. At the mill they had a brick erection into which they put the coal just to make tar.

Corn and oats were taken to Heybridge, then were taken to London by barge. Now the barges only bring up wood for Brown's Wharf, and they are propelled by diesel engines.

Mrs Betty Spalding also mentioned the AGM of the Canal Company, which actually took place in a barge on the canal travelling between Chelmsford and Heybridge. Meadgate Farm was required to supply a horse complete with harness to pull the special barge. Apparently this was a palaver because it was necessary to get the horse ready very early, with sparkling brasswork, then transported to the other side of the canal to get onto the towpath for the outward journey. A day later it had to be transported back from Heybridge. The practice stopped some years ago.

Local Employers Chelmsford

The printing trade changed radically with the advent of computers. Alan Willis talked of his time in the trade in the 40's:

> I got a job as an apprentice in a little printing shop in Tindal Street called A.Driver & Son (they are not there any more). They were general printers, printing everything except newspapers. I was a printer's compositor, which meant handling all the type, setting it up. It was an old fashioned concern. All the type was laid in trays, A, B, C etc and you had to hold a stick in your left hand and pick up the different pieces of type and place them on the stick. We laid out a line at a time, or for long items like a magazine, ten or twelve lines at a time. You would lift them all out and place them on a galley. You read back to front and upside down. When I first started the foreman would pick up a letter and say this is the way it goes into your stick. An 'n' looks like a 'u' and vice versa, so you used to get it wrong at the start.
>
> All the village churches produced magazines. There was a lot of postal work. Letterheads for business, cards, catalogues. They did every sort of printing imaginable bar newspapers. They would make books, they had a bookbinding department with half a dozen girls. I started when I was fourteen and worked there until I was eighteen.

Even when he later worked for the Essex Chronicle, new technology kept leading to redundancies.

(Photo 7-4 shows a press in a typical small printing shop).

Apparently many common phrases came from the printing trade:

1. A firm called Cropper made a printing machine capable of causing injury if you lost concentration and did not withdraw your hand quickly when loading paper. Hence you could 'come a cropper'.
2. Minding your p's and q's is possibly connected with printing. Another suggestion was that p's and q's referred to pints and quarts causing drunkenness in public houses.
3. Letters were kept in two cases, one above the other. Capitals were kept in the upper case, and non-capital letters in the lower case. Hence Upper case and Lower case.

In Chelmsford there were a good many, mainly engineering, firms where local residents spoke of being employed - Crompton's, Christies, Hoffmans, Marconi's being the major employers. Janet Chilvers told us that these firms weren't allowed to take each other's staff. You had to leave one place and be out of work for a while before you could move on. Staff was very valuable. Kathleen Steven's father was a draughtsman at Cromptons where he used waxed linen as drawing paper. When the drawings were finished with, Kathleen's mother would wash away the wax and cut the material into hankies!

At one time it seemed that every other person worked for Marconi's. Harry Clayden is typical. He joined Marconis after the forces, beginning in the repair section, then becoming a charge hand at Broomfield. Harry spoke fondly of his time saying:

> You got to know a terrific number of people, you could enjoy good sporting facilities and we even received a company magazine. At that time Marconi's built the EV 16 TV consoles. We built the televisions from scratch. During my thirty odd years of service, I moved to various sites, ending up as supervisor of contract services at Basildon.

Una Matthew's father Aubrey Hockley was a Marconi employee and remembered seeing Marconi himself walk through the New Street factory. (Photo 7-5 is an aerial view of the Research site)

Reg Bush and Derek Hurrell worked for another big employer of local people, the County Council. In the mid 40's Rosemary Hill worked as secretary to Sir Kenneth Cowan, the County Medical Officer. That period leading up to the start of the NHS in 1947 was a busy time.

Les Sparrow worked in the Chelmsford Rural District Offices in Waterloo Lane. He explained:

> I was appointed junior rating clerk under Mr J. Bales, who was a Rate Collector, and I had a salary of ten shillings a week, less stoppages, payable monthly. That job involved writing out details of every property in the Chelmsford rural district, which comprises twenty seven parishes, issuing demand notes etc. Also we attended as poll clerks at the local elections, compiling registers of electors.

Tony Horsnell was involved in the family building firm. He told us:
> After service in the RAF I joined my father's building business at Galleywood. He was a hard parent and a hard employer. Our work was mainly on old buildings but we built some houses as well. My father also bought properties, including about twelve houses in Roman Road, Chelmsford, where I now live. They then cost about £100 each. We had about seventeen employees who covered all aspects of building work. Each employee owned his own tools. When my father retired I took over the business (though father would look in nearly every morning) and I ran it for some twenty years, passing it on to my son-in-law. We got our raw materials from Browns or Sadds and nearly all the work was local.

Many people spoke of serving an apprenticeship. Tom Steggles, working for Chelmsford Corporation, served a five year apprenticeship, through doing evening classes at Market Road studying gas fitting to City & Guilds level. After the war Alan Willis was obliged to return to the printing firm where he had worked before army service in World War Two, since he was a 'bound apprentice'. He was 'obliged', therefore bound to serve out the rest of his apprenticeship.

Local Employers: Gt.Baddow

Local builder Laurie Russell was another supplier of building material, operating from Russell's barn and the shop that is now a delicatessen in Bell Street. The barn dates back to 1372. (Photo 7-6 shows the Barn rejuvenated as Russell's Restaurant).

Tony Pennack the undertaker is the third generation of the business that began life as builders and carpenters, with funerals as a sideline. As the village has grown, so the funerals have taken over completely. Tony Pennack's grandfather began his business at a time when Una Matthew's grandfather, Henry Hockley, was running an undertakers from the back of the Carpenter's Arms pub. (Hence the name - the carpenter worked in wood, making coffins and furniture for a living, and running the pub in his spare time). Tony Pennack's son will take the business to a fourth generation. (Photo 7-7).

Within the village there were firms that offered employment: Munnions were coach builders who operated in the industrial estate, off Church Street. Munnions made fire-engines on this site. (Photo 7-8). The office of Essex Radiators, in the green shed, was the headquarters of the fire brigade before it moved to Longmead Avenue.

Baddow Brewery, which closed in 1930, had been a steady employer of local men for eighty years or more. Les Sparrow can just remember, as a boy, seeing their horses and drays with the beer. Photo 3-7 in chapter 3 shows the Brewery and photo 7-9 shows a cottage in Galleywood Road (formerly 2 cottages) believed to have been let to brewery employees.

John Jackson was the third generation to own and manage a garage on Church Street, which employed thirteen people at one time. After World War Two there was about a month's waiting list for major overhauls at Jackson's garage. (Photo 7-10 is their pre-war recovery vehicle). They served quite a big area, to the far side of Chelmsford and out to Maldon, but the family gave up the garage in 1969 when further expansion proved impossible, partly as a result of the Baddow bypass removing the passing trade. John and his son went on to establish a coach business in Bicknacre which continues to create local employment around that village. They have fifteen coaches, five smaller ones for school contracts and ten full size for continental trips to Spain, Switzerland, Germany etc.

In Beehive Lane were two gravel workings: on the left going down, behind the terraced houses, was a pit started by Dora Norrington's uncle Mr Robert Jackson; on the right was Snow's gravel pit, now a light industrial site. Material from the pit was used in the building of the Marconi New Street factory. For a long time after it closed in the 1930's the rail track still ran down the side of the pit, and the gadget used to haul the gravel up remained. (Photo 7-11).

Jesse Pryke senior and his son Jesse (now semi-retired) ran a building firm, and it is possibly thanks to them (and Gavin Suttle) that Baddow House and Baddow Court did not follow the fate of so many other big houses in the village - demolition! (Photo 7-12 shows Baddow House converted into luxury apartments).

Jesse junior was involved with another village landmark. He helped build the base for the Marconi mast when it was moved from Canewdon after the war. It had formed part of the Home Radar chain in World War Two. (Photo 7-13).

Jesse also helped to build an extra Marconi factory building on the Research site, used to mass-produce radios. About this time he witnessed early experiments into colour TV with a pretty girl being filmed outside a laboratory. Of course this last episode was after World War Two, when the Marconi Research Labs had settled down to more agreeable tasks.

Tradesmen

Many men in the village were self-employed as tradesmen - painters, decorators, and plumbers. Derek Hurrell's grandfather Fred, despite having lost an eye as a young man in an accident, was a 'marvellous painter and decorator'. Derek recalled:

> He lay on his back painting a ceiling in one of the big houses for about three months one year. A bicycle was one of his main assets and he used to cycle to Burnham and places like that for work. He saw no fear and used to get up on a ladder to repair the holes in the church steeple. Boys with their small guns had fired pellets into the lead.

Den Harvey spent a lot of his working life as a plumber. He described his worst incident:

> Miss Potter, my old school teacher, lived on her own in Vicarage Lane. I was only a young man and she wanted a new boiler in her kitchen. It was a solid fuel anthracite boiler, which I fitted. I tested it fine, no problem. The next day a lady, who lived opposite her house, went over the road and found the dear old soul dead in the kitchen. I hadn't even been paid for the job. My first fears were 'anthracite; was the flu leaking?' I had checked the flu with smoke testing bombs to make sure it was fine but anthracite fumes were dodgy things. My first thought was, 'my God, have I killed her?' In fact I had done nothing wrong and her brother subsequently paid me. It transpired that she had died from a heart attack.

Women's Work

Apart from serving in shops, women often had to make money as best they could. In the 1940s Janet Chilver's gran, who was widowed and needed the extra cash, took in lodgers. She also took in washing at 2d a sheet. There was no electricity or piped hot water, so it meant washing in a big old copper, (photo 7-14) then putting it through a mangle outside and finally ironing it.

Women often worked in domestic service. H.Ely wrote that she would have liked to have been a schoolteacher, but in 1899 there wasn't even a High School to provide higher education. "I think most girls had to go into domestic service in those days," she said.

Of course, once married, running a home was a full time job. Harry Clayden explained:
> My mother had three boys and my father to look after. She was marvellous. In those days boys didn't have anything to do with running the house. They helped their dad but didn't do much inside to help their mum.

Jim Hurrell's mother started work at fourteen as a maid at Clumber Park, and ended up at Luxfields in Vicarage Lane (now demolished) in the home of Major and the Hon. Mrs Inchbourne, daughter of Lord Lucan. Major Inchbourne was a director of Walker & Hill's firm and when Mrs Hurrell left to marry he gave her a lovely cutlery set as a present. (Photo 7-15 shows Luxfields in 1905).

Conditions of Service

It's fascinating to hear how little people earned and how they managed to survive. H.Ely's husband was a skilled joiner and in the early 1900's he earned 7½ d (3p) an hour, so his weekly wage was 37s-6d. (£1-87½ p). His work started at 6.00 am, with half an hour for breakfast, one hour for dinner, finishing at 5.30 pm. In 1926, when Robert Norrington began work in the Co-op gent's clothiers, he earned 8s-9½d (=44p) a week. In 1937 Tom Steggles, a gas fitter, earned £2-18-9d (=£2.94) a week. A little later, possibly in the early 1960s, Kathleen Steven's husband earned £10 a week as a skilled engineer at Marconi's. The annual salary at Marconi's for a qualified engineer in his mid twenties in 1963 was between £800 and £1,000.

Many mentioned the strict discipline and codes of conduct at work. Robert Norrington remembered a reprimand:
> How fashions have changed: men all wore hats in those days. I got told off by my boss Mr Skinner for not wearing a hat. He called me into the office and asked why. I said mine was shabby, so he told me to choose another one, which was charged to me with a 33.3% discount.

Clive Barker's grandfather Sam went to work in a bowler hat because he was the site foreman. He built the front of the old Marconi building in the 1920's.

Careers

Despite the sometimes-strict conditions of service, it is noticeable how long people stayed in their jobs. After an initial period at the printers A.Driver & Son, Alan Willis spent over thirty years working for the Essex Chronicle, which eventually became part of the Daily Mail group. After early work as a cowman, living in Duffield Farm, Don Brown went on to spend twenty seven years working for the Sutton Trust in general building maintenance. Harry Clayden served thirty three years from 1946 to 1979 at Marconi's.

Other residents had far more itchy feet! John Kemp began work at Carter's, the bakers, then went on to their farm working the threshing tackle. He then became a miner in Kent for five years. Next he opened a greengrocers, before moving on to Wallace's potato merchants at 100, Beehive Lane. After a brief time as a car salesman, he ran Russell's DIY in the village. There followed spells as a humper driver on the lorries and a painter and decorator and finally he opened a sports shop in Chelmsford, which he decided thirty years later was probably a successful move! All Sports in Chelmsford is still flourishing, run by John's two sons.

Bert Collis had an equally varied career and it is fascinating to see how one job led to another. His father got him his first job on the Essex River Board because of his interest in maps and drawing. When he could progress no further without taking Civil Engineering exams, he decided to sit the exams for entry to the police force. Preparing for the education paper, he read a book on scientific criminal investigation and wrote an essay on finger printing. He failed the exam but was offered a job as a civilian in the fingerprint department. While there he could not read some notes he'd previously made, so he taught himself italic writing. This led to a better paid job as deputy registrar of Births, Deaths & Marriages, where good hand writing was essential! Fed up with the bureaucracy, he finally moved into teaching and teacher training. A chance purchase of a glass engraving tool from a Green Shield Catalogue led to an enduring interest as an engraver, bringing further work making decorative glass and as a speaker on the subject.

Modern Jobs

Whilst there are still some jobs in local shops and businesses, most wage-earners work in Chelmsford in the service sector or commute to London and other towns. Sadly the big Chelmsford engineering firms have gone and Marconi's is constantly reducing its work force. But interesting new jobs do arise, illustrating modern ways of working. Philip Taylor's wife works three days a week for the Woodland Trust, aided by personal computers, doing two days in her office at home and one day at the head office in Grantham. She runs the Phenology project, collating data about when the first buds burst on oak trees, when the first migrant birds appear and disappear etc so that a track can be kept of the effects of climate change.

This relatively easy working environment, using a desktop personal computer in the home, compares with harsher conditions in days gone by. Incidentally, when Clive Barker's uncle John helped put in the first computer at Hoffmans, it took up a whole room! Later on, in the mid 60s, Marconi Research developed the Myriad real time computer to control radar systems etc. Myriad 1 was the size of a large desk with a 4k by 24 bit ferrite memory, which was a three feet cube, many thousands of times larger than current memories.
Reading of such advances, one wonders what changes will affect the world of work in years to come.

Children's Aspirations

We asked selected nine and ten year old children at Larkrise and Baddow Hall schools what jobs they aspired to and received some interesting answers.

Stephen said: "I want to join the RAF but I'm not sure whether I shall be a display pilot or a different pilot. I shall probably be a display pilot because you get loads of money and a big house".

Stephanie: "I would like to be a gymnast, a teacher, or a shopkeeper. My cousin went to different countries, in a hotel, doing the children's disco, face painting and things. I would like to do that as well".

Lauren: "I want to go out to America and be a dolphin trainer. I would also like a shop to sell fashion clothes".

Alex: "I want to be either a footballer, a tennis player or an artist".

Eleanor said: "I would like to be a choreographer. I want to go to Los Angeles and teach Pop stars how to dance".

Clark's plans were: "I want to be a motor bike mechanic. I know quite a lot about motor bikes. My dad works for a motor bike race team and my mum caters for it. I normally go every other weekend".

Olivia: "When I'm older I want to be an athlete and I want to be in the Olympics. Hurdles and sprints are my favourites".

When asked about plan B when her career in athletics is finished she said: "When I was little I always wanted to be an ice cream seller". I wonder why?

Daniel was quite adventurous, saying, "When I get older I would like to move to Australia and become a crocodile hunter". When asked whether he thought that was a long-term career, he decided it was probably quite a short-term job and he would probably be 'broke' most of the time, so he would probably become an engineer.

Conclusion

Many of our older contributors had little choice of career. They did what they had to do, sometimes unwillingly, but with the sure knowledge that if they did not work they did not eat. Thankfully we have moved away from those hard times and do not need to worry too much about where the next meal is coming from. Also it is good to know that we don't have to worry about the younger generation. Those we interviewed were very sensible and had clear ideas of what they wanted to do, though we noticed the influence of the media on their thinking.

Photo 7-1
Mr. Bush,
Blacksmith,
at work

Picture 7-2   Dustcart

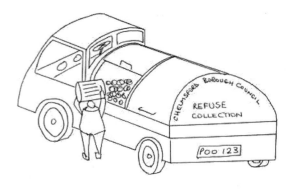

Photo 7-3
Chelmer and
Blackwater Navigation

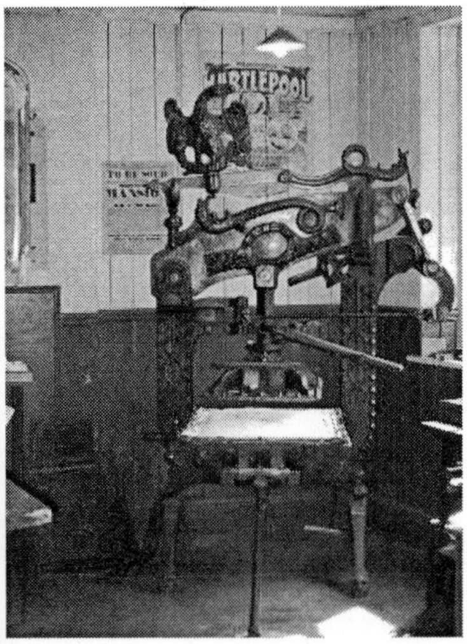

Photo 7-4
Printing Press

Photo 7-5
Baddow Research

Photo 7-6
Russell's Barn

Photo 7-7
Pennacks

Photo 7-8
Munnion's
Fire Engine

Photo 7-10   Jackson's Recovery

Photo 7-9   Brewery Cottages

Photo 7-11
Beehive Lane Quarry

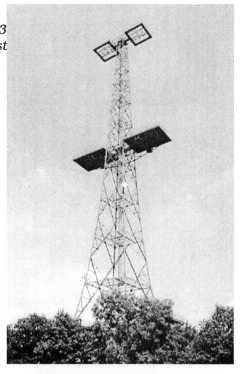

Photo 7-13
Baddow Mast

Photo 7-12
Baddow House Luxury Appartments

Photo 7-14
The Copper
(Water
Heater)

Photo 7-15
Luxfields
1905

Chapter 8 - Leisure

Introduction

This chapter looks at children's games, adult pursuits, sport and holidays, as remembered from fifty to seventy years ago.

Children's games

Older people often speak of the 'simple pleasures' of their childhood. Certainly there was little ready-made entertainment - no TV, computers, videos, DVDs or 'play-stations' - and generally little money to spare. As Tom Steggles says, "we had no money so we amused ourselves". A view echoed by Clive Barker, " we couldn't afford the cinema and there was no television to keep us indoors. We played outside until dusk". There is a sense, rightly or wrongly, that life was safer for children then. Certainly Gillian Crowe thought so, "children used to play for hours in the woods and fields up Vicarage Lane with no worries about safety". The village in the 1930s and 1940s was still largely rural, and children could amuse themselves in the countryside and on the farms.

Peggy Bradley's memories sound idyllic:

> I have very happy memories of Gardiner's Farm in Beehive Lane, which was a lovely farm with lots of land, which went out towards Watchouse Road. We were allowed to play in the farmyard, which I don't suppose one would be allowed to do these days. At hay making time we were allowed to ride on the hay carts. Mr Harvey, who was a lovely character, put a swing up for us in the barn, which was very kind of him.

Una Matthews has similar memories:

> In my childhood there were mostly girls living in the houses in Beehive Lane from Dorset Avenue (though it wasn't there then) down to Winchelsea House. We would meet them in the field that was behind our homes, for playing in the hay, picnics and other country activities. The fields extended to the Recreation Ground, and through to Bells Chase, which was then an unmade narrow lane.

The recreation ground and the park at the top of New Road were other favourite playgrounds, as Den Harvey told us:

> There were a couple of swings and some lovely trees for climbing. We also had our own speedway team and cinder track. We were on pushbikes and called ourselves The Baddow Hornets. We wore black and gold hooped tops. I was probably only a wasp not a hornet - I hadn't got my full sting! It was very well organised. We had caps, and hammers to bang for the start of the race. We had competitions amongst ourselves. There would be fifteen or twenty of us as there wasn't much else to do. We would play until dark and then go home.

With less traffic it was also possible to play in the street, as Janet Chilvers explained:

> We used to just play in the streets or in the fields. We played hopscotch. I had a bike, when I was seven and in the junior school, having learned in the fields to ride on my dad's bike with no stabilisers. I enjoyed riding round the Hanningfields. Children today would not be allowed to do that.

Children invented games such as "Fox and Hounds", with one child as the fox and the remainder as hounds who chased the fox until they caught him.

These games could be quite elaborate. Les Sparrow has vivid memories of playing Cowboys and Indians:

> At the top of Longmead Avenue near where the fire station is now was Pitt Meadow. It had been a pit, then was left disused and became overgrown with brambles, and all kinds of plants had grown up. Kids used that area for Cowboys and Indians, which was a real treat, especially when we enacted what we had seen at the cinema 'tuppeny rush' (the matinee) on a Saturday. We had gangs of cowboys and tribes of Red Indians; I was a Red Indian because my father kept chickens and I could get feathers for the head-dresses. We played the parts, complete with chicken feathers and painted faces. I used to raid mum's pantry for cocoa to make face paint. The cowboys had bandoleers of conkers and six-shooters, which were made out of wood, or used cap pistols. We used to have thirty or forty in these gangs in Pitt Meadow on the weekends and we really had a good old go. On the rare occasions when we were allowed to play there on a Sunday the parents came up and watched us.
>
> We were very realistic in the game and the Red Indians had their squaws, the cowboys had their wives. We had bows and arrows, which could be lethal. For arrows we used to fire dead chrysanthemum sticks with a bit of lead on the end. We took 'prisoners', and one particular time we had captured some cowboys' wives and (doing what we had seen at the cinema) we staked them out on the ground with pegs and string around their wrists and ankles, 'hoping that the ants would get them'. One day we packed up after a good game and I was at home having tea, and there was a knock on the door. A parent of one of the girls said, "You haven't seen so-and-so, have you?"
>
> I said "Oh yes, she was playing with us in Pitt Meadow".
>
> He said, "She hasn't come home". In those days we wouldn't have been too concerned, not like nowadays.
>
> Dad said to me, " Can you go to where you last saw her".
>
> Me, "Certainly I can".
>
> So we all trooped up there and I led them saying "we captured the prisoners here, then we led them through here, and we tied them up round the back of this bushŒ" and there she was, still staked out, crying her eyes out. We'd gone home and forgotten all about her, poor girl.

Colleen Yaxley's pleasures were more sedate:

> I loved the garden because my grandfather had built a summerhouse there for my youngest aunt. I inherited it and I spent many, many hours in there drawing, painting and reading on my own. My best friend, Sheila, lived across the road and was also brought up by her grandparents. She came round a lot and we started a book club, called Colwyn library. School friends came round and borrowed books at 2d a time, with the money going to Christian Aid at the chapel.

(Photo 8-1 shows her by the village pump with friends).

Peggy Bradley enjoyed handicrafts:

> We used to go into Dorset Avenue, on the right hand side, for sewing classes and embroidery. We loved going there to Miss Howes, who was a lovely lady with very rosy cheeks. About five or six used to go, but I don't remember who the others were. I presume Una Hockley went. We did some embroidery, and it was a very pleasant evening, and I loved the house.

But she also liked to be active:

> My garden overlooked the quarry in Beehive Lane and we used to love playing there. After the gravel had been taken out there was still the rail track going down. The gadget

they hauled the gravel up with was still there, but it wasn't operational at that stage. We used to pull it up to the top of the pit and let it run down. We had great fun. They had traction engines there. We really were not allowed down there but we had some fun clambering up and down.

Clive Barker remembers "Old man Tipping" (Peggy's father!), who used to chase them away when they slid down the slope of the pit.

Rather like Den Harvey:

There was a wall all the way round the Vineyards, with broken glass bottles stuck on the top of it to prevent access. As kids we still got over it to go scrumping, and got caught coming out near Ducking Stool Cottage.

Some of Les Sparrow's games were downright dangerous:

I remember going onto this big flat building (which had belonged to the Brewery before it closed) and doing what we called a parachute jump. Every Saturday children went to the Select Cinema in Chelmsford to the 'tuppeny rush'. Once we saw "Hells Angels", a First World War film about air fighting aces, where we got the idea of doing a parachute jump from a ramp. The take-off point was this flat roof, about 10 ft from the ground. What could we use for the parachute? I volunteered to supply my mum's linen basket to sit in. Another lad said he could get a blanket. Someone else brought some rope. To cut a long story short five of us shinned up this drainpipe onto a flat roof. We tied the four corners of the blanket to the two handles of the basket. We tied a rope to one of the handles so we could pull the basket up again and away we went. Being the leader of this gang I went first, and we got this basket balanced just on the edge of this flat roof, half way over, I sat in it with my knees hunched up under my chin, and they pushed me over the edge. I remember seeing the sky above and the other four looking down before I hit the ground. All went well with the others until the last boy, who had no one to launch him off the roof. He rocked himself at the edge, and fell out of the basket, hitting the ground first. None of us were hurt, falling onto a patch of grass, but looking back there's no doubt it was a bit dangerous. I also remember getting hauled over the coals for taking home a smashed linen basket. The lad who brought a blanket got hauled over the coals too because the blanket somehow developed a split in it.

He went on:

Baddow Hall was a grand old house. It had a big iron fence all round it, and a shrubbery in the front, in a lovely setting with the farm at the back. We used to play in the field at the front. It was a very good field for mushrooms. On the parkland, which now backs onto Jeffrey Road, was a former gravel pit. In those days if you wanted some gravel and you had some on your own land you just dug a hole and extracted it. So there was a deep hole with paths down into it which we used for toboggans in the winter. There was one steep path in particular called 'Devils slide' which followed a path, then took a short cut halfway down where the toboggans leapt into the air, jumped over two other paths then came down to earth again at the bottom. It sounds dangerous, which it was, but not too dangerous. In summertime we poured water onto the path until it was muddy, then slid down on the mud. I remember one time we were playing there and one boy who shall be nameless hit the bank on his sled. He flew into the air and landed with his head stuck between two bars of an old bedstead. We couldn't get him out; he was all right, just hollering a bit, so we went across to Jeffrey Road, where they were just building the houses, and asked a workman for help. A Mr White came across and managed to prise the lad's head out. He was all right apart from two bloodshot ears!

In summer swimming was a favourite pass-time. Colleen Yaxley speaks for many:

We walked to Baddow Meads through Lovers' Walk, across the fields to swim in the river. We also cycled to Maldon to swim in the lake, buying rolls for a picnic at Nan's Pantry.

Bert Hunt also used to head for the river:

Lovers' Walk (also called the Twitten), opposite the recreation ground in Baddow Road, was used as a footpath to the river for swimming. It led to a footbridge opposite the lock gates. On Sundays three to four hundred people would meet there to hire boats and have tea at the café.

Les Sparrow added some more details:

We all went swimming in the Chelmer down near Baddow Meads at Sandford Mill. There were two places where you could swim down there, one called the Diver and one called the Navvy. The Navvy was where you could wade into the water before you could swim. The Diver you dived straight in, this place was really for the more capable swimmer. Girls and boys swam together in those days. The boys used to swim around Sandford Mill, going across the bridge to undress the other side of the river, the Springfield side. The girls used to stay on the Meads side. There was a little coppice there where they used to undress and then swim on their side. (Photo 8-2).

In winter skating replaced swimming:

"Mr Smithers, owner of Baddow Court, let people remove gravel for their own use. A shallow ornamental pond was formed after removal of the gravel, where we used to swim. In winter it was used as an ice-skating rink and ice hockey matches were played between the Village and Maltings Estate", said Bert Hunt.

The countryside afforded many other simple pleasures. Peggy Bradley enjoyed fishing, but was not always lucky:

We tried to catch tiddlers in the pond near our house. Once I caught some in a golden syrup tin. Making my way back to the house, I slipped on the side of the pit, and the whole lot went down the front of me. It was a Saturday, and my other school clothes were in the wash, so I was sent to bed since there was nothing else for me to wear.

She could also remember picking mushrooms and blackberries across the fields at the back of number 22, Beehive Lane. The fields went across to Moulsham Lodge and up to the back of Taylor's fruit farm (Lathcoats).

Janet Chilvers did a lot of walking:

We used to meet in the evenings, and have trails through the woods round the back towards Sandon. There was a lovely copse there with bluebells and all sorts of wild flowers: - celandine, cowslips, primroses and violets. We used to listen to the birds and have fun making 'eyes' and natural markers so other people could track us down.
There were always plenty of birds about - thrushes, finches, bluetits and I think we heard a nightingale as well down there. If we came back along the river Chelmer, by Sandford Mill, we would go fishing with our nets. There were always swans and plenty of ducks around. A lot of the boys would swim there as well. We used to come back across the Meads and collect mushrooms.

As always, Les Sparrow has vivid memories of wild life:

Another childhood memory was the bridle way in Vicarage Lane. It is still there and it used to have two ponds on the left-hand side going up, the remains of them are still there. One day during a summer drought Mr Hedges, who was a Romany and lived in the Bridle Way in a caravan, came down to school at Baddow and asked if he could have some help. One of the ponds had dried up and many fish were in the mud at the bottom, struggling to survive. About a dozen of us were persuaded to go up there and help Mr Hedges get the fish out. He was a nice old boy and he had collected together baths, tanks and tarpaulins, all full of water. We scooped these fish out, I think there were about sixty to seventy fish altogether, but not all were rescued on the afternoon we helped. They were still alive in the mud and were mostly mushy carp.

Across the other side of the bridle way, as you enter it from Vicarage Lane, is the field called Moors Wood which was one of the sources of springs which took the water to the back of Vicarage Lane and through the village. In my childhood it was full of adders and local farmer Mr Carter kept cattle there. He would give you perhaps a halfpenny or a farthing if you caught an adder and took it up to him - depending on how he felt at the time. We would catch them with a long stick, about six foot long with a fork on the end. We would pin them down, kill them and take them back to Mr Carter at the shop where he would take you into the outhouse. He had a big pole with all these adder skins on it. If they were in short supply we used to keep him engaged, by talking, and if there was a fresh looking one on the pole we would rip it down and take it to the other shop and get paid twice. I'm sure he knew. (Photo 8-3).

The main organised activities for children were the cubs, scouts, guides and brownies. Les Sparrow was a scout:

Sometimes we went camping at the weekend in a field at the bottom of Lovers' Walk in Baddow Road, which belonged to Reg Spalding. It was just before you got to the Meads proper on the banks of the River Chelmer. We had a summer camp with the Scouts, which was usually down on the East Coast somewhere, at Beccles on a farm, which also belonged to Reg Spalding and was close to the sea. Also we used to camp in the village of Winterton near Yarmouth, which had coast guard and fisherman houses and there was a quarter of a mile of dunes.

"I attended Scouts church parade once a month at St.Mary's" said Tom Steggles. "I was assistant scoutmaster until the war. The Scouts met in the Recreation ground. Our scouting activities included camping at Boreham near the river at Wheaton's farm, with Jimmy Jameson as scoutmaster".

Alan Willis spoke about the Boys Brigade:

We had quite a strong company and Tom Newton was the officer in charge. He was the son of Mr Newton, the Sunday school teacher. The vicar Reverent Holmes played a big part in it. In the summer of 1939, when the war broke out, we went to the Isle of Wight, camping in great big marquees with lots of others from all over the country. It was a bit like a Boy Scouts Jamboree. This was the August before the war broke out. Even amongst the boys there was always the talk of "When is the war going to start?" People were talking about it for months ahead. Everybody seemed to know a war was going to start, it was just a matter of when.

In the Boys Brigade the activities were similar to boy scouts and included parades. Where the petrol station is near the Beehive there used to be a church hut. Everybody knew it as the Tin Hut. It was a large building. We used to play there once a week and perhaps on Sundays. We had little uniforms with a little side cap, a belt and a white sash. If it had carried on there were various badges you could qualify for. Unfortunately it didn't last very long, only about two years. The war came along and put paid to it.

Janet Chilvers described her time in the Brownies:

> Mrs Maslin used to run it and she was a lovely person. She taught us a lot about wildlife and handicraft. We went to where Sandon Youth Club is now for our meetings. We used to walk through The Bringey but not in the winter. We met on Saturday mornings so that we could get there safely. We used to go for our badge testing in Dr Pirie's lovely old house on the Southend Road. It was quite a treat to spend the day there. We had various badges to work for like they do now. We practised quite a lot of household type things: handicrafts, knitting, needlework and a little bit of cooking. It was probably quite primitive to what they do nowadays.

The Youth Club was a popular activity as children grew up:

> "When I was a bit older I joined the youth club, which was held at the Sandon hut opposite to where Sandon School is now. We walked through the Bringey to it. We produced the show 'Oklahoma' in the Parish Hall. We borrowed check shirts from a girl who had a horse, and made little skirts with cut edges at the bottom. We sang in the chorus. There were boys as well as girls, which is why we went there, I think! It was a nice happy time, with simple pleasures", said Colleen Yaxley.

Rosemary Hill joined the village youth club and learned various dances there including the 'jitter bug'!

When pleasures were so simple we can imagine the excitement caused by the visit of a circus, as described by Dora Norrington:

> A circus came and went into a meadow behind where the Army & Navy public house is now. It often went to Maldon first and then came down the road. There was an old chap, with a broom and a pail, who followed the elephants. He wanted 'it' for his garden! They had some nice shows but they weren't very big. It was a penny to go in. I think there were only two elephants, a big one and a small one. It was great fun.

The children of Larkrise and Baddow Hall Junior Schools were asked about their leisure activities in 2002, for comparison with childhood leisure of fifty and more years ago. Thankfully they still enjoy the outdoor life as well as the many indoor entertainments now available. Here are some random comments from Zara, Marcus, Jade and Max:

> "The park is good because there's the tennis courts, playthings, the pond and there's usually football matches or cricket".
> "The May fair every year, that's good fun".
> "There's the jumps for the bikes".
> "We play loads and loads of football matches, or we just practise on our own".
> "I go down town with my friend and we play out the front or in the back garden".
> "I like watching telly with my brother and sister".
> "And reading, I love that".
> "I play computer games sometimes".
> "Every Saturday I go to the river and go canoeing".
> "I play in the garden on my bike, chasing my brother around and throwing tennis balls at him".

Adult pursuits

Just as for children, adults' leisure activities were unsophisticated. Colleen Yaxley recalls how they spent their spare time:

In the living room there was a piano and an organ in the parlour which grandma played every day. We didn't have television. There wasn't much to do in the home except read and listen to the radio. My grandfather made photograph frames out of wood with two pieces of glass. He cut out little fretwork crinoline ladies and these were stuck on either end of the photo frame. I used to paint the crinoline ladies. We used to collect seashells and make necklaces. He used to drill a hole through them and then we thread them. I painted those. My aunt used to sell them at Hoffman's and to all the relations. The money for that went to Christian Aid at the church.

My grandmother was the pianist for the Woman's Institute and I also used to recite poems for the WI. It was a bit nerve wracking. I had to learn them by heart, but I can't remember them now.

At Christmas time we were entertained by lantern slides and fretwork that my grandfather had made. All very simple entertainment but we used to laugh until we cried over these silly figures. It was the same thing every year.

People played cards a lot to entertain themselves in the evenings. Listening to the radio was a big thing in D.Hurrell's day, before television, to get information and news. People would rush home to listen to the serials, as they do today to watch soaps on TV.

Adults were as happy as children to spend their free time in country pursuits. Dora Norrington and her friends formed a hikers' club:

We used to get a rowing boat and row down the river, to an island, half way to Maldon. The rowing boat would hold six and we would row to the island to have a picnic. It was 3d to have the boat for a whole afternoon and evening.

Horse riding was Peggy Bradley's passion:

I remember going out on horseback with Mr & Mrs Loftin (he built Loftin Way). They were very keen riders, and didn't know the area, so I went out with them around Galleywood. I can remember one of the Carter family coming too, who I think had been a scout mistress. She knew how to ride and was proud of her ability. However she had a fall when the horse pitched her off.

One morning I can remember getting up very early. We had some of the horses turned out on the Baddow Meads. My father wanted to go cub hunting, so I went as well. Have you heard of cub hunting? When the young fox cubs appeared, they used to try to kill them, so there wouldn't be so many running around. It was very early in the morning when we set off. I think it started at Boreham, and we had to be there at six o'clock in the morning. It was very difficult to round up the horses on Baddow Meads, if they didn't want to be rounded up, as it was a big area. Luckily we didn't have a kill that day and I decided I didn't want to go cub hunting anymore.

When she was a girl, Peggy would ride one of her father's horses from Beehive Lane to the Dolphin Pub in Tindal Street (now demolished). There was a blacksmith's in the yard behind the pub. The publican's wife would supply a gin to comfort Peggy after her strenuous exercise.

On another occasion her father had lent a horse to a family in Little Hallingbury, near Bishop's Stortford, for their daughter to ride. After a week, Peggy was driven out to collect it and ride it back. En route she stopped at the Spotted Dog for a lemonade. Her father almost sent out a search party to look for her as she was away so long!

According to Derek Hurrell his father was, "marvellous on birds in the garden. He knew the breed of each bird exactly. He and my uncle collected bird's eggs, which you wouldn't do today. He also used to go shooting in the area and was quite a good shot".

For many gardening was and remains an enduring hobby. Once a year the gardeners got a chance to show what they had grown (as they still do). Les Sparrow narrates:

> Our major amusement in the village was the annual flower show and fair. The flower show was held in the recreation ground and the fair would be on the field opposite at the side of Lovers' Walk in the grounds of Baddow Lodge. The field on the right of Lovers' Walk used to belong to Mr Britten in those days. Nicholl's Fair always used to be put up there on the day we had the Flower Show. Everybody entered in the flower show - the W.I., church organisations, the horticultural society and the school. It was a gala day up at the recreation ground and in the evening there was the fair.

Another activity which brought the village together was the annual fête:

> "There used to be annual fêtes in the village held in the rectory gardens. Dr Spencer-Phillips used to have clock golf, brought from his own home I daresay, and he always used to win it but he never took the prize", Derek Hurrell told us. (Photo 8-4).

Whilst the children went to the Scouts and Guides, their parents had bingo, whist drives, cards and billiards in the old Reading Room in Bell Street; the Young Wives Club met in the tin hut in the Vicarage grounds. There were also whist drives in the Parish Hall, along with concerts, which Les Sparrow describes:

> I used to be in various concerts, held in the Parish Hall and some schools and I was in other British Legion activities. Then I was asked to join the Baddow Minstrels, which was a black and white troupe, as we used to call it. The troupe used to tour round all the local villages and the songs were adapted to suit the local names and personalities e.g. Mr Seabrook who was a farmer. There were fifteen in the troupe, a pianist, two banjo players, two comedians, chorus etc. There were two soloists - Jack Thomas, tenor in the church choir and the cathedral and also Charlie Simpson who had a lovely bass voice. He won a Richard Tabor Scholarship and eventually appeared in many of the London Musicals under the stage name of Vincent Charles (or it could be Giles).

Children were not allowed into pubs and Florence Hardwick remembered that her grandfather's pub in Suffolk - the Lime Burner's Arms - had a bar plus a separate room where the women used to sit. The only game played in the pub was cribbage.

The Marconi Club was a popular venue for many of the activities mentioned above. Harry Clayden was a keen member of the Marconi Sports and Social Club, which was then located in the former girl's school on the corner of New Street and Victoria Road in Chelmsford.

> I went there for nearly two years, when we lodged at Rainsford End. The billiard and snooker sections of the sports club were based at the Three Cups in Springfield Road. They had two tables upstairs. Then the new club was built in Beehive Lane round about 1957.
>
> Every Wednesday afternoon we went, and still go, to the Marconi club. We play whist, bingo or snooker. That's for the retired people of Marconi's. I used to be on the committee, and at that time, we had between one hundred and one hundred and fifty people there. It's decreased seriously now, because people have passed away, and nobody is retiring from Marconi's.

Many employees, like Kathleen Stevens, whose first husband loved ballroom dancing, enjoyed their social evenings and especially the dances. Janet Chilvers met her husband at a Marconi dance.

The British Legion also held dances and Les Sparrow's parents looked forward to the Christmas dance, with the big raffle to raise funds for the legion, held in the Parish Hall.

Of course many of these activities still thrive in the village, in many instances in the same venues, such as the Parish Hall, or the recently renovated Reading Room, along with newer venues such as the Bell Centre and the superb Millennium Centre in the Recreation Grounds. The modern new library affords much pleasure and with its computers helps the residents who take up research. Bert Collis did an Open University course, studying local history; Alan Willis has hand-written over one hundred history books since he retired, including a study of all the places in England that Queen Elizabeth 1st visited. "I think English history is wonderful," he said. The books are liberally illustrated with the excellent photographs he has taken on his tours around the British Isles. Several of his local photographs are included in this book (with his permission).

Increased wealth and leisure, and better health have brought a wide range of activities within the range of our older residents, who enjoy Scottish country dancing, the Women's Institute, drama, folk dancing, rambling and cycling to name but a few. The Baddow & Galleywood University of the Third Age (U3A), formed in the village in 1998, has brought an even wider range of activities to the village. These include Bird Watching, Bridge, Calligraphy, Canasta, Chess, Computing, a Discussion group, visiting Essex Churches, a Gardeners' group, Local History, Music Appreciation and Music Playing groups, Needlecraft, Painting, Poetry Appreciation and Poetry Workshop, Reading, Scrabble and Walking. A monthly general meeting usually includes a speaker to educate and entertain members. The current membership is about two hundred, with ongoing recruitment of new members and new activity groups starting. (Photo 8-5 shows the walking group in Wales).

Eileen Hance said:
> Gt.Baddow village is a thriving community, and the U3A lets you meet people. I've met so many who said they knew me, but until then I did not know them. It's so nice to go to the village and be able to say "Hello" to someone you have seen around but did not really know.

Politics

For the more serious minded there were organisations like the Rotary Club or the young Conservatives, to which Alan Willis belonged:
> After the war I took up politics quite a lot. There was a very strong movement of Young Conservatives formed in the village, of which I was secretary for a considerable number of years. Secretary of the Young Conservatives could be a full time job. You would be elected onto other committees, and it was just a matter of how much you wanted to get involved. I retired at forty from the Young Conservatives before I got involved with the senior Conservatives.

> We were associated with canvassing to get the local MP in. We had a very strong movement in Great Baddow, as did most of the villages. There was a shield to be won by the best village group, which we won quite a number of times. Various points were awarded for all sorts of activities. We had meetings with other branches and parties and we had a quota of money to raise, which we did. We joined with the senior branch at the summer fête. We also manned one of the polling stations at election times, which was quite enjoyable.

There was quite a strong rivalry between the Conservatives, Labour and the Liberals, at that time in the village. Politics was very strong for twenty years or so just after the war. Everybody displayed his or her colours at election time. I can remember going round a lot of the villages seeing how many blue or red posters there were in the windows. It was quite a strong thing at election times. Today nobody seems to do that.

As secretary I tried to enrol as many new people as possible. We had a meeting every Thursday, and we had committee meetings to plan the programme for the week. I got elected on to the town committee, and I also went to meetings in London. I think politics today is totally different from what it was twenty or thirty years ago.

Reg Spalding provided the earliest mention of the subject, referring to the early 1900s. He said:

I just remember the coming into birth of the Parish Councils, which took over the powers of the Vestry. I believe that was circa 1892. As Church was Tory it had ruled the parish. However the Chapel congregations were Liberals and with the introduction of Councils the Liberals made progress.

Major Rasch was a Conservative member for Chelmsford at this time.

The Conservatives would go round with blue wash, which they splashed on the houses of their opponents so Mr Charles Burgess Snelling (a strong Liberal) always ended up with his house Dynes on the High Street splashed blue. (Mr Burgess Snelling was a freeman of the City of London and a jeweller. He always rode a tricycle). The Liberals replied with a yellow wash.

'Protection' versus 'Free Trade' was one of the arguments then, (and remained central to Left and Right wing politics for most of the 20th century).

Palmer the Horse Slaughterer in Chelmsford sent six starved old horses, labelled Free Trade, and six beautiful horses, labelled Protection. The Liberals had a ditty 'High over the fence jumps Sunny Jim, Free Trade was the power that rises him'. When a man named Dence (Liberal) put up against Rasch a poster was printed stating 'Rasch is going to be lost in a Dense fog'.

There was no local Labour party presence as yet. (The Independent Labour Party was formed in 1900 from trade unions, which were probably less active in this area compared with more industrial counties. It may have taken a few years to reach Essex).

Mrs H Ely remembered:

The most exciting election time I remember was the time we returned a Liberal candidate from Chelmsford. I don't remember which year it was, but it was before 1910. The man's name was Dence. The young men used to stay out quite late, to hear the results. 11 o'clock was very late in those days.

In more recent times Jesse Pryke has been involved with the 'Grey Party', which he told us is a relatively new political party looking after the needs of the elderly. Len Overy-Owen was the candidate fighting in Colchester recently. The Grey Party believes that the State should pay for care and pensions after retirement. They compare the UK Pension, which equals 17% of average pay, with a Germany pension equal to 60% of average wage. Their policy embraces free prescriptions; free dental care; free opticians' charges. Their policies also cover occupational diseases in building, roof tiling, carpentry, typing, forklift truck driving and mining.

Sport

Another great way to meet people and socialise is through sport. Football, Cricket, Bowls, Tennis, Quoits, Table Tennis, Badminton, Snooker, Billiards, Pool, Golf, Dominoes, Kung Fu, Tai Chi, Rambling, Scottish country dancing, Folk dancing, Darts, Swimming, Horse riding, Motocross, Scrambling, Cycling, Rowing and Wrestling have all featured in our interviews of Baddow residents.

The Millennium Centre is an important headquarters for sporting activities, and the halls are hired out many times in the week for some activity or other, such as ballroom dancing, bridge, Kung Fu or Tai Chi. Other sporting venues include the Bowls pavilion, the Tennis courts in Ladywell Lane and the former RC hut in Longmead Avenue used for table tennis. Swimmers can sometimes use the facilities at some of the local schools. The Marconi Social Club also hosts many sports, and horse riding stables can be found at the Chelmsford Equestrian Centre in Beehive Lane.

Football

Over the years many people have enjoyed playing football in the village. There is even a photo of the village team in 1902-3, (photo 8-6) when they played in the Brewery Fields off Church Street before they moved to the recreation grounds in the 1920s.

Les Sparrow remembers his father:

> My Dad was keen on football, and he was a very good footballer in his time. He played for the village team and later, when he gave up playing, became the treasurer of the village team and then the president. I think that if he had been about today he would have been a professional footballer.

Clive Barker told us that he got his Essex and England colours for football whilst at KEGS.

Bert Hunt was also much involved in the village side for 40 years. Around 1951-52 he played then captained the team. Subsequently he was secretary of the club and he has the records of everyone who ever signed on.

Den Harvey has had a life-long connection with village football:

> We started the first boy's football team in Baddow. We called ourselves the Baddow Minors and we played in the minor league, ages between fourteen and eighteen. I started it with my brother in law, my sister's first husband, Brian. He was a bit older than me and managed it. Our first couple of friendlies was with the Sandon House boy's school, a big old boarding school on the Maldon road. We played in the Bringey where they are now building houses. We changed in the hut at the top of Molrams Lane and walked to the Bringey. We were in the minor league for three years. To my knowledge there was no other youth football team in the village. There are now lots. We played up to eighteen and then transferred. I signed on for Baddow men's team in 1959/60 season. They played in the recreation ground. The better players transferred about sixteen. I played some twenty odd years for them, then managed them. I've been chairman, played and managed at every level. I'm still involved now. I make the teas every Saturday afternoon.

He can remember a time when the Parish Council said 'No' to Sunday football in the Recreation Ground, and he recalls the old wooden pavilion and changing rooms which pre-dated the Millennium Centre. (Photo 8-7 shows the 1950's men's football team and 8-8 the ladies' team).

Cricket

Cricket has given similar pleasure to a great many residents. There is a photo of the village cricket team dated 1892, with the players resplendent in top hats. (Photo 8-9). They had their ground in Baddow House said Harry Clayden, in Mr Beale's land in Galleywood Road on the left. When Mr Beale sold up they had hoped to buy the ground, but in fact it became the Eastern Electricity (Estrics) cricket ground. The Gt.Baddow team then moved to the Recreation Ground.

Harry Clayden told us:

> I was playing when they moved to the recreation ground, and I helped them move. We moved the pavilion ourselves. We stopped playing during the war and we restarted in 1948. There was less than half a dozen of the old side remaining that had played in the recreation ground, mainly because of getting married and moving. (Photo 8-10).

"At one time Mr Amoss, the headmaster of Baddow School, almost ran the cricket team," said Harry.

> Mr Amoss finished playing but was our umpire for years. We used to play Little Baddow, they still do, and my wife Mary and other ladies made the teas. When we played away, if it was local, we cycled. Nobody had private cars. The only person who had a car, which we used now and again, was Mr Silas Jackson. He lived in New Road and ran taxis. His son Les became our scorer.

One day when the team played Danbury a haughty Baddow lady said: "Such a pity Danbury has not a gentlemen's team". John Simmond of Danbury somehow knew that her brother had been a spendthrift and had only paid 9s-0d in the pound on his debts. He heard her remark and replied, "There may not be any gentlemen in Danbury but they all pay 20s-0d in the pound".

In his youth Tony Pennack was scorer for the British Legion cricket team that played in an area behind Longfield Road in the 1950s. They had a Nissan hut as their pavilion, and the outfield had to be cleared of 'pancakes' before the match could start.

Bowls

The Bowls club is another thriving group in the village. Bert Hunt explained its history:

> It was originally formed in 1927, on the green under the tree, where the first tennis court is now in the recreation ground. (Photo 8-11). I believe that there was also a bowling green in the grounds of the old Vineyards. (Shown on a map in The Country Life article dated Jan 1911 seen in the Essex Record Office).
> It originally consisted of local people, but now has a membership of about 150. Bert Baines is the secretary of the bowls club. The Bowling Clubhouse used to be wooden. It was burnt down in the 70s, when the club was playing away at Burnham. The new hut was built from the contributions of members. Later Harold King made two extra rinks. Bowls was not allowed to be played at Great Baddow recreation ground on Sundays in the early days.

John Kemp is another keen member and said:

> I started playing bowls after I retired at about sixty two. I'm now a very keen bowler and I play as often as possible, at club level, in Chelmsford and District. Great Baddow Bowls Club is brilliant, with fifty or so players on the rinks at any one time.

Quoits

Another local sportsman represented his county and England in his chosen field. Aubrey Hockley, father of Una Matthews, grew up in the Carpenter's Arms in Baddow Road, where his father was landlord. Baddow Road Quoit Club held its matches on a ground laid out behind the pub, and afterwards the landlord's wife would provide teas for all those taking part. Aubrey was a member of this club and represented both Essex and England in matches around 1937. (See photos 8-12 to 14).

So little appears to be known about this sport, but it was very popular in Southern England and Wales until 1939. The English Quoiting Association, established in 1887, lists 52 clubs in London, the Home Counties and Somerset in its 1938 rulebook, which Una Matthews lent me. She remembers quite clearly going to the ground as a small child. From her comments and the rulebook we discover:

> It was a rectangular space, with a bed at each end, eighteen yards apart, and benches for spectators to sit on. Each bed had to be between 4ft square and 4ft 6ins square, filled with clay to a depth of 8ins. An iron HUB or PIN had to be firmly fitted in the centre of the bed, at which the quoits were aimed. The quoits were flat metal rings, which 'could be any weight, unless stipulated. They must not exceed 2 ¼ inches in height, or 8 5/8th inches in diameter, and had to have a circular hole of at least 4 ins in quoits weighing 10 lbs per pair'. The clay must have been quite soft, as on one occasion I visited the ground with my father, and went home with my cream silk dress splattered with clay.
> The last information I have about the game is on a programme of an International match between England and Wales. This was played at Ilford, on August Bank Holiday, 7th August 1939. My father and Mr J. Moss of Albert Terrace, Baddow Road, played for England.

Apparently quoits could be quite dangerous, possibly fatal, as a badly thrown quoit could do serious damage if it hit you in the head. Scoring was somewhat like bowls, each player having two quoits, the object being to throw nearer to the centre of the pin than your opponent. Hence you could score up to 2 points per end. A game consisted of 41 points, or 61 points for a final in a multi-round competition.

Tennis

Clive Turner, the Chairman of the Great Baddow Lawn Tennis Club, tells us that the club was founded in 1902 on a site in Galleywood Road, on the corner with Bells Chase:

> The records show that in 1929 six dozen tennis balls cost £3-15s-10d. Saturday afternoon teas were an important part of club life in the 1960s; all tennis would come to a halt (whatever the score) when the time came to serve tea.
> In 1966 the club moved to its present site in Ladywell Lane, onto land purchased from its first president, Lionel Maude. The six courts were laid with red shale rather than grass, which apparently needed a lot of maintenance, with regular sprinkling and brushing. Further repair was needed after frost damage, with a top dressing, rolling and brushing. Eventually the red shale was replaced by a hard acrylic surface and later by artificial grass.
> Additions were made to club facilities in 1968 (bar area) and in 1970, when floodlights were installed to permit evening matches.
> The men's team enjoyed success in 1990 when they won Division 1 of the Essex League for the first time.

Holidays

John Jackson gives some indication of how little people travelled before and even after the Second World War. He said:

> In the early 1930s, when I was 7 or 8 we had a visitor to the youth club who had been round the world. He gave a film show. He was a missionary I think, but a rarity someone who had travelled far and taken many photos.

For the most part people did not have holidays and certainly not exotic ones to foreign parts. Florence Hardwick's father was a farm worker and his annual 'holiday' was typical - Good Friday and Christmas Day! Les Sparrow's father was self-employed and was loath to take holidays because he was not earning money.

Holidays were also difficult if you ran a shop, like Dora Norrington's family:

> It was not easy if you were working shop hours. When I had a holiday my eldest sister used to take my place. She had to sign on with head office to say that she was capable of selling stamps and that sort of thing. She stayed with mother while I had a holiday. Mother used to stay at Westcliff with her sister for a week. My sister and I then managed the shop between us.

Peggy Bradley sometimes got away:

> We did not have family holidays when I was a little girl, unless we went to Southwold with the Duffield's, for whom my father worked as a chauffeur. That was lovely. A neighbour who was quite a lonely lady took me to Clacton once. She wanted a few days away, and she thought a trip to Clacton would do me good. I was about six or seven years old, and I wasn't very impressed with it.

Colleen Yaxley told us of one special trip to the seaside. (Photo 8-15 shows a sweet group in their Sunday best).

Most people would be content with a day out, perhaps on the yearly outing to Walton-on-the-Naze for a shrimp tea with the Church choir. Derek Hurrell remarked that an outing was the big event of the year, to go to Maldon or even Southend one day a year.

Reg Bush even ventured into Surrey:

> An annual outing went by charabanc to Epsom races. On one occasion, when the time came to return home, one man was missing. They found him on London Bridge; he had got onto the wrong coach, and had been turfed off that coach when the strangers realised that he was not one of them. He was extremely lucky to be spotted by his friends passing in the Baddow bus. Needless to say he did not venture to Epsom again! (Photo 8-16 shows a typical holiday crowd in a charabanc all ready to leave the Kings Head pub in Great Baddow).

Sadie Gemmell went to Clacton with her cousins and stayed in a boarding house, taking over the whole house.

Bert Collis told us:

> Before the war we went by train to Great Yarmouth and stayed in a boarding house. There was a magnificent beach there. We had boat trips up to Norwich on the broads' steamers. That was more or less a routine.

Gradually people's horizons have widened. When he first retired Alan Willis had some lovely holidays touring in Scotland.

Rosemary and Roland Hill also liked to visit Scotland, the Lake District and Cornwall, but their big adventure was a motorbike trip to Spain in 1952:

> This was before the boom in tourists' attractions. We went through France, the Pyrennees, Pamplona (where they race the bulls) then on to Barcelona. At the time it was under Franco and they had guards about. We had to be careful. They quizzed you a bit at the borders. We went to a village called Rosas, which had about three hotels. The Americans had a base there later and it developed into a big place. We saw very few tourists. The bike was a Vincent Comet. When we stopped we were surrounded by young men who were fascinated by the motor bike. My father was horrified that we had spent our money abroad instead of saving it to have a house built. He said we should have had gone on holiday on Baddow Meads! However, Spain was an experience, and we didn't have to spend much money.

John Kemp, typical of so many nowadays, has travelled far and wide:

> I've managed to keep skiing, though I've had a few injuries. I went to France last year, but for a number of years I have skied in the States in Vail in Colorado and hope to go back in the winter. I like travelling and I'm keen on cruises, seeing lots of places and taking your hotel with you.

Of the modern children interviewed about their leisure in the 21st century, Adam enjoys fairly local holidays, at Butlins, Great Yarmouth or Camber Sands. Zara usually goes to visit her father in Cyprus, but Marcus has been lucky enough to go to Disneyland in Paris.

John Jackson has set his sights even further! He enjoys 'travelling' in Space, thanks to his new telescope, observing Jupiter and its four moons, then a trip around Saturn. But most of all he appreciated sailing in home waters, away from the crowds, at a leisurely pace. His account makes us appreciate how much beauty there is near to home, in our lovely country:

> I was off Clacton about four years ago, with very little wind, a lovely sunny day, no one about, so I shut down the engine and drifted for two hours. I sat in the cockpit with my feet up on the bench seat, drinking a cup of coffee, when there was a whoosh, the coffee went flying and a seal popped up out of nowhere. I could have touched him he was so close. A local said he was old 'so-and-so', he waits for the fish. He had a big moustache and I could feel his breath. I thought how lovely it was for a wild animal to come up and see me. You see the migrating geese in the spring and autumn who have travelled thousands of miles to or from Russia coming to the same spot in Essex each year. When I'm returning to the creek at low water, I pass geese feeding 30 yards away. As I pass they stop and look up then carry on. The sunlight in the winter is beautiful too. I recall my son Michael in his boat netting some herrings one evening as the sun was setting. I was a quarter of a mile away in my boat and the fish were glistening silver and gold in the sunlight as he was pulling them in over the side. It would be good to be an artist to paint such a scene. That's what sailing is all about. (Photos 8-17 and 18 attempt to conjure up this scene).

The simple pleasures described in this chapter with such obvious nostalgia by our interviewees are priceless. Like John perhaps we too should value them.

Photo 8-1 Village Pump 1940

Photo 8-3 Adder

*Photo 8-2
Sandford Mill*

*Photo 8-4
The Vicarage*

Photo 8-5
U3A Walkers in Wales
2002

Photo 8-6 Baddow Rovers 1902-3
season in the Brewery Fields ground.

Top: J.Brown, W.Barker, C.Quilter,
W.Cook, W.Auger, H.Richell, E.Finch.

Centre: J.Clark, A.Richell, A.Brooks,
J.Newman.

Front: W.Brooks, M.Rawlinson

Photo 8-7
Great Baddow Football
Team 1950s

Photo 8-8 Great
Baddow Ladies
Football Team 1950s

Photo 8-9
Great Baddow Cricket Club
1892

Photo 8-10 Great Baddow Cricket
Club 1948 with Tea Ladies

Back Row: Frank Gowing,
Eddie Ritchie, Tom Bax (or
Backs), Jim Preston, Cyril Payne,
Bert Clayden, Reg Arnold,
Jack Cooper, Percy Cook,
Reg Stebbing,
Mr E.A.Amoss(Umpire)

Middle Row: Les Jackson,
Mrs Gladys Ritchie,
Mrs.Mary Clayden (wife of
Harry), Mrs Margery Clayden

(wife of Bert), Mrs Ivy Watson, Mrs Gladys Arnold, Doug Bloomfield,

Front Row: Frank Watson, Harry Clayden, Dick Partner

Photo 8-11
Great Baddow Bowls Club
1920s

Photo 8-12
British Quoits Team 1937

Photo 8-13
Quoits Ground
behind Carpenters
Arms

Photo 8-14
Quoits Winners
North Essex League
1934-7

Photo 8-15
Colleen's Outing

Photo 8-16
The Annual
Charbanc Trip.

Photo 8-17 John's Boat

Photo 8-18 John's Seal

Chapter 9 - Wartime Reminiscences

Introduction

Many of our interviewees provided vivid memories of World War Two, which we are happy to relate. This chapter gathers together many of those reminiscences, plus some notes about relatives who served in World War One (the Great War as it was called). The soldiers' families who were left behind, and those who served their country without leaving the village, are also mentioned. We have also included a few experiences of Baddow men who 'did their National Service' between 1945 and around 1961, when it ceased.

Men at war

Many fathers went to war when their children were very young. Perhaps dad did not return or maybe they did not recognise him when he returned. Possibly he was severely traumatised by the war and it was difficult for him to adjust when he came back. Moreover, many women performed tasks previously regarded as 'men's work' and resented returning to 'women's work' after the war.

Some Baddow men were directly involved in the hostilities of World War Two. Colleen Yaxley put it into perspective:

> The war was a bit sad for us and it did affect us. My father wasn't at home. He was at war. He was billeted in this country quite a lot, as he used to drive. Then he went abroad. My aunt's husband was away the whole time. She sat and wrote letters to him every night. He was away four years. They married in 1939 as he was going away, because he wasn't in a reserved occupation. It was quite sad for ladies whose husbands were away for such a long time. You can't imagine it now, can you?

Les Sparrow told us of his experiences in the services:

> I was in the first 5th Essex Territorial Army before the war and we went all over the British Isles before going abroad in 1942, to Cairo for six or seven months and Iraq through to Lebanon, and I was part of the spearhead into Italy. We travelled to Sorrento and carried on through to Foggia and pushed forward to the River Trento. Unfortunately only a few got across and we were taken prisoner and eventually shipped back by train through the Brenner Pass via Innsbruck, through Germany to Neusburg which was a big transit camp near Munich. There I spent the rest of the war. We were very near the concentration camps in Germany. There was a huge transit camp where there were about 25,000 prisoners of all nationalities and this particular day a train came in from the Russian side. When they opened up the cattle trucks in which the prisoners had travelled, some of the prisoners were frozen solid.
>
> A short time before the war in Europe was finished about 6,000 of us in our column were sent on a march by the German powers that be. They were trying to get us back to Salzburg to hold us as hostages against the final reparations when it came to the Armistice. They never got us to Salzburg, as we used to keep overlapping, the back would overlap the front, so we did not do more than five miles a day. The Americans eventually liberated us. Our guards were old Austrian guards, who had little time for the old 'Nazi' Germans. Normally the SS would take the prisoners from one area to another but one day the Austrian guards took all 6,000 of us to various farms and hid us. Somehow the Americans knew we were there and rescued us. Eventually we all

came home in Lancaster bombers to Oxfordshire. I weighed 7st 5lbs. In Oxfordshire they kitted us out in civvies, then I had seven weeks leave, during which I got married. That was the end of my Army career. I wouldn't have missed my Army experience; we used to moan about it, but there was a wonderful spirit; we all looked out for one another. You don't get that today!

Tom Steggles joined the Territorial Army in April 1939 and the RASC on 1st Sept 1939. He said:

> We went to Diss, then to France in December 1939. It was a poorly equipped, ragged army, without overcoats, and in a vehicle with no windscreen. Eventually they gave us an extra blanket. No wonder we had to evacuate from Dunkirk!
>
> We were picked up by the destroyer HMS Anthony, but instead of sailing straight home she shelled a coastal road to stop the German army. We were subject to air attack all day before we got to Dover, and we were frightened. First of all we were billeted in stables at Newbury, then I was posted to the 9th Highland Youth in Scotland, Beau de Garten which was made into the 51st Highland, an independent brigade. I was posted to Northern Ireland and I stayed there twelve to eighteen months. Then it was back to France for the invasion, starting at Gosport, then Deal, then across the channel, but I was not in the first batch. I stayed in France until the war ended.

John Jackson also told us what happened to him:

> Dad had the garage, my brother Ted was called up into the Airforce, so it was best I left school to stand in for my brother and help Dad. I had an apprenticeship for two years until 1941 and I joined the ATC (Air Training Corps); I think we were one of the first groups, which formed about the same time as the Home Guard started. I was in the ATC until I was called up in August 1942. I was on the reserve to start with, then called up at eighteen.
>
> I was interested in aircraft and boats, and in the ATC you could do both. My ambition was to get into the Royal Air Force on the marine side, which I preferred to being in the Navy. However, when I had my interview they asked me what experience I had had with boats, and as I had only got experience of dinghies I could not get into the marine side.
>
> I had six months training on aircraft engines at RAF Cosford after "square bashing". They had instructors from Rolls Royce, as Merlin engines were used on about 50% of RAF planes, on Spitfires, Hurricanes and Lancasters. We did not have many aircraft with radial engines, unlike the Americans, who did not have many inline engines. I can't think why we preferred inline engines, as they are more susceptible to damage. I've known an American engine come in with one cylinder hanging off, but still running on seven cylinders. A bullet had gone through one cylinder and locked the piston. This broke the con-rod off and that broke the cylinder off.
>
> After training I went to South Africa then India. I was only about two months in Africa, waiting for a ship and based in a transit camp in Durban. We were supposed to be going up to Egypt, but this was the time the Japanese were trying to get into India. They were on the Burmese border, so rather than send us to Egypt, where that war was nearly over, they thought they would send us to India. I was then sent to a posting in India 1,000 miles from the sea. I was three and a half years there. What good we did I don't know! We certainly wrote off a few aircraft!

The aircraft I worked on were mainly Dakotas plus occasionally Hurricanes and Spitfires. (Photo 9-1). The worst aircraft we worked on was called Vultee Vengeance, which was a dive-bomber. We were the only squadron in the Royal Air Force with dive-bombers. The Royal Indian Air Force tried to copy the German Stuka pilots. We used to see them practising over the desert, and sometimes they wouldn't pull out of the dive. There would just be a big hole in the sand. I don't think they did much good. The Australians also had one or two squadrons as well. (Photo 9-2).

In India there were about 100,000 British army and airforce, roughly half and half. We were there to repel the Japanese. Hitler wanted to come down through Egypt via Suez; the Japanese wanted to come from Burma and meet up with Hitler in the middle of India. Thankfully it didn't work out quite that way.

There was trouble with the Indians; they wanted independence, they weren't much interested in us, yet they were helpful, and the Indian airforce was a very good airforce. So together we stopped the Germans and the Japanese doing what they intended, which was to encircle us. If they had joined up that would have been just where I was stationed. We were stationed with the Americans on Dakotas, mainly flying supplies to Burma. The Americans were "going over the hump" to China. We serviced American aircraft, and we had US specialists from Pratt & Whitney and Wright Cyclone specialists. We also had Australians and New Zealanders on the base. The Indian airforce was quite a big airforce. At the height of the war there were 300,000 service people of which 200,000 were Indian. They included a lot of Sikh pilots, who were very good. The Indians were very helpful, so presumably we were joined together in a common aim. They did not want the Japanese to succeed any more than we did.

I was there until the end of the war. The Japanese war ended in August 1945, the European war having ended in May of the same year. That's when the atom bomb was dropped. Lucky for me, as I was just about to be posted to an aircraft carrier. I was in Bombay then, clearing up after the war. There was talk of us going onto an aircraft carrier with the Fleet Air Arm. I didn't think much of that, as it meant going out to the Pacific. When they dropped the A-bomb it all finished and I didn't go east.

There were one or two interesting stories relating to my time in India.
There were some brand new surplus engines in the stores, which after the war ended were taken out into Bombay harbour and sunk. They used landing craft to transport them, and I think it went on for weeks. They were brand new eighteen cylinder Cyclone engines, in two banks of nine. They were wrapped in cellophane, and greased. They were worth £3,000 each in those days, worth £300,000 or more now. They took them out, three or four at a time and dumped them.

A large variety of items including complete aircraft were thrown away, and I could never understand why. Perhaps it had something to do with the commercial market; they did not want to flood the market with cheap war surplus. No doubt Dakota parts would have been very handy for civil aircraft. After all, Dakotas or DC3s are still flying.

Many people got rich quick out of World War surplus. I know of three people very near us in Essex, one about three miles away, one about ten miles. I don't blame them; it made more sense, better than throwing goods away. I remember on our base we had ten tons of photography paper on our base, which was burned. It had six months to go before its expiry date, but it would probably have been OK for another ten years. It was all done up in tins.

I left India and was posted to the Royal Artillery aircraft-spotting squadron at Andover, equipped with little Auster aircraft. The war was over, we were sent up on top of Salisbury Plane. We had tanks up there with radios, doing direction finding. We had a fitter and a rigger and a wireless operator, in an old jeep. We put out a canvas landing strip and the planes came in at about 30 mph against the wind. You could almost shake hands with the pilot as they landed. It was so different to handling big aircraft. I was there until October 1946 when I got demobbed.

Harry Clayden, on the other hand, had by his own account a fairly uneventful war:
I went into the Royal Engineers to start with. I was called up on July 15th 1940, which is St Swithin's day. I had to report to Carlton Hall, Saxmundham. I was in the RE to start with and we did six months training before we became part of the RA (Royal Artillery). I was on the searchlights to start with. We went all round Suffolk and the seaside areas of Essex. From there I went to Birkenhead, just outside Liverpool, and then we were drafted over to Northern Ireland. That was as far as I went, during the forces, and I consider myself very lucky. I came out in 1946.

Alan Willis avoided the worst of the fighting but still managed to have memorable experiences:
I went to Brentwood for my first six weeks primary training (square bashing, rifle training etc), then we were sorted out, some into the Infantry regiments, some into the Royal Army Service Corps or the Royal Artillery. I went with a dozen others up to Chesterfield in the Royal Engineers and learned to drive. I was there for two months in the winter of 1943/44, on the Derbyshire moors, where we often got bogged down in the snow, which was very interesting!

I drove all sorts of lorries such as the 15 cwt Bedford, 3 tonners, or a large truck called a Carrier, like a troop carrier. They were very high off the ground and there was a very high pitched whine to the engine. That was the vehicle on which I took my test. From there everyone was posted to his or her regiment. I was posted to a holding unit just outside Oxford for a fortnight, then I was posted on my own to a group of Royal Engineers who had come home from Gibraltar and who were reassembling to go out to France. I joined them in May 1944. We went up to Wimbledon Common, where we did our invasion preparation, then to just outside Gosport.

The invasion was planned for June 6th. We were on the south coast for a month. There was some bad weather and the Mulberry harbour was broken up, so we weren't sure when we were going over. We finally went over to France in the middle of July.

In August 1944 we were in Brussels. We followed the infantry into Brussels, and were the first engineers into the city. We were in Monty's[1] 21st army group, part of his headquarters' staff so we were billeted in one of the King's palaces, where we had quite a nice time. That winter was very bad but we were comfortable there until the following March, when we moved into Germany. On May 8th 1945 the war finished, and a month after that, being one of the youngest I was posted to another company in Belgium that was going over to Japan, because the war in Japan was still on. We came home on

1 Field Marshall Montgomery of Alamein

embarkation leave, but while on leave the war finished, so when we returned back to our unit, instead of being posted to Japan we went to Italy for two years. The young people were going out to replace the older ones who were coming home.

I had two years in Northern Italy, which was very interesting. I was in the motor department, driving to the port for diesel or petrol, anything to support the Sappers and the other battalions. This was in Trieste and there were many companies of infantry in the area, and anything they wanted doing we had to do, erecting huts, laying water supplies, etc.

I went there on my twentieth birthday and by the following March or April six of us were posted onto the Austrian border in what they called a Forestry Group. In the morning we used to parade with the Italian Alpine troops, which was very colourful. I was there for a couple of months.

At that time there was a considerable amount of trouble in Palestine and being part of the First Armoured Group my group were posted there, with tanks, to keep the peace between the local fraternity and the Jews who were trying to take over the country. They were trying to set up the state of Israel at that time. Like in most wars the poor English Tommy was in the middle, getting shot at from both sides. I did all the training; the advance party went with all the equipment, and I was left standing in the clothes I had on, one set of everything. All my kit went. Two hundred and fifty of us paraded just outside Venice, ready to go to Egypt, which was the practice in those days to get acclimatised before moving into Palestine. I was called out by the officer in charge to say that because I had already done three years overseas I wasn't to go, so I said goodbye to the other two hundred and forty nine. I was posted to another unit just outside Venice, where I spent two months going into Venice nearly every day. I really loved that. For your leave you could either go to Rome or to Cortina, skiing; I chose Rome for two week's holiday.

At another time the English had opened a school in Austria. This college was set up for soldiers returning to England to catch up on their trade - building, plumbing, painting, etc. They wanted a certain number to get the college going, so they asked for volunteers to go to Austria for six weeks on a course of their choice. I jumped at the chance, and chose painting and decorating. My friend Albert chose plumbing. While I was in Austria the sergeant asked for anyone with knowledge of printing. In the army you don't volunteer for anything, but two days later he called again for volunteers, and said it would involve a trip to Vienna, so at that my ears pricked up and I volunteered to go to Vienna.

The destination was a new college, and they wanted a logo. I had a little more than a week there, and had an enjoyable time. I cycled round Vienna on a bicycle, which I hired from the NAAFI (Navy, Army and Air Force Institute). When I talked to the ladies behind the counter and said I had been round the Blue Danube, they said that's in the Russian sector, you were lucky you weren't arrested. Many other British soldiers had been arrested going there. I saw the notice saying Russian Zone, but this did not mean much to me so I cycled over one bridge, along the riverbank and back over a second bridge, but they wouldn't believe what I'd done. And I stood in the middle of the road taking photographs! I got away with it all right.

So I managed to see a bit of Italy and a bit of Austria. I had a good time. Of course we were in the Army, but provided you behaved yourself the Army was a wonderful experience in those days when the war was over.

I was also handy at painting and drawing, and when the officer found out he got me to do some entertainment posters. They had Bingo nights and dancing in the Officers' mess, events to which they invited the local people.

I spent a lot of time in Venice, as much as I could. I had a week's leave on the Lido at the Excelsior Hotel, where the film stars and royalty used to stay before the war. Another time I went on an education course where, instead of parading, you could have civilian people take you round different galleries and churches and show you the local places, which was very interesting. I did anything but work, taking every opportunity to see the sights.

Another very odd thing happened to me. My kit bag, with all my equipment and clothes, went to Egypt with the advance party and all this time all I had was what I stood up in. After three months I was told I had to return to England, and I was taken to the railway station. As I stood waiting for the train to come in, up came a lorry and the driver said, "Are you driver Willis?" "Here's your kit, it's come back from Egypt". Within less than an hour I was on the train to come home. So I had been without that kit all that time. It had been to Egypt and back and arrived just as I stood on the platform to come home. I finished up at Portland Bill, near Weymouth. I was there for two weeks, and then I was demobbed.

Robert Norrington was recruited into the Military Police. He told us how that happened and his wartime exploits as an MP:

They actually formed the Military Police in Chelmsford. During the war my wife was a secretary at the Automobile Association (AA). They made the boss of the AA into a Captain in the Military Police. There were only four men in the AA, and my name was put forward, so I was recruited into the Military Police through my wife's boss. They asked me if I could ride a motorbike and read a map, which I could. I was already in the Fire Service in Market Road, but got fed up with fire drills every week! I joined the Military Police (known as the Red Caps) at the Drill Hall on Market Road.

Military Police were proper policemen. It wasn't difficult, most enjoyable. I went abroad quite a lot. I was actually too short, but I stood on my toes when I had my medical, so the doctor put me down on the form as taller than I am, which got me in!

I was always called "Chayter", which is Egyptian for "Shorty". I went to Egypt, Palestine and Syria. I went by liner via South Africa and Suez Canal then to Alexandria. In South Africa we had to keep British troops out of area 6, the Coloured Area. While I was there the Officer Commanding the troops took me up to Table Mountain. It felt very good going to all those places.

I mostly got escort jobs because of being short. In the western desert I did 'field punishment duties'. After the war when I came back to England I was regarded as too short for Military Police duties. I got a transfer to the MPSC (Military Police Staff Corps), which is the prison service, as I had done prison work in Egypt. Later, when I was at Hoffman's I was approached to do prison work, but refused. I believe in discipline, and I might have done it if I could have been employed locally, but I did not want to move from Chelmsford.

I went through the war without a scratch. I went right up the western desert; I was with Montgomery; visited by Churchill. I'm still in touch with some war colleagues. There are a number in Chelmsford.

Although this section is entitled 'Men at War' we must not forget the women of Great Baddow who also served in the forces.

Extra Work

Adults who remained often did extra work to cover for the missing workforce, plus tasks such as Home Guard, Air Raid Warden or Fire Brigade volunteer. There was also a National Plea to 'Dig for Victory' by growing your own food in the garden. The Land Army consisted of teams of young women who farmed the land to provide food. Remember the British Isles was under siege, with U-boats sinking many of the vessels that were trying to supply us with imports.

Several of the men destined to become soldiers, sailors and airmen were occupied in preparations for war prior to 'joining up'. Alan Willis gave us a very detailed account of his time in the Home Guard and the part he played in the 'Spigot Mortar Group':

The war started when I was thirteen or fourteen. When young boys were seventeen they had to do some form of war work. You were either a runner for the ARP or you joined The Home Guard. I wanted to join The Home Guard, so I became a member of the Great Baddow Home Guard. By that time the war had been on for three or four years. Although we laugh about the Home Guard today as portrayed in 'Dad's Army' on the television, at the time I joined it, it was quite a considerable fighting force. There must have been about two hundred men in the local group. We paraded at the village hall on Wednesdays, and on the Sunday mornings we paraded on the Carter's field where the fire station is now. Our captain in charge was Captain Blyth. There were several officers and sergeants. We did all the usual 'Home Guard' things. At the village hall we did map reading. After about six months they formed a spigot mortar group which I joined. There were about six of us. There was a corporal in charge and four or five other ranks. It was a mobile mortar weapon to be used against tanks. It also could be mounted on a fixed swivel, which was situated at the Blue Lion. A trench was dug down with a mount for this mortar. There was a base plate, three legs and the mortar was fitted onto the base plate. Each person took a particular part to manoeuvre it about but also it could be on a fixture. It was quite a large anti-tank weapon with a base plate as big as a dustbin lid. There were three legs fitted into this and hammered into the ground. The mortar was placed on the top, which could be moved round to any direction. The actual missile, which was fired, was about two feet long with a bulbous front end; this was slotted on from the front and fired from the back. We could either fire up into the air or face it down towards the town, up the Maldon Road or up the High Street as it was on a swivel. It was placed in front of the Blue Lion on the corner, right opposite the Vineyards, where the road sign to Maldon and Southend is. However, it was portable and it could be taken anywhere with a crew of about five. The base plate wasn't a fixture, everything was mobile, but every part was very heavy. One person could move the base plate. Three others fixed a leg, which was slotted in, to make a fixture and one or two people would carry the actual firing mechanism. This would be in 1942/43. They were quite serious about invasion even in those days.

We also did exercises, and there were 'call outs'. During the night, perhaps at 2 or 3 am, a sergeant perhaps would go round the village and knock on the doors to call us on parade at the Blue Lion. Others would parade at the Kings Head or at various locations round the village. The captain would come round with one of the officers, to see how many had turned out. Everybody had to work during the day, at Marconi's or Hoffman's for instance and they were also in the Home Guard. At my little printing firm everyone had to do fire watching one night every week. You would go to work at 8 a.m. and work until 6 p.m. We would have a couple of hours off and then we would start fire watching at 9 p.m. until 7a.m. the following morning. You then had to go to work again at 8 a.m. Then there was the Home Guard duty to fit in. We might have several nights without sleep. Remember I was only a boy of fourteen or fifteen at the time.

Another resident told us there was an anti-tank gun at the corner of Molrams Lane and Maldon Road, where the petrol station is now. On the plan for defending Essex it was anticipated that the route for invasion would have been from the direction of Danbury so this gun was pointing towards Danbury. All the pillboxes in the area were on a line more or less parallel to the route of the A130 to Southend. At the Molrams Lane gun emplacement the local people used to take it in turns to provide a hot meal everyday for the soldiers. So even the civilians were involved in the war effort. The whole country was on a war footing. Everyone was doing his or her bit.

Alan Willis also described his father's efforts:
There was a group of people called The Royal Observer Corps. My father was a member of that. There must have been about twenty chaps. They would man their post 24 hours a day, reporting all aircraft that were flying in the vicinity. Hence the RAF knew where the enemy aircraft or our own aircraft were. The reporting centre was at Colchester. About every five miles or so, there was an Observer Corp. Their post in Baddow was first of all at the top of Galleywood Road not far from Readers Corner. A lot of the present houses weren't there in those days. It was open countryside. After a time it was moved to the top of West Hanningfield Road, way past Marconi Research (as it was then), almost opposite Great Sir Hughes, in a field. I suppose the reason for that was because if you got away from the houses you got better visibility. Also they were higher up. They had to plot aircraft with their instruments. Most of the people on that were elderly people, of Dad's age. Mr. Sparrow, who lived next door, was part of it. Billy Jackson, from the garage, I think was in charge.

Alan continued:
My father was involved in the First World War. He was in Egypt and the Holy Land for four years. He was on the Gallipoli affair, which was quite a disaster.

John Jackson's father carried out special war effort:
Dad had been involved during the war making small quantity runs of special items, which the big factories did not want to tool up to deal with. He made batches of two hundred or three hundred "bomb rings", which were intricate and involved very precise engineering. You were left with a wall 20 thou, (0.02 inch) thick, which was prone to split.
That kind of wartime work was apportioned out so that no one knew much about the final picture, and final assembly was usually done at a Government establishment.

Chris Woollard's father Arnold Woollard was also in the Home Guard. Arnold was born in 1900. He worked at a flourmill for T.D.Ridley & son as the Head Maltster. He was attached to the 6th Essex Home Guard headquarters. Due to his occupation it was inconvenient to fire his allotted issue of ammunition. He took the opportunity to go to Jackson's pit, off Baddow Road, to fire at china disc targets.

It is understood this was behind the Beehive Public House, in the old quarry area. The pit was the rifle range for the Home Guard. We believe that the US forces used it too. Chris, aged nine, went with his father, and a friend Peter Howlett aged thirteen or fourteen, to Jackson's pit to observe. His father used a heavy gun, a Brownings automatic rifle (BAR). He also watched his father at other ranges.

Rash Chan, an Indian officer, was in charge of the Home Guard. He lived near the Blue Lion pub and died in 1945.

Women weren't excluded from war-related duties. Peggy Bradley was in the Fire Service before working on the land:

> I joined the fire service in 1940 so I was in it during the war. I wasn't operational, I was stuck down in the control rooms, in Market Road. I eventually went to the headquarters in Springfield Road. I wanted to get out of the fire service, as I wasn't happy. The only way I could get out of the fire service was to take a job on the land. So I went to Little Sir Hughes fruit farm, on the West Hanningfield Road. We were living by that time in a cottage quite near there.

Flossie Steel's father was involved in a different role in World War One. He had to set up a canteen for the soldiers who kept their horses in the area now occupied by the recreation ground and Chelmerton Avenue. German prisoners of war (POWs) were housed next door to Orchard Villa, that stood where Chelmer Lea now stands.

Farmer Reg Spalding was also affected by the Great War. He wrote in his journal:

> In 1914 the First World War broke out with Germany. Soon all the spare sheds at the farm were taken by the army for horses. I think we had twenty, plus all their wagons and stores; I think we were paid about 1s-8d (= 9p) a day all told. Later on I was called up and went for a medical, but I was graded C3 so the tribunal sent me back to the farm. I would have liked to have gone into the forces but Mother had nobody to help her carry on.

Reg Bush could also recall World War One. Apparently in 1916 a Zeppelin was spotted in flames in the skies above Sandon and crashed a few miles away. Young Reg's dad quickly harnessed up the pony to their trap so that they could inspect the wrecked airship. It turned out to be a longer journey than they expected, the crash site being at Great Burstead.

Dora Norrington remembered an officer called Captain Young who lodged with them before the war. (Photo 9-3). The caption is: Captain Young telling me a story wearing my sun bonnet. My sister Phyllis is wearing Captain Wilkinson's hat and sword. Captain Young's name for me was "screw eyes". Captain Young was killed in 1915 leading his men. I was heart broken, I loved him.

The photograph was taken at "Brambles", Little Baddow, in 1913.

Baddow House used POWs in World War Two. Jesse Pryke told us:

> There was a prisoner of war camp at Writtle. My dad (Jesse Pryke senior) managed to borrow some Italian prisoners of war to help with sorting out the stream. During the war it got choked up with bamboo and things growing in the bed of the stream.
> I can remember some POWs in Chelmsford but I don't think there were any in the village. I think they were doing something by the river in Chelmsford.

Bangs, Bombs and Blackout

Great Baddow received its fair share of bombs and rockets. Anderson shelters were in use. Daylight raids disrupted children's lessons and homework, play and sleep were disrupted by night-time visits by the Luftwaffe. Some people lost their lives when their houses were bombed or when they were hit by shrapnel. When a bomb dropped nearby or a plane crashed there was often some excitement and people visited the site and even collected memorabilia. Streetlights were not lit, and it was an offence to show even a chink of light through your curtains after dark as it could possibly provide guidance to an enemy aircraft.

Peggy Bradley says:

> I can remember Dorset Avenue being bombed. I can remember my father at number 22 putting steel shutters up at the downstairs window, for protection. There was quite a lot of blast at times.

> I can remember only one air raid shelter. A few months after we were married we shared a house on Baddow Road, opposite Chelmerton Avenue, with some friends. Then we moved to Vicarage Road in Chelmsford where we lived with an elderly lady. She had an indoor Morrison shelter and she had rather a smelly dog. We weren't worried about raids, but as soon as she heard the siren, she would knock on the door to get us to go down in the shelter. We didn't want to get in the shelter with her and the smelly dog. All we wanted to do was sleep.

> Prior to getting out of the fire service I recall we were both on duty at times. We had twenty four hours off and forty eight hours on. To go back to the little cottage my husband and I occupied on Little Sir Hughe's fruit farm for twenty four hours was absolute bliss, a bit of peace and quiet. We had a landmine land in the field at the side of the cottage. We were away at the time. My father rang me, after investigating, to say there didn't seem to be any damage. I think that it was such an old cottage that it moved with the blast. Not even a window was broken.

Colleen Yaxley recalled a bomb dropping near New Road during the war, which left a large crater:

> We used to cycle up and down this crater. Our children also played in it, as the crater was still there when *they* were young. Thankfully the bomb missed Jeffery Road and Baddow Hall Avenue.
> Another bomb dropped in Great Baddow behind Dr Lyster's surgery in The Yews. It was a big old house, with a long garden, which was fortunate because the bomb dropped there. The pond is still there at the bottom of the recreation ground. We were told to keep away, as the water was very, very deep.

> In our garden my granddad and uncle built an air raid shelter under what was the rockery. Then they rebuilt the rockery over the top of it. During the war we spent much of our time in one or other of the brick built air raid shelters. One is still there. There was no proper lighting so we passed the time by singing or being read to. When the siren went we went in it and when the 'all clear' was sounded we practised crawling out of the rear escape exit. I was far more frightened of the mosquitoes flying about than the bombs.

In the latter part of the war we had a Morrison table shelter indoors. My aunt, who worked at Hoffman's on night work during the war, used to sleep on top of it during the day. If the siren went we all had to bundle in there at night. My grandmother used to take her box of legal papers in there but it was always taken out during the day.

I can remember standing in the garden with my granddad, and a couple of soldiers, and all the planes were flying high overhead coming to bomb London. One of these silly soldiers said, "come on then, drop them". My granddad said, "don't be so daft".

Reg Spalding wrote of the damage at Meadgate Farm in his journal:
At Meadgate we had been very unlucky. A big landmine landed seventy yards from the front of the house. Luckily the blast went upwards, but it blew all the windows in and blew off the roof. Then when the vacuum filled up the windows came outwards. I was picked up and thrown right across the lane and into a ditch, landing on my head. After that I spent twenty seven days in bed in a Chelmsford hospital.

Jim Hurrell witnessed a blast too:
During the early part of the war a bomb dropped in the Recreation Ground. We were sitting under the kitchen table. The house was shaken, greenhouse glass was broken, which destroyed the crop of tomatoes. The blast went down Longfield Road causing much damage. My Mother's bone china tea service was damaged even though it was packed away in a drawer. Everything in the house jumped one foot. The air-raid shelter was delivered next day!

John Kemp's record of events goes thus:
A land mine landed in the Recreation ground. It was a parachute mine. Everybody who saw it thought it was a torpedo. I was staying with Mr Willsher, who I called Buller. (He was nicknamed Buller after General Redvers Henry Buller, who commanded the British Armies during the relief of Mafeking in the Boer War). He saw the mine in the air. He said it was attached to a parachute that had not opened properly. I was young and under the stairs at the time, which we used as a shelter.
I think it was aimed at Hoffman's, but I don't know how a bomb with a parachute can be aimed. It had to be a hit and miss attempt as the wind was in the wrong direction. It was lucky for us it landed in an open space. It made a very large crater. Large amounts of it went through what was then the Co-op grocery shop, which is now Robert Michael Interiors. One large piece went through the back room of number one Valley Cottages where Mr & Mrs Moore lived, and chopped the back leg off the sofa. We were under the stairs in 2, Valley Cottages (Mrs Moore as well).

There was much damage. The fallout and debris came over the Blue Lion and landed in the road. It's difficult to pinpoint where the crater was. There are now lots of trees in the recreation ground. I still feel that hole, other than the other two man-made ponds, is part of the original crater, although some people say it was filled in. I remember several air raids. As boys we used to find bits of incendiary bombs on what was the farm chase, on Manor Farm. They were collected and hidden. I suppose it was a bit dangerous, but it was interesting to us as boys.

[Ed: In the Essex Record Office the official map of the area dated 1894 shows three ponds in the Recreation ground, all of which formed part of the garden of Noakes Place. The crater could be the pond alongside Palmerston Lodge or it could have been further into the Recreation Ground and filled in later].

Rosemary Hill remembers a different explosion:

> The loudest noise in my life was a land mine that exploded a few feet above ground in Southend Road. Father was on duty in West Hanningfield Road, and the explosion occurred between his post and our house, and he agonised over whether we had been hit, and wanted to come home and verify that we were all right.
>
> There was another explosion in a field near here, an area they called the 'bomb-hole' on the right hand side.
>
> I remember some bombs being dropped in Molrams Lane. There were six or eight. I was home with my mother and lying on the floor under the table, or else we went in the cupboard under the stairs if there was an air raid and listened to the bombs getting louder. They weren't huge bombs. They dropped them in Molrams Lane on the other side to where the houses are now. I don't know whether they were just dotting them. It was at night. We had Marconi Research Labs here which was a target.
>
> Hoffman's was unlucky. My husband Roland was at Hoffman's later on but not during the war. The V2 rockets landed on it. I can remember watching the doodlebugs coming over from the east, as we had a lovely open sky. There was then an awful silence before they came down. We didn't experience any bombs landing very close.

[Ed: At the end of the war they found scale models of the Hoffman and Marconi factories in German Luftwaffe stations].

Eileen Hance recorded:

> I worked at Hoffman's and Marconi's during the war years. I lived close to Hoffman's, so we were affected by the bombing. We lived opposite Archer's suet factory in New Street, next to the Cathedral school.
>
> We were bombed one night, when fire bombs (incendiaries) hit Archer's. That went up in flames and the fire engines dealt with that. We had one in our bedroom that had come through the roof onto the bed. Unfortunately my mother had a family bible and that was destroyed. We ran upstairs and threw the burning mattress out through the window. We had just managed to put it out when the door was thrown open, firemen rushed in with a hose and they were covered in suet from the factory. The firemen did more damage than the fire. However, we lived to tell the tale. I could not understand why people had to come and gawp. All the windows were broken, but we were still living there, but as the workers passed on their way to Hoffman's they stopped to glare in. Afterwards there was lots of community spirit. I remember a line of people passing on pails of water. My father was in the line; he knew everyone and would stop for a chat, and stopped passing on the water.

John Parkinson gave a first hand account of RAF action when he was a pupil at KEGS:

> During a daylight air raid we pupils hiding under desks saw a German bomber in a low-level attack on Hoffman's being chased by a Spitfire.

Bert Collis was at KEGS too. He tells us:

> Entry to the school in 1939 was delayed. The term started three or four weeks late as they were waiting to complete the air raid shelters. We only used them for a few months. The Headmaster said it wasted too much time going down to the shelters. Nothing happened and we were trying to work in impossible conditions. They changed the routine. Instead of the electric bell ringing for the change of lessons a hand bell was used. The electric bell was connected to the spotters on Marconi's roof. If the sirens

went we just carried on working but if the electric bell rang we got under the desks. We were in the hall one morning, which was then where the library is now. The electric bell rang. We all went down on the floor apart from Tom Harden. He typically put his head out of the window. He said, "it's alright, it's one of ours". Then six bombs landed on Swiss Avenue! I think he was duly chastened, but it was difficult to chasten Tom.

I remember when one morning we were regaled by the Headmaster, because he had a phone call from the Head Mistress of the girls' school. She said the boys were being cheeky to the girls in the shelters. Anyone who was there got a Saturday morning detention of two and half-hours. I was there so I got a detention. I can't remember having any truck with the girls though. It was a different atmosphere then. Any boy who was even seen by other boys with a girl from the High School got endless ribbing.

Tony Horsnell was also at school at the time and recorded:
Various bombs hit the village. It used to be one of our regular activities in the mornings, to rush round the playing fields to try to collect parts of things that had dropped off bombs or aircraft.
On Galleywood Common every now and again the undergrowth would be burnt off. They didn't want the Germans to set light to it, as it would light up Chelmsford and mark it for bombing.
I saw a V1 or V2 came down by Howard's farm but that was the only one I remember.

Derek Hurrell said:
We had bombs in the village during the war. We were evacuated to my mother's mother at the bottom of Beehive Lane. We had to leave all the windows open in Baddow Hall Avenue, because of the bombs that dropped in the park opposite and in the allotments. The next day we looked down the hole and then we were told afterwards that they hadn't exploded. Last year I walked through the village, with a friend who lives in Oxfordshire, but I was at school with him in Baddow. It was June and a hot day. When we walked through the park we could still see the different colouring in the grass where the bomb hole was in the park opposite Baddow Hall Avenue.
I used to walk to the school up Crescent Road and Jeffery Road and through to the school from that direction. There would be shrapnel around of course and flying bombs and all sorts of things.
We had blackout and we had a dugout in the garden, but we didn't have a shelter in the back room. My mother was there a lot on her own. My brother and I used to go down to the dugout that was made before the war. My father didn't do it personally as he was at work. He got local people to do it. After the war he used it as his compost area. As we got older it looked smaller and smaller. As children we used to able to lie flat out in it, but when we became adults it looked no size at all. My brother can remember when the siren went off at the beginning of the Second World War. He asked my father "what does that mean?"
Dad said, "it means we are at war".

I can't remember back to 1939, but I do remember the doodlebugs flying over. I wasn't old enough to know about the Battle of Britain, which my brother remembers. When the siren went we would all troop down to the dugout. My brother would take the canary in the cage. When we came out the first thing mother did was to put the kettle on. That went on for quite a long time. We always went down there, though it was quite nasty of course, but fun for kids. We slept down there, as it was big enough for two boys to sleep in. Mother used to sit in a chair. I expect in the summer it was quite pleasant but in the winter it couldn't have been very good - damp and cold and horrible.

Alan Willis reminded us that it was very difficult to get about after dark:
> It's very difficult for people today to imagine what it was like. Everywhere was blacked out. There were no lights at all. Finding your way home from work, in the dark, was quite an activity.

Rationing

There were general shortages of food, clothing, sweets and toys. There was a 'black market' in many commodities, but most people were too poor to afford these things. (Aside: women painted a fine black line down their legs to simulate sheer nylon stockings, which were virtually impossible to buy). There has been the suggestion that our diet then was healthier than our current diet. We had less meat, no junk food and more fresh vegetables. We worked harder and spent less time sitting down.

With many of the staple foods in short supply, Baddow mums still managed reasonably well to provide balanced meals to their families. None of our interviewees claim to have come near to starving in the war.

Even after the war rationing continued for several years. Peggy Bradley says:
> Soon after the war, in 1946, we were still rationed for various things. You could only be registered with one milkman; you couldn't get your milk just anywhere. At this time, the milkman always left our gate open. My father got so cross because the milkman had let the dog out into the road, so Dad asked him not to call anymore. The milkman said, "you won't be able to get your milk anywhere else". My father, not to be outdone, went to Danbury Park and bought a Guernsey cow. Beyond number 22, Beehive Lane was a space, just before the gravel pit. He virtually built a cowshed round the cow. It shows how Beehive Lane has altered; there were grass verges then, as you went towards Galleywood. Each morning he would tether the cow on different areas of the grass verges, to graze. My mother had a busy time making butter. My father didn't like to be short of sugar, so a bit of bartering went on. Eventually the cow was sold.

Colleen Yaxley confirmed that the health of residents was good:
> I can't remember there being any shortage of food in our family. There were five of us, and sometimes six, when my father was home on leave. I suppose it was just stretched. You can do that with a family. Apparently I was a bit greedy with cheese and butter. My grandmother made me have my ration separately, which was two ounces of each per week. I used to eat celery so I could get more cheese if I had eaten up my entire ration. I didn't like celery! They gave me cheese if I had celery. I expect it was to teach me a lesson. It hasn't worked because I still eat lots of butter and cheese. Grandmother used to make a lovely stew. There were lots of vegetables and big fat dumplings in it, but not much meat. I seem to remember us always having a joint at the weekend. I don't remember there were too many shortages or that we were ever hungry. We had dried egg and scrambled dried egg. I suppose it was a healthy diet. I do remember not tasting or seeing a banana until after the war. Then I didn't particularly like them.

Colleen reminded us that there were some places you could not visit during the war. For instance you could not go onto many beaches because of the barbed wire placed there to hinder any invaders.

Janet Chilvers:

When eggs were on rationing they were only available every two or three weeks. There was a dairy behind Jones's garage in Baddow Road. You were allowed two or three eggs each. They put them in blue sugar bags. We very rarely got them all back home whole. I can remember looking out at the orchards, at the back of the houses. The trees are all gone now it's been built up. Later on I can only remember sweets being rationed. Though when I was a bridesmaid in 1952 we were lucky to get dresses made as the material was still on coupons.

Jim Hurrell:

Mother was a good cook and eked out the rations in war. Luckily her father was a poultry farmer and gave her all the cracked and soft-shelled eggs that could not be sold. Dad had an allotment so we had plenty of vegetables. That was on Pound field, now the bypass, so we did not go short of food.

Florence Hardwick:

When one looks back I just wonder how we existed. We had 9d worth of meat and two ounces of butter. It was incredible really. The fact that people grew their own vegetables made a difference. You had to make clothes out of curtain material and things like that. 'Make do and Mend' was our motto. Yes and there was Spam! We actually sacrificed one or two ration points for a tin of the spiced luncheon meat, which was bland and extremely unexciting. We just accepted it I suppose.

People sometimes say that children were healthier then than now. I don't know if that's possible but I sometimes think that there are a lot of old people about now, and probably, they are the people who existed during the war. It was a very restricted diet without too much sweet stuff and convenience foods. Sweets were rationed and we didn't have the soft drinks we have now, or the tins of drinks.

Another Baddow feature mentioned by many contributors was the British Restaurant. Florence Hardwick told us:

The British Restaurant was an organisation set up by the government to supply food for people during the war. You could go there to get a meal. You had to pay. If I remember rightly you had to give up a ration coupon too.

Den Harvey:

The Bell Centre during the war was the British Restaurant and at the end was the only fish and chip shop open at night. There is a door, you go in from Bell Street, then steps down to where the counter was. The whole building is one level but you stepped down to that end, as Bell Street is very high at the top. The local people complained about the smell, so it closed down. (Photo 9-4).

Derek Hurrell:

One of the tasks I had was to take the weekly order to my old aunt in Bell Street. I'm talking about the end of the war when the rationing was about a half an ounce of this and that. The bag I used to take to her had hardly anything in it. I'm sure my father didn't let her go without.

National Service

Some of the men of Great Baddow born too late to serve in World War Two spent two years doing their National Service, which was eventually stopped around 1961. Some of their experiences are worth recording.

Clive Barker told us of his service career:

I went into the Royal Artillery. Same as my father. I did all right there. My headmaster didn't think I was officer material, so I went into the ranks, and I was a sergeant in eleven months. I thoroughly enjoyed it really. I was only in for two years. My friend Peter Sincock, another Baddow Road lad, came out three years ago as brigadier, MBE, a very famous man. He was born and bred in Baddow Road. He now lives in Warminster. When they held some hostages in the desert recently, he was on television. I was the first one to ring him to congratulate him on the interview he gave. We both went to KEGS. He went to Sandhurst straight from school.

I have happy memories of the forces. I was very keen, and when you are labelled a *Sports Person* you 'fly', don't you? Fortunately I was in the cadet force at the grammar school, so I knew how to 'bull' (i.e. highly polish) boots, how to march and carry out rifle drill. Also I was a marksmen (i.e. I had achieved a high standard at shooting), so they didn't have to teach me much. I was an instructor at school. I was fit and could do nine miles in full kit.

I could put together a Sten (machine gun), blindfolded, and Bren half blindfolded. We used to teach how to assemble these weapons and I could beat the kids blindfolded. The Sten gun was a totally inaccurate gun, but the Bren gun was quite accurate. It was almost as accurate as the old .303 rifle.

In North Wales we had a .303 range at Llangollen and we used to fire the 25 pounders at Trawsfynnydd, which ended up as an atomic power station. It was all War Department land then.

Bert Hunt's Father was in the Army and was at Dunkirk. Bert also 'did his bit'. He said:

I served two years in National Service and played football. I joined the Royal Corps of Signals and was posted to Port Said, Egypt. I connected telephone lines to ships, and worked in telephone exchanges. It was an interesting two years. It broadens one's views.

Bert Collis went into the army just as the war finished. He told us:

In 1946, two days after my eighteenth birthday, I got my calling up papers for the army. A week after that I was reporting to Bury St. Edmunds, where I did my basic training. Then because I was working on surveying I was allocated to the Royal Engineers, which was exactly what I wanted to do.

My father had also been in the Army, between the wars. He was in the Grenadier Guards for three years just at the beginning of the 1920's. He was born in 1903 and so he probably went into the army in 1921. He was mostly on guard at Buckingham Palace and Windsor Castle and so on. He spent several months when he was just an ordinary guardsman as batman to a Lord. When I applied for officer training a panel of officers interviewed me. The central one was a Colonel from the Cold Stream Guards. He said, "was your father in the army?"

I said, "Grenadier Guards, sir".

"Really, what was his rank?"

"Guardsman, sir".

"Oh!"

That was the end of the interview in 1946. I hope it's different now.

Evacuees

Many children from cities were evacuated to the country, to places like Gt.Baddow. Many evacuated children suffered from isolation from their parents. They were usually billeted on volunteer families. There was overcrowding in the country schools, and local children sometimes resented the incomers. Some evacuees settled in the area to which they had been sent.

Strangely enough, although the Chelmsford area was a target for bombs, plus V1 & V2 rockets, people were evacuated to the village from London. Apparently, there were so many evacuees here there is now a society for former evacuees. One of our interviewees, John Kemp, was one of the evacuees who came to Gt.Baddow in 1939 from Tottenham. He tells us:

> Originally I stayed with a Mr & Mrs Avis in Crescent Road, Great Baddow, but only for a few weeks. Then I went to a Mr & Mrs Willsher at 2, Valley Cottages, which is opposite the Blue Lion.
> I was very lucky in that, though I was only a boarder, they kind of adopted me and I stayed until 1953 when I was twenty-one and I married.
>
> I attended the village school by the Church the majority of time. When we first arrived in Great Baddow the school was already full. I think there must have been a hundred evacuees and we were distributed around. I went to school at Foxon's, next to the old brewery, in the front room (i.e. Baddow Place). I went to the Parish Hall and to what was, eventually, the British Restaurant and then the library. As the other evacuees drifted back to London we got into the main school.

Kathleen Stevens was most put out when she was sent from Great Baddow as an evacuee:
> Father asked my aunt and uncle, who were moving to High Wycombe, to take me with them to avoid the war. Meanwhile my father and brother stayed in Chelmsford. I felt jealous of my brother for being allowed to stay.

The Village in Wartime

So how did Gt.Baddow cope with the war?
In many ways life went on as usual - children went to school, mums did their washing every Monday and their ironing every Tuesday. Shopping still needed to be done, albeit under the constraints of rationing. People still attended church as they had done pre-war, but no doubt their praying was more intense, with a common purpose. Everyone wanted the war to end, and for their loved ones to return safely home, but there were other feelings too. Many women had been released from the boring routine of household chores to carry out exciting worthwhile wartime duties.

Peggy Bradley:
> I used to drive the tractor at Little Sir Hughe's fruit farm, and do some of the spraying. That was quite a happy time. It was nice to be outside, and enjoying the country air.

However, for many there were extra duties necessitated by the war, which had to be fitted into 'normal' daily life. Den Harvey talked about his Mum's landlord:
> Old Laurie Russell, the landlord of my mum's place, used to be the fire engine driver during the war, not that I remember that, obviously. I do remember him driving the fire engine after the war just before 1950. He knew the village well, and when the blackouts

were on, he was the man to drive the fire engine. It was voluntary then. The siren would sound and off Laurie Russell went in his fire engine.

Philip Taylor's parents had a novel additional duty apart from apple farming. He says:
We have a photograph of the garden lawn covered in rabbit hutches. It was a means of producing protein in difficult times. We have some very interesting photographs that were taken by the government at the time, as a way of showing people that the country wasn't starving; it was being fed. They showed lots of activities going on the farm, picking apples and so on, and food being produced. (Photo 9-5)

Although it was not part of their contract local firemen laid on a party for local children. Gillian Crowe (née Russell) remembers that they made jam tarts as big as dinner plates.

Bert Collis remembers special duties for his parent:
During the war our house on the Maldon Road was the police station. The lounge was used as the police office. It was the reporting place for twenty-four special constables every night. I usually had to do my homework for the Grammar School under the table, as it was the only place I could get. There were two war reserve constables, one a Mr. West from Sandon, who was a retired barge skipper and a very fascinating character.

During wartime the Collis family earned a little extra (and helped the war effort) by dismantling dud and broken radio valves provided by a local manufacturer, salvaging the OK parts and supplying the bits back to the supplier to be remade into new valves. They got 1d per hundred.

There were other stories that could not be told at the time. For instance a Mr Peterson was sent from London to work at Marconi's during the war, working on secret projects. He lived with his wife in Baddow Hall Crescent. When his masters in London wished to speak to him they rang the police station. I had to run to his house to get him to the phone. Everyone had to go out the room while he answered his call. I became quite friendly with Mr & Mrs Peterson, who had no children of their own, so they sort of adopted me. They taught me how to play chess. Mr Peterson had been a Marconi-trained radio operator on ships pre-war. He had many momentoes of South America, including butterfly wings. He spoke several languages.

The gun emplacement at the end of Molrams Lane was disguised as a shop, but built in a concrete bunker. The anti-tank gun poked through the shop window and even had a Wall's ice cream advert pasted on the barrel to disguise it. There were six soldiers based there, and when they were equipped with rifles they managed to get an extra one for my father to use in an emergency. Dad was ex-grenadier guards and could handle a rifle.
Derek Hurrell:
My father and his brother, my uncle Jack, ran a shop in Great Baddow called Hurrell's Stores, opposite Crescent Road (now Crowe's). They were there from 1936 until about 1956. My father had served in the back end of the first war. He wasn't called up for the second war, he was forty-ish but he had to be a special constable. He worked all day in the shop and was out most evenings. He was out when the bombs were all round the Blue Lion pub, where the lake is now. A landmine dropped there and he was there the night it happened.

Dora Norrington recalled an infamous character of the time. From other contributions it is believed that this man was William Joyce, Lord 'Haw-Haw'. He was living in Gt.Baddow before the war. He renewed his passport in August 1939 and travelled to Germany in that month to offer his services to Josef Goebbels' Nazi propaganda ministry.

> Dora: During the 1930s and the early part of the war we kept a post office and grocery shop at the corner of Baddow Road and Beehive Lane. There was a black shirt (British Nationalist) living on the corner of Chelmerton Avenue. He was a very nice gentleman. He used to come in and buy all of his groceries. He was very polite.
>
> Some months later, after we had sold up the shop and the war had started, a detective came to see us. He wanted to know all about this black shirt. I said, "I can only tell you that he was a very nice gentleman. He never spoke anything about the war". The detective wanted to know so much, but I couldn't tell him, and I didn't want to be involved. The man we were discussing had disappeared shortly before the war started. "That's what we want to know," the detective said. "We want to know where he is and what happened. Did he have meetings? I had been told that there were lights on nearly all night". They suspected that there had been meetings going on in his house. There were always closed dark curtains at the windows. He was thought to hold meetings there and entertain many visitors as he bought large amounts of groceries from the shop, always calling first thing in the morning. Dora remarked to her mother at the time that he was a customer to be valued. He always wore a black shirt - was very good looking, polite and well spoken. (Sir Oswald Mosley also called in the shop).

He also sent telegrams from the Post Office and Dora remembers one in particular, going to London "Saw G.P last night". What did he mean by GP? A doctor? Working it out much later he meant 'German Plane'.

His arrest at the end of the war by two British Officers on the German Danish border was bizarre:

Two British officers were collecting firewood when a civilian called in French to draw their attention to useful branches. Not understood, he repeated his remark, but in English. One officer told the other he thought he recognised that haughty drawl.

But how to cleverly unmask the man? They evolved a master plan, worthy of Blackadder. "I say" said one officer, approaching the civilian, "are you by any chance William Joyce?" At which Joyce made a snatching movement towards his pocket. The second officer fired his revolver, wounding Joyce in the hand and backside. It transpired that he had not been reaching for a weapon, but for a passport declaring him to be a German civilian. Denying that he held British nationality during the war did not save him - the transcript of his Old Bailey trial reveals that it took the jury just twenty three minutes to find him guilty of treason.

Another interesting fact is that William Joyce was escorted back to England by a Military Policeman from Great Baddow. (Photo 9-6 of William Joyce).

Jesse Pryke was living with his parents in Baddow House at the beginning of the war:

> An anti-aircraft gun was 'posted' to Gt.Baddow. A hole was smashed into the wall of Baddow House grounds in Vicarage Lane and the gun positioned in the garden. Many times my sister and I ran to hide when the gun started firing at German planes and rockets.

The Prykes knew of a Russian 'boffin' who used to cycle to the Marconi labs during the night if a brilliant idea came to him. A US company poached him. Jesse has a memory of a barrage balloon which had broken free from its Chelmsford mooring drifting to the grounds of Baddow House, the wire getting caught in trees, and a rescue team winching it in and taking it back to Chelmsford.

He also recalled that the Gibcracks farm in Danbury (formerly owned by Jesse senior) was commandeered by the MOD (Ministry of Defence) in World War Two and Baddow Road hospital was an army barracks.

Sadie Gemmell also mentioned troops billeted locally:

There was a large army camp on West Hanningfield Road, opposite Pontlands (there are houses there now). Sadie walked her brother to school past the army camp. A young officer was billeted with the family and he asked if his wife could stay with them. She became part of the family. She had a camera and took many photos. She was so appreciative that she helped Sadie's mother. As they lived on a farm they had good food during the war.

At the end of the war Sadie remembers sitting on the officer's lap listening to the church bells. "That means PEACE" he explained. It was wonderful.

Rosemary Hill remembered the troops in the village:

During the war a number of soldiers, who were billeted here, took over the old brewery on the Southend Road, which had been derelict for a while. We used to get different groups coming in but not Americans. The 'Yanks' just used to come to the village for dances. There were quite a lot of soldiers about. We went to church on Sunday mornings and there was always a church parade when the soldiers were here. I don't know why they were billeted here. Several of the girls got married to the soldiers when they were billeted in the district. A friend of mine married a soldier who came from Cumbria. Then the soldiers were posted abroad.

Colleen Yaxley:

I know that soldiers were billeted here because my aunt married one of those soldiers. They used to march up and down New Road. Children used to march up and down with them. We had soldiers billeted with us too but I don't know where they slept. I had to sleep at one stage in a cupboard under the stairs. I liked it. I put pictures up on the wall and took my toys in there. I think it was an interim period after Dunkirk. A lot of them were young soldiers from the North Country. We couldn't understand anything they said!

Entertainment

Thankfully wartime was not all doom and gloom. In Great Baddow people managed to enjoy themselves, mainly by making their own entertainment. The 'wireless' was an important standby, giving up to date news, but especially for the uplifting programmes such as Tommy Handley's ITMA (It's That Man Again). The theatre and cinema provided escapist entertainment, once Gaumont British News had given a taste of the harsh realities of warfare and the latest propaganda to lift our spirits.

Peggy Bradley:

I remember the Ritz, which was then called the Odeon. I remember 'Mrs Minivere' was one of the big films, during the war.

Den Harvey:

The old reading room in the Bell Centre was the nearest thing we had to a community centre.

Mum used to go to bingo and to the young wives' club, held in the tin hut in the vicarage grounds. There were also whist drives. There was the library, which is now the Bell Centre. Before it was the library it was the British Restaurant and a school.

John Jackson made his own cinema:

> During my early days when the war started I was in the youth club as were most boys and girls. I used to give a film show at the Parish Hall. I used to hire a film from Body's the chemist in Chelmsford for 1s-6d a spool. I used to have it for three days. They were mostly First World War films and I remember one with U-boats and Q-ships. The children got very excited with that one, which was a 5-reeler, lasting one and a half hours! There was no sound. I had a radiogram with a speaker behind the screen in the Parish Hall. You might forget to wind it up. Sometimes it would blow up and the children would cheer and clap. The projector fuse would blow and the transformer would smoke, and I would have to wait for it to cool down. It was all in black and white, with no talking. I used to choose the music. For Q-ships I chose 'Dance of the Hours' as it had exciting music in it. There was dreamy music too. In the dark you had to pick out the right track to go with the scene.
>
> I remember the children in Baddow really loving these old films. They all went quiet, then they used to cheer when things went right, and cheer when the projector went wrong! They hissed the baddie and shouted out, "he's behind you". They shouted at the screen as if it was a play.

Colleen Yaxley:

> I had rare treats when my aunt took me to London during the war, to see shows. We saw 'The Dancing Years' and 'Merry England'. I remember hearing the sirens go in London. We used to come back on the train. Nobody seemed to bother much then. We got blasé about it all. I was lucky in that way.

Alan Willis remembered:

> There were cinemas and dances and they were well attended by the Americans troops from Boreham. Most of my life, prior to being called up, revolved around the church, Sunday school and in later times Sunday school for older boys. The older boys met at the tin hut, on Sundays, instead of going to Sunday school. We could go to church if we wanted to.

Conclusion

So, in conclusion, Great Baddow suffered in the wartime, but it survived remarkably well. Villagers carried on with their life, they helped one another, and as far as they were able, they enjoyed life. Many even enjoyed the experience!

Photo 9-1   Spitfire Mk VB 'LF'

Photo 9-2   Vultee Vengeance

Photo 9-3   Dora & Phyllis
with Captain Young

Photo 9-5 Apple Stacking

Photo 9-4   The Bell Centre

Photo 9-6 William Joyce

Chapter 10 - Religion

Introduction

For many of our older interviewees church and church-based activities were an integral part of life. As Rosemary Hill said, "I've always been involved in the church. I like my Sundays, I like church, it's part of my way of life." Alan Willis felt the same. "Most of my life, prior to being called up, revolved around the church," an involvement which continued after he was demobbed from the army.

Village Worship

In the village we find a variety of places of worship. For the Church of England congregation, St.Mary's is the established church and dominates the area with its tower and steeple. (Photo 10-1). Reg Spalding, in his diary, wrote of its vicar, Reverend Alfred Noel Colley, who he described as "A Welshman, a really good man". Apparently the church clerk Mr Harnden "sang loud amens!" Mr Mallet, the lay reader, is nicknamed 'Zam-Buk' because when he stands on his box in the pulpit delivering his message, he 'rubs it in'. [Ed: Zam-Buk was the proprietary name for an ointment like Radian-B]. He mentioned the overbearing Crabb family who owned the living of St.Mary's Church and used to sit with their watch in hand, and woe betide Mr Colley if he did not preach his sermon for forty minutes. Reg also mentioned the little bell on the outside of the spire, which was rung just before the end of the sermon in the morning service to warn the cooks in the big houses to get the dinner on. (Photo 10-2).
[Ed: We understand that the proper name for this bell is the Sanctus Bell, rung to call attention to those unable to attend that the most solemn part of the service has been reached].

The first vicar that Den Harvey could remember was Canon Kingham, who was held in high regard by many in the village. The modern old peoples' homes on Maldon Road are named after him.

Further down the High Street opposite Rothmans was the Congregational Chapel, now the United Reformed Church, which seems to have catered very well for non-conformists. (Photo 10-3). Les Sparrow described the building, saying, "It was smaller than it is now. It was an extra village hall, used for little functions and social activities". He remembered upright, cast-iron, gas-fired radiators were used for heating. As a so-called responsible person he had the job of lighting the boiler. The routine was flap up, gas on, count to twenty, light up. Result minor explosion! Dangerous but funny. The chapel has been extended and is now a pleasant building.

Colleen Yaxley explained further about her grandparents' involvement:
> It consisted of one room, and I think there was a kitchen and two outside toilets. The church was their life, and my grandfather made a beautiful table and a hymn board. He was the treasurer and lay preacher. My grandmother was the organist. She taught us new hymn tunes and carols. It was their life, and my life on a Sunday, because we had to go three times a day: morning, afternoon Sunday school and the evening service. I remember changing clothes and black patent shoes three times a day. We had to change clothes each time when we came home.

Dora Norrington's family also had ties with the chapel:

My grandmother used to preach in that little Congregational Chapel in Great Baddow. My mother used to play the organ. Grandfather used to stop at home. He didn't go very often, just sometimes, when she got round him. I don't think he wanted to hear her preaching. He had enough of it at home! At one time the chapel was led by John Lewis Sparrow, one of the village blacksmiths.

Dora Norrington:

Along Baddow Road on the Chelmsford side of the Beehive pub was the Congregation Church, in what was known as the Mission Room. It was used as a church and as a parish hall. The Boys Brigade used it as its headquarters under Mr Newton who was the Sunday School Superintendent. Some people called it the Tin Tabernacle. The congregation sat on forms and plays and concerts were held there. Mrs Boreham, my mother, fitted out the hall and provided refreshments for these occasions and for visiting clergy. A Mr Spurgeon normally rang the bell, though on one occasion during a storm it rang unaided.

In Bell Street opposite the Bell Centre, there used to be the chapel belonging to the Peculiar People, a religious sect who broke away from the Methodists. (Photo 10-4). (The chapel is now used by St.Mary's Church). The 'PPs' were very pious and demonstrative in their worship, which occupied most of every Sunday. 'Peculiar People' in this context means 'Specially chosen by God'. They did not have parsons, and one of their leaders or elders in the 1930s and 40s was George Collins, who ran the local taxi service. He lived in The Hollies (now called Brick Walls) opposite the new library. Other Baddow families involved were the Flacks and the Rayners.

Reg Spalding wrote about the Peculiar People's chapel:

If it were a Sunday morning about 9 am there would be a lot of soberly dressed men and women going in. They would be carrying a bag made of American cloth containing food for the day. They would have enamel mugs containing tea, and would spend the day in Religious Worship. They were very devoted and honest people.

The sect seems to have been largely based in Essex and East London and lasted for over one hundred years.

Mention was also made of St.Paul's Church in Beehive Lane, which was formerly a tin shack in Baddow Road before being rebuilt in today's modern style.

The main church for Roman Catholics was Our Lady Immaculate in London Road, Chelmsford, which was under Monsignor Wilson. In the 1960s he created various parishes in the area; the Baddow parish being based in The Church of the Holy Name on Moulsham Lodge. The building is an unusual shape, with a glass tower, and is irreverently referred to by some Roman Catholics as 'the Mosque'. (Photo 10-5). Gt. Baddow village was part of this parish and for some years local Roman Catholics met in the Tin Hut or Reading Room, next to the Bell Centre, with a congregation of forty to fifty. (Photo 10-6). London Road or Moulsham Lodge provided the priest. Apparently mass was celebrated around the billiard table, and one young man who shall be nameless, sometimes knocked over the billiard cues to provide a little diversion during services. In the late sixties the local Roman Catholics acquired an ex-RAF hut, which was installed on land at the top of Longmead Avenue. It only had a planned life of ten years, but has given valiant service as a Roman Catholic church until recently, with a congregation of one hundred plus. The resignation of the incumbent from Moulsham Lodge has caused some recent rationalisation, and Moulsham Lodge is now 'linked' with London Road, rather than being a separate entity. Following a reduction in facilities in Writtle, Roman Catholics from there join Great Baddow Roman Catholics for mass in 'the mosque' on Saturday evenings.

Some people went to church outside the village, perhaps to the London Road Congregational Church, or like John Parkinson, to the Trinity Methodist Church in Chelmsford, or to the Cathedral, where Eileen Hance was Church Warden for eleven years.

Sunday School

Nearly every child went to Sunday school. Dora Norrington went to Sunday school, then to Bible class at St.Mary's, taken by Miss Colley, the only daughter of the Reverend Colley.
As they grew older some resented having to go to Sunday school, as Colleen Yaxley admitted. "As I got older I resented it as I had to become a Sunday school teacher. I didn't particularly like that as a teenager."

The Church Choir

Many people spoke of singing in the church choir. Les Sparrow was one such, and used to go every Friday night to choir practice. All day Sunday was given over to services and the Sunday school. Sunday afternoon, after Sunday school, was the only leisure time he had as a choirboy.

Alan Willis gave a similar commitment:
> A lot of the boys in my class at school were also members of the Sunday school and the church choir. We had choir practice on Wednesday nights and again on Friday nights, when it was the full rehearsal for the Sunday services. We had the 11 o'clock service on Sunday morning and 6 o'clock Evensong service in the evening. Although I didn't sing in the boys' choir after about fourteen, I continued in the adult choir until eighteen when I was called up, by which time my voice had fully broken. The choir was mainly comprised of young people in those days; the trained male singers had been called up so they were pleased to have anybody.

Derek Hurrell like his father and grandfather, sang in the choir - his grandfather served for twenty three years.
> Christmas and funerals were busy times for choir members. Being in the choir you had to attend the funerals, so you were let off school, went across to the church to put on your cassock and surplice. They had the choir in attendance and they would all march out for the actual interment. In those days there were no separate cemeteries, it was all in the graveyard. You used to get paid extra for attending, I can't think what it was but it didn't buy a row of houses anyway!

Carol Singing

Derek Hurrell's father would go round carol singing at Christmas time, when they would go round to individual houses and sing in the main hall. They were very well catered for in all these marvellous old buildings in the village, with mince pies, cake and perhaps a small sherry (well, they were on 'duty').

Church Parades

On Armistice Day there was always a church parade which was well attended, especially after World War Two. Les Sparrow said, "I was in the cadet corps playing the bugle. Every Armistice Sunday I used to go into the belfry at Baddow Church and with Mr Skipman, who was a First World War bugler, we used to blow the Last Post and Reveille at 11 am". Rosemary Hill remembered, "There was always a church parade when the soldiers were here in the wartime".

Church Groups

Many of people's social activities were connected with the church, perhaps through the Woman's Union, and for youngsters the Campaigners (like the Boy Scouts as Den Harvey explained) or the Boys' Brigade.

Church Fêtes and the Annual Outing

There were Church fêtes to be enjoyed and for many children the high point of the year, the Sunday School outing. Reg Spalding wrote of the church treat, held in Gilmore Park, where children would be taken by wagon and horses, lent by local farmers. Jim Hurrell travelled to his outings in Walton by coach. A convoy of Ashdown coaches lined up at the Vineyards to transport the children. Florence Hardwick used to go to Southend for her Sunday school outing, "the only time we ate out," she said.

Continuity

With the exception of the Peculiar People's Chapel, the other churches mentioned are still flourishing. People may not now spend as much time in church as those interviewed here, but most people still attend services for births, deaths and marriages. Let us hope that no one suffered the fate of John Jackson's grandfather in the 19th century. When his parents took him and his brother to be christened the parson took the two children in his arms and asked "What names?" Mother said "Solomon and Samuel", meaning one son to be called Solomon and one called Samuel. The parson misheard and said "I christen this child Solomon Samuel". When mother corrected him and said "one boy is Solomon and one is Samuel" the parson replied that it was too late, he had christened one boy. They had to think up another name for the other son, so he was called Herbert! (Photo 10-7 shows Canon Kingham performing a more recent baptism).

Note. This chapter is relatively brief concerning details of the various churches. For further reading the reader is recommended to consult the detailed notes prepared by the churches about their respective buildings.

Photo 10-1
St MAry's Church
East View

Photo 10-2   Bell for Lunch

Photo 10-3
United Reformed Church

Photo 10-4
Peculiar People's Chapel

Photo 10-5
Roman Catholic Church
of the Holy Name

Photo 10-6
Reading Room and Part-Time R.C. Church

Photo 10-7   Canon Kingham
performing a Baptism

Chapter 11 - Transport

Introduction

As you look out at the cars parked nearby you may find it hard to picture Great Baddow village without cars. Yet many of our older residents like Les Sparrow can remember a time in their childhood in the 1920s or 30s when motorised traffic was virtually non-existent.

Trade and Working Traffic

Les recalls:

It was all carts and horses in those days. In the early days the greengrocer came round with his horse and cart. One in particular was Mr Chapman from Galleywood who came round with his seasonal produce, (such as peas). You could always tell when he was about, as he used to shout out: "Pea all, pea all" and anyone who wanted peas would come out with their dishes. There was the milkman who came round, not with bottled milk in those days, but with a churn of milk. He used metal churns and had his quart, pint and half-pint measures to ladle out what you wanted. You never went out to the cart; he knew what you wanted. The milk horse knew the customers' houses, so he would be up the road ahead of the milkman to stop at the next house. He knew the route by heart as well as the milkman. Almost uncanny it was.

Harry Clayden has similar memories:

When my father was a baker at Carter's he had a horse and cart. He used to deliver down at Sandford Mill, Brook End. There is a brook there and when there was a lot of rain you couldn't get through. There used to be a little walk bridge, that was all. With the horse and cart he just drove through. (Photo 11-1) When the weather was very bad, and the water was too high for his cart, he used to have to come back into town and up Springfield Road to get to Brook End. I don't think he got paid for overtime! You didn't in those days.

The carts and horses belonging to Carters' were kept behind Brook House, which is at the bottom of Foxholes Road behind the old bakery (now a Design office and Dace's piano shop). Richard Carter spoke about the family business:

My father's sister, Elsie Carter, lived in Great Baddow until the early 1970's, and had been involved in the family business, as it was then. It consisted, initially, of delivering milk and bread by pony and traps, and bread vans. (Photo 11-2). My aunt developed at that early stage a great interest in ponies and became very successful showing harness ponies. She won a number of national competitions over the years. She moved to West Hanningfield in the mid 1970's, and continued to keep ponies and traps there until five or six years ago.

Jim Hurrell, born in 1938, recalled that his grandfather took his decorating equipment from site to site on a handcart. (See sketch). This was little more than a flat piece of wood five or six feet square mounted above two cartwheels, with a long handle.

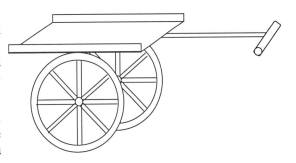

Traction engines used to trundle around Baddow in the old days. They were the motorised equivalent of heavy horses when pulling carts, but they were also hired to the local farmers at harvest time to provide the motive power to threshing machines, which separated straw from grain in the days before combine harvesters. Peggy Bradley reminded us that Mr Herbert Jackson owned the quarry off Beehive Lane (behind the old eastern Electricity Offices) and he kept traction engines there.

> Les Sparrow remembered that the traction engines used to shake the ground when they went along. They really used to rattle the High Street and Maldon Road. If anyone was ill in a particular house the farmer used to come along and put straw down 50 yards one side through to 50 yards the other side of the house so that when the traction engines went past they were muffled and did not make a noise and disturb people. It was quite a common occurrence, and as children we would know who was very ill from the straw in the road. The straw was taken up again when the people got better. (Photo 11-3).

Tractors were in evidence from World War Two onwards, and they replaced both horses and traction engines.

Horses

Horses were not only used for deliveries but also for transport. Better-off people (such as Henry Carter) kept a good horse and a fine carriage. (Photo 11-4). Dr. Spencer-Phillips initially did his rounds on a horse, or used a pony and trap, and the stables can still be seen between Yew House and Thomson's shop. (Photo 11-5). People who were not quite so well off had a donkey cart. (Photo 11-6).

Les Sparrow has a vivid and delightful memory of his very early days:

> Grannie took me one Christmas (probably around 1920) by pony and trap into town in a pitch-black night down to the Regent Cinema, then called the Regent Theatre, to see Aladdin. I remember going down in the pony and trap with the oil lamps on its sides. Baddow Road had no houses from Ebenezer Terrace until you got to the Beehive, when you came across all the terrace houses and you went along old Baddow Road until you got to Baddow Road corner. On the right hand side was a tannery, which had a big yard. When there was anything on at the Regent Theatre the pony and traps stopped at the yard. There was a man on duty and when you pulled into the yard he would look after the trap while you went into the theatre. It was an open yard, had high walls and there were some buildings on which they had some hooks to tether the horses. Some horses were taken out of the traps and just tethered and the shafts went down to the ground but most of them were left in the traps. The theatre only lasted about two hours like it does today.
>
> I do not remember much about Aladdin except about the vision of colour and lights and a lot of laughter that sticks in my memory. But coming back was a memorable journey because as we came back from the theatre it was snowing. When we got back to the tannery yard, the trap was all right as we had a big leatherette rug over the front, but as we came back towards Baddow it snowed and snowed. There was no one about except for several ponies and traps with their oil lamps flicking. I don't remember any streetlights but there must have been some.

Mrs H.Ely, born in 1885, was also taken out by her grandmother she wrote:

> I often went to London with my Grandmother, and remember riding in a hansom cab, and on top of an open horse-drawn bus.

In 1934, aged fourteen, Peggy Bradley was working in a shop in Stock. She told us:

> It was very difficult to get to Stock, in time for the shop to open. So I rode the horse out there, and stabled it around the corner from the shop. It was quite a hard ride. There were buses, but I don't think they ran very frequently. Rather than be late for work I rode there on the horse.

Aeroplanes

Peggy seemed to like adventure. When she was a girl she went up in a two seater open plane during an airshow in the fields between Beehive Lane and Watchhouse Road. It was so small that the other passenger, a policeman, had his arm and shoulder hanging over the side of the plane.

Outings

In the 1920s and 30s for most people the choice for transport was walking or cycling, and consequently the majority seldom ventured far beyond their own village. Annual Sunday School outings to Southend by charabanc might be the only time in the year when they ate out, and were a big event according to Florence Hardwick, who also enjoyed occasional trips to the other side of Ipswich! She says:

> We somehow went to Chelmsford and picked up the train. How we got to Chelmsford I don't know. Then we had a carrier from Ipswich out to the pub. There was no bus transport in those days.

The village carrier was Mr Collins, father and son. The carrier was a crucial figure in providing transport to and from Baddow. Mr Collins senior had a wagon and horses that was used to carry goods from Chelmsford to Baddow, (photo 11-7) and his son George Collins had one of the first cars in the village, which was the local taxi.

Christine Vernon, George Collin's daughter, remembers her father telling her that his fares included many important people, usually from the railway station to houses in the district. One passenger she remembers was a Mr Maud, who was connected to the early Labour Party. Another was one of the Sitwell family.

Jim Hurrell confirmed that the first village taxi had been owned by George Collins who lived at the Hollies (now called Red Bricks, opposite the library). (Photo 11-8). He remembers that the vehicles were kept in a yard at the side of the house, where Reynards Court now stands.

As people gradually acquired cars travel became easier. Una Matthews acknowledges this fact:

> My grandfather's brother, Edward Hockley owned the garage in Beehive Lane, opposite Jackson's Pit and central between the red brick houses and those we called the concrete houses (just above the Cabin Newsagent). He was early in owning a car, which made a great difference to the family, when they travelled to Sewards End near Saffron Walden, as he could chauffeur them. The alternative was several changes of train, or to cycle. The latter could be quicker than the train.

However, for many the only access to a car would be the village taxi (and only then for special occasions). Peggy Bradley, born in 1920, spoke of her father, Mr Tipping:

> My father had been chauffeur for the Duffields, at the house called Hampton (next to the Marconi Social Club). He eventually started his own private car hire business. Also, when things were quiet, he started up a small riding school. We had horses either side of Beehive Lane, one lot in Jackson's gravel pit, and more down in the pit we called Mr Snow's pit.

He would drive people on holiday to Devon or Cornwall. He once picked up Wilfrid Pickles and his wife Mabel from Chelmsford Railway station. (Wilfred Pickles was a popular figure on the wireless in the 1940s and 50s, the host of 'Have a Go').

According to Harry Clayden:

Nobody had private cars. The only person who had a car, which we used now and again, was Mr Silas Jackson. He lived in New Road and ran taxis.

Den Harvey remembers when he played soccer for Gt.Baddow, and the taxi journeys to football matches, in the 1950s using the big Austin taxi owned by Mr Silas Jackson of New Road (who also kept the market garden).

We used go to football matches from St Mary's school in that car. All eleven would get in that old big Austin six taxi on a Saturday morning. We would go to Melbourne, Rainsford, Moulsham or out to Little Waltham. As soon as we got in he said 'You must all sit on your hands and do not touch anything'. There were eleven boys and a master in one taxi. That taxi is in Beaulieu now. It was given to Beaulieu (Motor Museum), to Lord Montague.

[Ed. Beaulieu were asked for a picture of the taxi, but they do not have the vehicle any more].

Cars

In the early days, as Peggy Bradley told us, "there were not many cars about at all on the roads, and it was great for driving". It all sounds very relaxed!

When Sadie and Robert Gemmell learnt to drive there was no proper instruction:

Their father turned them out into the meadow in front of the house and they taught each other. Sadie has never taken a test.

Mary Parsons learnt to drive aged seventeen in 1938:

I used an Austin 7 made in 1928. It was a two seater with a dickey seat. No brakes, and a clutch that was either in or out. Women often drove in the 1930s. Over seventeen, you had to get a licence but did not have to take a test. She took her test in 1948.

Peggy Bradley learnt in 1937 in the gravel pit off Beehive Lane:

I was about seventeen when I learnt to drive. Mr Ship had a garage on Baddow Road, as you turn right at the bottom of Beehive Lane (Tower Garage). He loaned me a bull nose Morris car, to run up and down the gravel pit, to learn to drive. We had great fun. I used to put my sister and Una Hockley, who was my sister's great friend, in the dickey while I drove up and down. I was quite good at reversing the car in those days.

Unlike Sadie, she actually took a driving test, in a Humber Snipe 24 HP (which she remembers with affection).

Because it was my father's pride and joy, when I went for my test, he sat in the back. He tried to make signals in the mirror, but I didn't take any notice of him. He gave up half way round and thought I had failed. I hadn't, and I was pleased about that. I was then able to help him on occasions, when perhaps there was a wedding or a funeral, and they needed an extra car.

Stella Carruthers mentioned that Miss Peggy Bradley (néeTipping) was the first woman in Chelmsford to get a Hackney Carriage licence. She used to drive auctioneers out to Rochford and Wickford cattle markets.

John Jackson remembers working on his old Standard, which he described as 'the Standard with the dodgy big ends':

> I had an old Standard 12, which I bought off a scrap heap. I spent a year doing it up. I remember we were going off to Swanage with my son who was three. The car had cable brakes and a cable snapped with a bang coming from Danbury to Baddow, so I spent much of the evening before we set off replacing a cable, and we still set off at 6am. the next morning. Two years later the big ends went. I remember one big end started to rattle like anything. I took the sump off about 8 o'clock. I did not have time to do a proper job, which would have meant melting them in, and would have taken several days. I took out the shims and filed the caps off to make them tighter. We went to Devon and just got home before the big ends went again. That was just a bodge to get there and back. You wouldn't dream of doing that now, and we had to keep the speed down. In any case the car did not do much more than 40 mph.

He also remembers:

> My grandfather lived at Walton on the Naze. We had an old Erskine, which was a Studebaker 1928. Top speed was about 60mph, but you couldn't do 60 because of the gravel roads. However, we used to go to Walton in one hour and a quarter. You can't do it now in much under an hour, even with fast cars. There was no traffic then; you just wound it up to 50mph and just went. There were no bypasses. You went through Kelvedon and Witham through the main streets.

Richard Norrington never owned a car. He rode a bike and also had motorbikes and scooters:

> I had a round tank BSA 2 ¾ horsepower. There used to be a garage opposite St.John's church in Moulsham Street. I remember fuel there was 1s-11d a gallon (=10p). I used to buy half of that for a shilling (=5p). I was once told off for taking passengers on the back. I had a cushion on the back. A pal of mine wanted a lift to Galleywood but the bike was only made for one. There were no crash helmets and I only did local trips. I took my wife to Southend once, but she said "never again". She didn't like the ride.

As late as the 1940s and 50s Janet Chilvers says:

> There was only one car in our street. The person who worked at County Motors had a car. He occasionally took us to where he used to live at Woodham Walter on a farm. We thought it was a long way. What a simple life!

Kathleen Stevens recalled:

> No-one had cars in my area until about 1975. My first husband had an old Ford Anglia. Everyone now has a car except me and one or two others.

Garages

John Jackson inherited the garage on Church Street (where Dale Hire now is) from his father. The business was started by John's grandfather Solomon Samuel Jackson in the early 1900s as a general workshop and cycle shop. It expanded into a motorcycle workshop before branching out into cars when they were fairly uncommon. (Photos 11-9 shows a 1920's motorcycle with an uncle of John Jackson on board). The garage was a going concern for three generations of Jacksons (including specialised engineering work on bomb parts for the war effort in the 1940s).

John recalled:

> After the war we had about a month's waiting list for work. We hadn't got enough staff or capital. We were quite busy. We had thirteen people there at one time. We could fit in a service, but major overhauls had a waiting list. Cars were less reliable and needed

more servicing. A Morris Minor had thirteen grease nipples, at 1 ½ d a nipple; it cost £3 for a 'decoke' and service. (A 'decoke' involved removing carbon deposits from the valves, the top of the piston and around the cylinder head. This was a common servicing requirement in the early days of motoring before clean petrol was developed). A car wouldn't run much more than 10,000 miles before it needed a 'decoke'. The average man was doing about 5,000 miles per annum then; nowadays it's nearer 10,000 miles. The business was sold in the late 1960s when the Great Baddow bypass took much of the traffic away from the High Street and with it, the customers.

Tower Garage in Baddow Road was named after the water tower which was erected over a spring and bore-hole behind the Carpenters Arms (in the area used by Chelmsford RDC for storing their refuse lorries). For many years Mr Jones owned the garage.

The petrol station further down Baddow Road below the Beehive pub is built on the site of a Mission Hall, and the petrol station at the junction of Maldon Road and Molrams Lane used to be a mock-up shop during the war, housing and disguising an anti-tank gun.

Cycling

For many people cycling remained the best option. Peggy Bradley spoke of working in a shop in Stock when on Saturday afternoons people used to cycle in from quite a distance, because there was a chance of having something a bit cheaper. They came in for a bargain.

There were many stories of cycling to school or work, bikes being the only form of transport. (Photo 11-10 is of Fred Hurrell on his bike). One resident, Bert Collis, the son of the local policeman, recalled cycling home from KEGS during the early days of the war and riding straight into an Air Raid Warden. This was in the winter after dark on a bike with no lights (because of the blackout). Both of them ended up on in a heap on the road. The warden said, "Why don't you look where you are going?" forgetting that he was in the wrong, walking down the middle of the road in the pitch darkness, trying to spot enemy planes.

Harry Clayden kept fit most of the time by riding:
> When I was fourteen, I knew a chap who went to Baddow School named Percy West who lived in New Road. He did a paper round on Sunday mornings and he asked me if I would like to take it over, as they were moving. I went down to Radford's in Baddow Road. I got the papers from there, and went as far as Tanfield Tye, East Hanningfield reservoir, cycling on a Sunday morning. I got two and six pence. That would be 1928. I didn't think anything of it.

But he wasn't always lucky ...
> It was walk or cycle. My brother, when he was fourteen, got a job in Thompson's in Moulsham Street. He hadn't been working long, before he bought a bike, a drop handle bike. He let me ride it. I was dressed up in my Sunday best, and I rode it up Vicarage Lane. It was a gravel road. When I got past the back way into Baddow House, with its big gates and a wall all the way round, I turned, lost control and flew over the handlebars.

More recently Janet Chilvers (who was born after WW2) speaks of cycling to work at Boots:
> The Army & Navy was a very small roundabout originally. It was quite easy getting round on your bike. There were no sub ways of course. I don't do it very often now, though I do venture sometimes.

I can remember my uncle coming down from Derby, just visiting, and going to the Friday market in Chelmsford. He was amazed at how many people came up New Street on their bicycles.

If you worked in London, of course the train was the best option. Kathleen Stevens describes her journey to work forty or fifty years ago. She caught the 7.37 am from Chelmsford, arrived at the shop in Oxford St. at 8.45 am. The trains then were very reliable and not too crowded. Ah! Happy days.

Traffic

The increase in the number of cars on the road has been relentless. Eileen Hance complained:

> When I first moved here to Baddow Road in 1950 I couldn't get out of my drive to go to church because of the traffic.

Janet Chilvers described how the queue from the Army & Navy along Baddow Road was right back to St Mary's Church in the morning rush. Mrs Hance was grateful when things improved when the Gt.Baddow bypass opened in 1963, because then hardly any traffic used Baddow Road. Since then traffic has built up again, but she feels that the new traffic lights at the Army & Navy roundabout (installed in 2002) have definitely helped to improve traffic flow.

Conclusion

John Jackson, who has been involved with vehicles all his life, described the many benefits brought by the internal combustion engine and certainly most of us enjoy the ease of movement provided by the motor car. Munnions, who produced fire engines in Church Street, also produced the two elegant vehicles shown in the photograph. (Photos 11-11 & 11-12).

But as we wait to cross our busy village streets nowadays, it is hard to imagine Beehive Lane with grass verges where Peggy Bradley's father grazed his cow, or a child playing with a hoop in the middle of Baddow Road.

Aubrey Hockley recalled (via his daughter Una Matthews) that when he was quite young (in the early 1900s), he would be in the garden of the Carpenters Arms in the evening, and hear the sound of the horn as the coach made its way to Colchester.

*Photo 11-1
Fording the River
Chelmer*

*Photo 11-2
Delivery Van*

*Photo 11-3
Fowler Traction Engine
1905*

*Photo 11-4
A Fine Carriage*

Photo 11-5
The Doctor's Stable & Hay Loft

Photo 11-6
Lathcoat's Donkey Cart

Photo 11-7
The Local Carrier's
Wagon

Photo 11-8
The Hurrell Family in
Mr. Collins' Taxi

Photo 11-9
Mr. Jackson, Motorcyclist
1920

Photo 11-10
Fred Hurrell on his bike

Photo 11-11
Munnion's Bus

Photo 11-12
Munnion's Car

Chapter 12 - Health

Introduction

Over the years Great Baddow seems to have had a reputation as a healthy place to live! James Hodgson suggests that the village was just far enough away from London to provide a haven from the plague. So when in the Middle Ages the plague struck in London the rich would seek refuge in places like Great Baddow. In more recent times, the early 1930s, Bert Collis's father was moved from West Thurrock to Gt. Baddow. Bert tells us:

> My father was the village policeman in West Thurrock. We were there until 1934 when my father had chest problems caused by the dust from the cement works. The doctors suggested that the police force moved him to a less polluted area.

Presumably this area was chosen in 1893 for the old Isolation Hospital because it was thought to be a beneficial spot.

The days before the NHS was created

Rosemary Hill was closely involved with the early days of the NHS, since she was secretary to the District Medical Director of Health in 1948, who was responsible for implementing the NHS in Essex and making it work. Many of the older residents of the village remember the days before the NHS was created.

Colleen Yaxley's grandmother Mrs H.Ely wrote an article in 1965 which made the point that pre-war one did not call in a doctor until it was really necessary, because money was short and doctors' bills could be heavy.

Florence Hardwick:
> My father was a farm labourer in the early 1920s. I don't ever remember him being sick. It must have been the outdoor life!

Alan Thomson:
> Someone arrived unannounced at Dr.Spencer-Philips surgery to say that a casual worker in one of the Manor Farm fields was currently giving birth, and could he come quickly. When he arrived at the field there was no sign of any commotion. The young gypsy woman was pointed out to him and he found that she had given birth, attended to the infant herself, put it in a bag on her back, and carried on picking peas.

Clive Barker:
> Grandma Barker was the local midwife. She used to bring people into the world, and during their lives, she tended to their needs and their ills. When the poor people died she used to lay them out for burial. She was a very famous person in her own right.

Les Sparrow:
> You could join a hospital scheme for 2p a week, which covered your stay in hospital. The money was collected weekly into a 'slate club' into which you made weekly payments and if you were off sick you could draw a little benefit. The money that was left over at Christmas was shared out among the members.
> Home-made remedies were used in those days - to stop a cut finger from bleeding my granny use to wrap it with a cobweb. If you had a sore throat you either had a drop of

sugar and vinegar or sugar and eucalyptus oil. For a sore chest resulting from coughing you had brown paper smeared with goose fat wrapped round your chest. You went to bed with two soft bricks heated in the oven and wrapped in flannel, the idea being to sweat it out. It was also guaranteed to break a fever. For insomnia, not that children suffered much from this, granny used to say, "you should not go to bed on an empty stomach, always fill your stomach before you go to bed". Also lavender sachets under the pillow helped. For constipation you had sennapods or a cane of liquorice or a spoon of brimstone and treacle. [Ed: this brimstone was an edible form of sulphur]. Diarrhoea was treated with hard-boiled eggs. For grazes iodine was used and witchhazel for bruising.

He recalled:

Grandfather got bitten by a rat, and it went septic and eventually some weeks or months later he died from it.

There were evidently real dangers in putting off prompt medical attention!

The war years took their toll on people's health, though many had narrow escapes. Kath Brown was at home ill with bronchitis the night Hoffmann's was bombed, with a direct hit on the area where she worked. Eileen Hance was at work the day a small bomb fell, but simply tripped down some stairs and sprained her ankle.

Peggy Bradley told of her husband's frightening experience:

During the war we had a nasty raid, and my husband had been on the duty where they linked up the fire service pumps. They were all sitting in their various fire service vans, when he was overcome by carbon monoxide fumes. The other people in the back of the vans were being tended to because they were vomiting. They didn't realise that my husband was in the front, tucked under the steering wheel, unconscious. They took him to hospital, and brought him home, at five o'clock in the morning. They rattled on the steel shutters, which frightened everybody. He smelt of fumes, and was quite ill for a couple of days.

Local Doctors

Many residents have vivid memories of the village doctors, "old" Dr.Lyster and his son, "young" Dr.Lyster who served in World War One. There was "old" Dr.Spencer-Phillips and his son "young" Dr.Spencer-Phillips. Mary Parsons describes Dr.Spencer-Phillips senior, her family doctor when she was a child:

I can remember him very distinctly. He was a very tall man, slightly ginger haired, freckles and a huge moustache. I can still hear his voice. He always wore soft shoes which didn't make a noise. He had a good bedside manner. He was a marvellous man.

Derek Hurrell enlarged on this description of a well-respected pillar of the community:

Dr Spencer-Phillips was a well-known character and doctor in the village for many years. He died when he was about 97, I think, in 1980. My mother worked for the family as children's nurse before World War One. She kept in touch with them for years and years. When some of the children had children, and came back to see their parents, she would look after them as well, fifty years later.

Dr Spencer-Phillips was churchwarden, a bell ringer and was a very nice chap. He lived to a very great age, and the story is that **his** father was quite elderly when he was born. His father was born in the mid 1800s. (See photo 12-1).

Dr and Mrs Spencer-Phillips had three or four children. One of the sons, Patrick, followed in his father's footsteps and became a doctor.

Tony Pennack added that Dr. Spencer-Phillips was also a yachtsman, and even knitted clothes during World War Two to help the war effort.

From the early 1900s Yew House (sometimes known as 'Youse') was the home of Dr Lyster senior, and it was also the surgery and pharmacy. Like most doctors in those days Dr.Lyster used to do the odd operation and was also involved with the Cottage Hospital, as it was, in London Road, Chelmsford. In fact it was through an operation that Dr. Spencer-Phillips came to join the practice of Dr. Lyster senior. Alan Thomson explained:

> Around 1912 there was an opening for another doctor and Dr. Spencer-Phillips applied after graduating at Cambridge University. Apparently, when he arrived for his interview old Dr Lyster (who was then aged about 90) was in his surgery, about to operate on a young girl with appendicitis. Dr Lyster suggested that Spencer-Phillips assist him saying, "You can do the ether". Having started the operation Dr. Lyster apparently said, "My hands are not too steady, you can do the operation". So Dr. Spencer-Phillips had a "baptism of fire" and performed the operation successfully. Consequently he joined the practice, and the girl survived into her 80s.

Reg Bush can remember being operated upon by the two local doctors. When he was ten (i.e. in 1921) Reg needed to have his tonsils removed. The two doctors operated in the Bush residence on Church Street using natural light from the front window, with a gathering of local children looking on from the other side of the fence.

Derek Hurrell also had cause to be grateful to "old" Dr. Spencer-Phillips:

> I recall my father saying that when I was a baby I had a nightlight beside my bed plus a glass of orange juice. Somehow the paraffin from the nightlight got into the orange juice. I drank some of this and was very ill. We were living in Bell Street then and my father was at home, so he ran all the way to the doctors to get Dr. Spencer-Phillips to come and sort me out. I can't remember what the treatment was. It was pretty instantaneous and it was lucky a doctor was there. If the doctor had been on his rounds!

During the First World War Dr. Spencer-Phillips (senior) married the daughter of old Dr. Lyster and they had moved into Yew House. When his father-in-law died, the practice passed to Dr. Spencer-Phillips. Apparently (according to rumour and hearsay) this was not a popular move from the point of view of 'young' Dr. Lyster who may have thought the practice would be bequeathed to him. At this time he lived close by at Noakes Place[1], where he held his surgery. (He is said to have set up a practice at Sutherland House in Baddow Road in opposition).

At the time of writing in 2003 the surgery for the present doctors' practice is at 16 High Street and includes doctors Steven Russell, Peter Stern, Elizabeth Barron, Waseem Ahmed and Anja Vermeulen.
The practice at Sutherland House includes doctors Azmi Nadra, Miriam Edelsten, Gerald Cunniffe, Robert Climie, Joanna Birn-Jeffery and Hilary Ramsay.

Illnesses and Treatment

Many residents reminded us how dangerous the childhood infectious diseases were - scarlet fever, diphtheria, measles - in the days before mass inoculation, vaccination and antibiotics.

---

1 Noakes Place was formerly on Tabors Hill, just past the Blue Lion. The site is now occupied by Buckleys, named after Dr. or Mr.Buckley, a consultant surgeon living at Noakes Place around 1970 when the house was pulled down for development.

Florence Hardwick says:

> Diphtheria was a very nasty illness. My brother had diphtheria. He was sent to an isolation hospital. You had your house fumigated in those days. They used to seal up the windows to fumigate it.

And Dora Norrington tells us:

> There used to be a Mr Adams who had a black van - if anyone had scarlet fever he used to have to go and get the mattresses and steam them in a boiler house before taking them back to their owners.

Measles was treated with bed rest, with the curtains drawn because the illness affected the eyes, according to Peggy Bradley. When they caught scarlet fever many children ended up in the old isolation hospital. The hospital was situated behind the Beehive Public House and the quarry area off Beehive Lane. The hospital was approached via the lane between the paper shop and Steele & Co the building firm, on Baddow Road, and was a collection of separate buildings housing the various services and wards. It has recently been pulled down to make way for housing.

Mary Parsons:

> In 1926 aged five, I had scarlet fever and stayed in the Isolation Hospital for 6 weeks. I was taken in a khaki ambulance with a Red Cross to the Hospital, which had a small gatehouse. The Hospital was behind Granny's house and I used to wave to her through the window.

Many other former patients remember having no contact with visitors and only being able to wave at them. Children were understandably scared of the hospital and didn't even like walking near it.

Dora Norrington:

> We used to hold our noses when we walked up in the field because we were afraid of getting scarlet fever.

Robert Norrington, her brother-in-law, remembered that as children they were told not to touch the fences around the site for fear of catching something.

Perhaps the most dreaded illness was TB, often referred to as consumption. Bert Hunt told us that his mother was so concerned about infection she insisted they move house after a lodger developed TB and died. Another lady was offered a job in the late 1940s in the laboratory of Black Notley Hospital, which was also a TB hospital, but her mother would not let her take the job because of the risk.

Dr. Arthur E Lyster, Gt. Baddow doctor and District Medical Officer, published a book called "A Simple System of Treatment of TB and Other Diseases in Buildings Open to Air and Light" in the early 1900s. In the book he shows a series of photographs of what are really no more than canvas tents, with no heating, to be erected in the patient's garden. Some residents remember their relatives with TB being treated in structures like this. We have no records of the success rate! (See Photos 12-2 & 12-3).

We should not forget that cancer is not a modern disease. Bert Collis remembers his old headmaster at KEGS:

> Unfortunately he shot himself. He had cancer. This was just after the war when cancer was definitely a terminal disease, and painful. They didn't have the drugs then that we have now.

Hospitals

Apart from the Isolation Hospital in Gt. Baddow, Broomfield hospital also treated TB, and there was a small sanatorium in Howe Green, now two private houses. For non-infectious diseases there was the Chelmsford and Essex Hospital along New London Road, near the Essex County Cricket ground. Baddow residents have spoken of stays in all these hospitals. It was not always a happy experience. Dora Norrington recounts:

> I was three years old when we first came from Danbury. My mother's brother had TB and I used to sit on his bed, and talk to him. He was only twenty-one when he died. After he died I had a lump come underneath my chin, in the middle of my foot and in my arm. My mother took me to the doctor and I had an examination at Chelmsford Hospital. The doctor said, 'she's very fortunate because instead of it going to the lungs the TB has come out in these lumps'. I was taken into hospital. 90 years later I still have a dent in my arm and underneath my foot. They don't show so much now. They cut the lumps right out. They were butchers in those days. The Matron was a terror and I used to scream every time I saw the nurse coming. In hospital we had great big thick pieces of bread and margarine for our tea, no jam or anything else. My father came in one day when we were having tea. He kicked up such a row. He said he had never seen anything so disgraceful to be given to little sick children.
>
> My parents were allowed to come to see me because I was in there a month because of the places healing up. I couldn't put my foot to the ground. In hospital I was in a big ward full of children crying and screaming. I can remember that very clearly. I can today still see this trolley coming with all the bandages.
>
> Then I had to have my tonsils out when I was 13 years, at the same hospital, in the women's ward. We were taken down some stone stairs, with nothing on my feet, taken to the room and laid on a table and they put a mask on my face for the gas. I was kept in hospital where I was fed by tube for two weeks instead of a couple of days. I had developed some infection. Then I was in bed at home for three months and I was very weak. I could not eat anything solid for ages.

However, Les Sparrow was luckier:

> I did have a spell in the Isolation Hospital when I had scarlet fever - in fact it was called the Scarlet Fever Hospital in those days. I had a very nice time if I remember, except for the thick liquorice drink I had to take.

The main problem seems to have been that children in hospital were treated like adults. Kathleen Stevens remembered that in 1963/64 her one year-old son had been admitted to the isolation hospital after having convulsions, and she was unable to visit him for a whole week.

Florence Hardwick had a similar experience in the late 1950s. She said:

> I can remember taking my nephew in to have his tonsils removed. I had to leave him at the ward door. He had to walk down the ward all by himself. There was no connection between the parent and the child, once the child was in the hospital. Parents could only visit for two hours on Wednesdays, Saturdays and Sundays and sometimes young patients had to go into adult wards.

Changing Conditions

We can all bear witness to the changes made in the treatment of illnesses and patients during our lifetime. Some local residents are proud of being directly involved in bringing about change. In 1970 Florence Hardwick helped to establish a local branch of the "Action for Sick

Children", following her earlier experiences with her nephew in hospital. This organisation has led to better parental visiting with overnight stays where necessary, the establishment of children's wards and the creation of play workers attached to these wards. They are now working for a separate section in A & E (Accident and Emergency) for children to lessen the trauma experienced at these times. Florence also feels there is more work to be done to help old people in hospital and after discharge.

Other residents of Gt. Baddow are actively involved in Farleigh Hospice. There is a local support group that organises monthly lunches, tea dances and other events to raise money. Eileen Hance was Director of the hospice for ten years. She explained:

> I did voluntary work for the hospice before becoming a director. I am a firm believer in hospices because I had three members of my family who died of cancer, before the hospice opened, and I saw the difference between the hospital and the hospice.
> The philosophy with a hospice is to help people <u>live</u> until the last possible moment. Usually when people go into the hospice they are so happy because they are being well looked after. Not everyone can get in, of course. I managed to get my neighbour in; she had motor neurone disease. I actually got her in a week before she died, and it was wonderful to see her safe and calm.

John Parkinson, for many years the Gt. Baddow pharmacist, has witnessed many of the changes that have taken place in the use of prescribed drugs. He says:

> I mixed emulsions. I was apprenticed at University College Hospital. I was the last person to make a batch of pills there, about 2,000 of them, belladonna and phenobarbitone. Later it became much more technical, with more powerful drugs. In the old days tonics were made up, sometimes these had mainly a psychological benefit. We went through a period in the 1980s when people who were 'out of sorts' were given powerful anti-depressant drugs, and then they had immense problems weaning people off them. The general feeling was, "medicines must taste nasty to be regarded as any good".
> I was brought up to take a pride in making a medicine or emulsion or an ointment, and in the packaging and sealing it with wax.
> Nowadays one needs knowledge of the more powerful drugs, the interactions and side effects. The art of dispensing has disappeared. One needed skill to read the doctor's prescription or when one couldn't read it one used a two-headed penny! Modern drugs need greater knowledge of pharmacology.

> There were occasions you needed to correct some things said by the doctor to the patient; we were the last in the line, and if anything went wrong in dosage or concerning incompatibility we pointed it out. We worked very closely and had a good relationship with the local doctors.

> Computer programs now in use show up incompatibilities between drugs. Computers are useful, but 'two-edged'; they aren't always right. Computer programs ignore seasonal factors, which can result in insufficient stocks of medicines in the winter. I also anticipated that.

> My Father (who was the village chemist before me) was not in best health when I first joined the business, and he died in 1968. Three lobes of his lungs were removed in the early 1960s.

Nevertheless he was a live wire. He served on several pharmaceutical committees. In the early days of penicillin he prepared injections of penicillin for Doctors. He had to send these out to the doctors packed in ice in a vacuum flask.

With the advances in medical techniques, many previously untreatable conditions can now be treated. Robert Norrington has recently had a successful hip replacement operation and is to be seen shopping in the village and working in his garden.

Just before being interviewed Harry Clayden had undergone laser treatment on a cataract in his right eye. He was happy to report that it has been very satisfactory, and has greatly improved his distance vision.

No doubt Bert Collis would have been spared much embarrassment during his basic training for the Royal Engineers had such an operation been available in the mid 1940s. When he was eleven it had been discovered that he had had a stationary cataract in his right eye from birth. He recalled his army life:

We were sent to the ranges for firing. The character of this cataract is an opaque spot in the middle of my eye. Firing a rifle was all right because I can fire left-handed. I looked through the sight using my left eye. A Bren gun is different, however. It's impossible to fire left-handed because the site is offset to the left. If you are left-handed it's on the other (wrong) side of the gun. I had to fire it right-handed. The nature of the sight on a Bren gun is a small hole. Looking through this small hole I saw what I thought was the target, but I was actually looking at my cataract. I fired at it and shot away the number over the target next to mine. I was promptly put on a charge by the sergeant. The resultant conversations went like this:

Bert: "What is the charge?"

Sergeant: "I'll think of something".

I appeared before the commanding officer. "You are charged with conduct inappropriate of good order of military discipline. You fired at the wrong target".

Bert: "I couldn't see it as I have a cataract in my right eye".

Officer: "It says here you are A1".

Bert: "That's not my fault, it's the fault of the medical officer".

Officer: "You will have to report to the medical officer".

I reported to a different medical officer. He sent me to Aldershot to a specialist who was very interested in my cataract. He had worked with Dr Corner, who was the doctor in Chelmsford who had first spotted it when I was eleven. He had a theory that cataracts were caused by sugar diabetes. He said, "your mother probably had diabetes before you were born. That's why you have a cataract". He said I would need a urine test every morning to make sure I hadn't got diabetes.

Every morning, before parade, I had to go to the medical officer. I was downgraded to A3 because of the cataract. When I got back to my base camp I did this for the rest of my training. They eventually decided that there was nothing wrong with me. Before I came out of the army I had another medical and they upgraded me again to A1. This doesn't seem very logical until you realise the Army would have had to give me a pension if it could be proved that my eyesight had deteriorated during my service.

Funerals

Eventually, despite the best efforts of folk remedies, doctors and hospitals, we will all have to say our goodbyes to Great Baddow village for the last time! The chances are that Pennacks and Sons, who have been funeral directors in the village for three generations, will conduct the funeral arrangements.

When Dora Norrington was a child, funerals were very formal and sombre events. She still has clear memories of family funerals:

>I remember my grandfather's funeral. Pennack's did not have a horse and carriage; the bier with the coffin was pulled on by hand. Mr Pennack walked in front, the others walked at the side. The post office would not let us close the shop, mother went to his funeral and she came home to see if everything was alright and then I went up to see all the different aunts. Later I returned to the shop, as mother had to be present when the Will was read. I was dressed in black for weeks.
>
>Grandma had the same sort of funeral, no horse and carriage just the bier with the coffin on and she was the first dead person I had ever seen. I remember when my father died Mr Pennack, Tony Pennack's great grandfather, came. They got me out of the way because I was so upset. I was seven when he died. I was taken into the bedroom to see him just before he died. I was sent to my father's sister, Hilda Clarke, in Beehive Lane while the funeral took place.
>
>Now the funeral starts from the chapel of rest, which is much nicer, but in those days you went straight from the house. My relatives are all buried in Great Baddow churchyard.

Les Sparrow's recollections are similar:

>When we had funerals in the village of course it was quite a sombre occasion in those days. Everybody wore black apart from the children. Women always wore hats to church. Window blinds were drawn in the street in the immediate vicinity of the dead person, you rarely saw an open window and if you did it was frowned on as being disrespectful. There was no cremation in those days, all burials.
>
>I don't remember the horse drawn hearses myself but there must have been some. The very young children did not always go to the funerals, they stayed behind with a neighbour. There was generally a little bit of a 'wake', and you went back to the house for sandwiches, not like it is today with a 'bean feast'. No, it was a strange 'silence and sandwiches' experience, as they say.

From Pennack & Son's records dating back to 1889 a typical funeral arrangement included supply of a coffin in elm, suitably lined, plus attendance of the undertaker and bearers. This cost between £3 and £4 including burial fees. In 1890 an elm coffin was supplied, lined in swansdown, with best black furniture, nameplate in gold. There was a 'car' (i.e. a horse-drawn hearse since this is the time before motorised hearses) plus brougham (for mourners) and two pairs of horses to transport from Galleywood to Danbury, with a pony trap for the bearers, and re-fixing of a headstone, total cost £11-11s-6d.

In 1897 an upmarket funeral that cost £21-4s-6d was partially paid for in kind with hay and straw valued at £7-4s-3d.

Often the coffin would be transported on a hand bier, similar to the handcarts used for transporting builder's materials, but a bit posher with side-rails (see photo 12-4). The records also refer to a shilibere, a word no longer in use, which is another form of horse-drawn hearse (see photo 12-5).

Village residents who died away from Great Baddow would be brought back to Chelmsford station by train and transported from there to the church by the undertaker. Conversely a visitor to the village who died locally would be returned home via train with appropriate courtesies.

Conclusion

The experiences related above should perhaps prevent us taking modern amenities for granted. Even a bout of toothache can cause plenty of anguish, let alone a serious illness. How would we have managed before painkillers and other modern drugs came along? Perhaps we really have never had it so good.

Photo 12-1
Dr. Spencer Philip's
Family

Photo 12-2
T.B. Tent Partly Open

Photo 12-3
T.B. Tent Fully Open

Photo 12-4
Hand Bier

Photo 12-5
Shilibere

Chapter 13 - Historic Events.

Introduction

Sadly none of us was around to witness what was probably the biggest event in the history of Great Baddow, when many hundreds of peasants gathered in St.Mary's churchyard at the time of the Peasants' Revolt of 1381, an event of National significance. They wanted removal of the crippling Poll Tax, an end to servitude, equal treatment for everyone under the law, and the sharing out of Church property. Together with other peasants from the Home Counties they burnt many documents in Chelmsford town centre, then marched on London to put their case to King Richard. The peasants beheaded the Chancellor (Archbishop Sudbury, a former landowner in Essex) and Treasurer Robert Hales (of Cressing Temple). The Mayor of London executed the leader of the peasants, Wat Tyler, without trial. The revolt was put down by the London garrison and 500 local people who fought a last ditch battle against the King's army were slaughtered in Norsey Wood, Billericay. The king moved parliament to Chelmsford from 1st to 6th July 1381 while he sought out and hung the local ring leaders.

Simple Events

Life since then for ordinary folk has rarely been this rousing or worthy of a revolt! Events that have remained in our interviewees' memories are mostly family occasions perhaps a 21st birthday or a wedding celebrated in the Village Hall. Big weddings of local dignitaries were special, as when Dr. Spencer-Phillip's children were married and the church was full of flowers and people.

Christmas time was memorable, especially if you lived on a farm. Les Sparrow recalled:

> Well House Farm had a large inglenook fireplace in the lounge with a turn-spit on the side. I mainly remember fish or kippers being hung on it, though at Christmas they used to use it to burn 6 ft logs, which would burn right up the chimney and gradually get lower and lower. We would put the logs on at Christmas and the fire would not burn out until New Year's Eve.

Dora Norrington too was invited for Christmas meals at farms owned by relatives. She told us:

> Christmas Day was spent at Pound House, the Jackson household. Children were made to sing and play instruments. Uncles and aunts attended. We had lots of good food. The family gathered at Carter's farm on Boxing Day. They had a long dining room and a whole sheep was roasted with lots of food.

Derek Hurrell said:

> During the years of World War Two people had to make their own enjoyment near to home. They didn't go far, nor did we even after the war. If we went to Chelmsford it was a big event. If you were really lucky you might go to Maldon or even Southend once a year. Hence the popularity of the annual fêtes in the village. Harvest suppers were keenly supported and concerts in the Parish Hall when local people did their own thing were well attended, and they were very popular. I can remember one or two of the local people who thought they were stand up comics. The same people would always be there. In my father and grandfather's time you really would have known everybody's first name.

According to Florrie Steel the annual Flower Show was another annual event, held by permission of a Mr Britten in the grounds of Baddow Lodge, opposite the entrance to the recreation ground. Apparently there was a fair with roundabouts and competitions with tug-of-war teams, usually won by the Baddow Brewery team. Of course, similar events such as fêtes and flower shows still go on today in the village but small boys will be glad that "beating the bounds" has ceased. (Apparently boys were spanked at the village boundary posts to imprint the memory of the event on their minds. Reg Spalding commented on this practice in chapter 1).

Reg Spalding also used to be involved in the Chelmer Navigation Annual General Meeting, which was held on a horse-drawn barge while travelling between Chelmsford and Heybridge Basin.

Galleywood Races

Peggy Bradley can just recall Galleywood races:
> I can vaguely remember, I must have been very small, a lot of people coming up Beehive Lane to go to the Galleywood races. The racecourse went round Galleywood church. It's a lovely area. There is still part of the racecourse there now.

Tony Horsnell also witnessed the races as a child:
> My earliest memories of anything of interest would be the steeple chasing[1] on Galleywood Common. I can remember as a small boy seeing the horseboxes all being parked in Watchouse Road, Galleywood. They had taken the horses over to the racecourse, which went round the church. I think it's the only one in the country.
> I was only six or seven at the time. I can remember being with my mother at the post office, which used to be on the Stock Road. There was a jump alongside, and just as we got there a horse came over it and fell down and hurt itself. I remember crying so much. My mother took me into the post office and let me have as many sweets as I liked.

Apparently race-goers, jockeys and trainers were accommodated at the White Horse according to one resident, whose predecessor William Napper was the licensee between 1919 and 1927.

National Events

Of course, when events of national importance occur, the village participates to the full. An early memory of celebrations is that of Reg Spalding, who wrote:
> I was born on 15th June 1894 but my first memories of Gt. Baddow were of Queen Victoria's Jubilee in 1897. There was great rejoicing in the village. I think I can remember the Essex Show of the Jubilee Year held in Goldlay Fields in the Baddow Road.

He went on:
> From 1898 onwards the Boer War was in progress. At the relief of Ladysmith and Mafeking people went mad with joy, and we were given little flags.
> I well remember the new century coming in. My father called us at midnight to see the first year of the 20th century come in. It promised to be so wonderful.
> In 1901 at the death of Queen Victoria we all had black ties.
> Later on when Edward VII was to be crowned he was very ill and notices were put up in all churches to pray for him. When he recovered the coronation took place, with tremendous excitement.

---

1 Steeplechasing originates from cross-country races from one church steeple to the next. No doubt as the fields between churches were developed for housing the races were made more local, perhaps from Galleywood church around the course and back to the beginning.

Interestingly Dora Norrington tells us that she lived in "Mafeking Villa", Baddow Road. Her father bought the house from a Mr.Daly. When the relief of Mafeking was announced in the Boer War Mr. Daly decided to change the name from Baddow Cottage to Mafeking Villa. [Ed: I believe this end of terrace dwelling near the Star pub is now called The Cottage]

Several interviewees recalled Empire Day, as described by Les Sparrow:
> Empire Day was very well celebrated in the old days. We had a half-day off from school; we used to have to go into school in the morning and have assembly and go across to the church for a very short service. The rest of the day was our own.
> Girls as well as boys used to march across to the church. I believe in the very early days the infants used to carry cardboard Union Jacks, but I never carried one myself. The papers were always full of Empire Day news from around the world.

The Women's Institute have supported worthy causes all over the world. Occasionally they have been known to 'let their hair down'. A Pageant entitled "Britain Awake" was held at Mrs Beale's, Baddow House on July 18th 1933. (Photo 13-1). The ladies are asking us to buy British Empire goods, including South African oranges. The WI appears to be recruiting younger members than usual, judging by the front row.

Mary Parsons told us in her interview that a Mrs.Collins lived in a house by Chelmer Lea and sang on the wireless.

This complemented information from the records of the Women's Institute about Mrs Collins:
> A past president of Gt.Baddow WI with a unique claim to fame was Winifred Collins, who died in 1992 at the age of 95. In 1920 she was Chelmsford's leading amateur soprano when Guglielmo Marconi and engineer W.T.Ditcham asked her to sing over the air in the first-ever musical broadcast. She broadcast from a packing shed at New Street, and was heard by the captain of a ship 1,000 miles out at sea. She was paid 10 shillings (equivalent to 50p in today's currency). This making of history was six months before Dame Nellie Melba performed a similar role, for which she was paid £10,000. What it is to be famous! Nevertheless, Mrs Collins received a medal specially struck to commemorate the event, and on several occasions was a guest VIP at the Marconi Company's special events. (Photo 13-2).

More recently street parties were held to mark the Queen's Silver Jubilee in 1977 (photo 13-3) and then the Golden Jubilee in 2002.

Natural Disasters

People always remember severe weather conditions. Reg Spalding described in his journal a heavy snowstorm:
> In 1881 there was a terrific snowstorm. It started at 3.30 pm and by 4.30 drifts were over 6 ft deep. My father Fred Spalding then lived at Lathcoats in Beehive Lane and went to Jeffery's school in Baddow. He collapsed and fell into a drift but luckily one of his legs stuck out and a man on horseback who was hunting for him happened to see the leg. He was pulled out and taken into Sawkin's farm where they bathed him and rubbed him with brandy. After some hours he came round, but had to spend several days in bed.

Apparently in the year 1879 it rained nearly every day from February to October. Also 1903 was a very wet year, with a big flood in July. Hay in cocks came rushing down the Meads, also beer barrels. Dr. Bodkins had about ten acres of hay flooded before it was cut. My father cut it but it was full of mud. The doctor kept some very good horses, so to get the dust out he hired Mr. Belsher's threshing machine and the hay was fed into the drum. It made a very good job but there were terrific clouds of black dust.

Rosemary Hill (who was secretary to the County Medical Officer) told about the dramatic event of the East Coast floods of 1953:
> Canvey Island was almost submerged. It was the night of January 31st 1953. There was an enormous surge down the East Coast of England. Lots of places were flooded. Everyone was very concerned about Canvey Island. It was thought that there would be an enormous loss of life. We had an ambulance station there and Dr. Cowan wanted to visit and I went with him. I saw him wading off but I didn't get out of the car. I did get a glimpse of the devastation but not as many died as was feared. Our interest at County Hall was with the ambulance and fire stations.

The Baddow Flood

The event that was mentioned over and over again was the Great Flood of Friday September 5th 1958. One National newspaper of the period wrote:
> The storm appears to have developed over the warm sea near the Isle of Wight. It rapidly moved across Sussex accompanied by whirlwinds that brought down trees and caused other damage. It then moved across Kent. The storm became stationary over Chelmsford in Essex. During the four hours the storm lasted, between eight and twelve inches of rain is thought to have fallen. That is almost six months of normal rainfall.

Jesse Pryke had problems getting home:
> My wife and I weren't here, being on our way back from our honeymoon in Torquay. The trains had stopped; they could not come on the elevated viaduct, as they were worried about the foundations, so they stopped all the trains. We got a bus back home, then we found out what had happened. Chelmsford was flooded.

John Kemp had a similar experience:
> My wife and I came up from Ramsgate for a weekend at Baddow. We'd driven up and there had been lightning and a storm for hours and eventually we got to Gt. Baddow. My uncle and brother-in-law had arranged for the three of us to go out for a drink. We usually went to the Rodney or The Generals Arms in Little Baddow. On this particular night he said, "I don't think we should go tonight. It looks as if we might have a storm, and you know what happens when we have a storm. The centre of the village always floods". The water always rose because it could not get away where it goes underground through the middle of the village. So we were having a drink in The Blue Lion when it all happened.

The Essex Chronicle of Sept 6th gave the background to what happened this time:
> The water built up to a height of eight feet behind the wall at the bottom of Galleywood Road, opposite the White Horse. Although there were gratings at the bottom of the wall these were obstructed by many year's vegetation growth. At this point the wall collapsed. The wave of water passed to the rear of the White Horse, through Carter's bakery and behind the post office/general store. [Ed: Now Dace's piano shop].

The Chronicle of Sept 12th gave the following account:
> Friday, Sept 5, is a date which the 6,654 people of Great Baddow will never forget. For on that night of terror and disaster homes and treasured possessions were swept away by menacing floods.

It was a night of fear of black-outs as the electricity supply failed, of high winds and heavy hail storms. Then, by the light of almost continual lightning flashes, came thousands of tons of water.

The great tidal wave swept through the village carrying with it walls, huge chunks of concrete, cars and people.

Today, the gallant little village has earned itself the name of the "Little Lynmouth of Essex", and rightly so. [Ed: This is a reference to Lynmouth in Devon, devastated by a tidal wave pouring down from Exmoor during a storm in 1952].

Mr.George Wilson, of Manor Place was carrying furniture upstairs when the wall, like a great dam, collapsed with a roar. "I saw a wall of water racing towards the house at about 40 m.p.h. I raced downstairs to my wife and daughter and within seconds we were up to our waists. Then the door was swept away and the inside walls of the house went," he said.

A car parked outside the 'Blue Lion' was swept away. It crashed into the fence and gate of the Wilson's home and demolished it.

There were so many minor tragedies it is impossible to list them all.

There was the plight of Mr. and Mrs. Ambrose. Mrs Ambrose found her husband floating across the room on a mattress. She dragged him to safety in waist deep water. He was none the worse for it.

There was young Christopher Ward, who was swept along the street while trying to help Mrs Ambrose. He clung to the branch of a tree until he too was rescued.

Three elderly sisters, the Misses Edith, Mabel and Clara Josling had so much water in their immaculate little home that the walls bulged and finally collapsed.

A separate article in the same issue of the Essex Chronicle advised:

A coffee party is being held at "Foxholes" in Great Baddow, tomorrow, in hopes of raising funds for the Baddow Flood Relief. It is planned to commence about 10 a.m. and last most of the day. It is hoped that Mr.Hubert Ashton will be present.

Farmer Reg Spalding of Meadgate Farm told of his traumas:

Early in September 1958 we had a fierce storm, which started about 7 p.m. and poured for several hours. The river soon overflowed and the Meads were covered three to four feet deep. I managed to get my 50 head of sheep onto the high land around the locks where they always went by instinct. I got the cows and horses near home but the bridge was carried away, so we had to rope each one and they were pulled to the home side. All I lost were two sheep which the horses and colts had chased into the river.

Richard Carter told us more about what happened to the Carter household:

My grandmother, who was eighty-four at the time, was living in Brook House. Her daughter, Elsie Carter, was away on holiday and my grandmother was there alone. The floodwaters came into the house to a depth of four feet. My grandmother was standing in a chair, being swirled round and round in her sitting room, until such time that she made it up the stairs where she took sanctuary with her dog. The bake-house was in the flood. Brook House was made of lathe and plaster and seemed to stand the shock of the flood much better than the brick built bakehouse, which was next door. Although the floodwater took a long time to dry out, in Brook House it didn't do any structural damage.

Floodwater swept down the High Street and flooded the bottom of the hill at the Blue Lion. The water was level with the pub bar and bottles were floating. John Kemp's wife and baby son were staying at the house of his adopted uncle and aunt, the Wilsher's, at No 3, Valley Cottages. John goes on to say:

They were upstairs while we were downstairs, battling to keep the water out. We had the window open; the water was coming under the door, we were scooping it up with the bucket and throwing it out of the window. Then the fridge hit. This fridge had broken loose from Becky's shop, next door to no 1, Valley Cottages and next to Manor Place. It was a sweet shop and the fridge floated out of the shop, came under the archway between numbers 2 and 3, Valley Cottages and smashed the wall in. By now the bucket wasn't much use! The water rose to 4 to 5 feet so Buller (Mr Wilsher) and myself had to get upstairs. A little later someone managed to get a little rowing boat and rescued Auntie and my wife and Gary and took them to the Blue Lion, and they slept over there. The pub did not have very much extra accommodation but they managed to put up a few people. My brother-in-law Barry, Buller and myself slept upstairs at No 3. (Photos 13-4 & 13-5).

They did say that if the house had had normal footings it would have gone down, but because it stood on timber plates, 4 foot x 4 foot oak on the earth with no real foundations the rain washed out the earth but left the house intact. It effectively floated. One wall was OK, but the water took out about two feet of earth under the house. My car was flooded up to the dashboard and was a write-off. My stepbrother in London had arranged the insurance through Eagle Star and managed to arrange a write-off sum as compensation. Cars subject to flooding are renowned for causing trouble for years. My brother-in-law did not get any success with his own insurance company and he had trouble with **his** car for a long time. My car was my pride and joy and it was ruined. It was a Vauxhall Cresta, a very nice car.

Other cars suffered too, as Den Harvey explained:

Mr Edey the milkman lived in the little cottage between the White Horse and the Carpet Centre. He used to park his milk float round the back of the White Horse. His little Austin seven car came floating down, past Carter's, and went off down the High Street. (Photo 13-6 shows the White Horse, near where the flood started).

In one instance the water carried a resident away:

"Poor Miss Wallis was swept down. She lived at Well House at the bottom of where Foxholes is now. She was caught up, and swept along the High Street and ended up at the United Reformed Church," said Rosemary Hill.

Another local, Jim Hurrell's great grandfather, had shared the same fate in the floods of 1888:

Great-grandfather James Hurrell was night watchman when a sewer was being put in at Baddow. The same thing happened: the wall burst and he was swept down the High Street in his night watchman's hut as though he were sitting in a boat - ending up in front of Manor House. It is in the records, but they only put 'a man', not his name.

Jim Hurrell was living in Ebenezer Terrace in September 1958:

My parents had just bought a new mattress for their bed, so the old one was rolled up and put across front door; they sat on it to prevent water coming in, but then the water came in through the cable duct and air bricks. We lifted the carpet and moved as much as possible up stairs. After this experience Dad realised that the 1888 floods had caused the mark 18 inches up the wall. The floods appear to come every 60 or 70 years.

The Parish Council organised help for those affected and Bert Collis's father, clerk to the P.C. organised relief collections, and did a lot of work getting donations.

Den Harvey gave help at the time of the flood, since the cellar of Miss Bryant's shop was flooded:

> My brother and I rescued her bacon and cheese. On the other side of the road, opposite Carter's, are some old garages. They were store sheds for Sutton's warehouse, which was at the top of the hill. They used to keep all their tinned stuff down there. They were flooded, the tins got wet, and all the labels came off. They sent for new labels. They told us to keep the peas, plums, pears, everything separate.
>
> We took them to old Mr Sutton's greenhouse up Galleywood Road to dry the tins off. Somehow we got the tins mixed up! I don't know what people found in the tins!

It was not just people in the village centre who were affected. Parish Councillor S.Sosin gives a vivid account of his scout meeting that evening in the hut in the Recreation Grounds:

> At about 8pm the storm broke and the outdoor activities were moved inside. The storm soon intensified. The noise of torrential rain on the roof, continual lightning flashes and thunderclaps made it very difficult for the leaders to give instructions to the scouts. Before 9pm, when the meeting would normally end, the power failed. Not only in the scout hut, but throughout Great Baddow. With the storm at its full intensity we were in pitch darkness except for the illumination of the lightning flashes. The leaders took the decision that the scouts should stay in the hut until the storm abated, or help arrived. After 10 p.m. my father arrived at the scout hut. He said that he would escort the scouts who lived on the Rothmans estate. They would have to wade through the flood at the southern end of the Recreation Ground. The stream had grown to be about twenty feet wide and one or two feet deep. My father told the scouts to form a chain, with each holding each one's wrist to ford the stream. He checked that each scout had the correct hold before he led the party across the stream to the forecourt of the garages behind Rothmans Avenue.

He went on to describe the aftermath of the floods:

> On the Saturday morning my friend, Terry Starkey, and I cycled through the village to see the effects of the storm. Up to that time the centre of Great Baddow was full of high walls (like the wall still evident on the east side of Vicarage Lane) that made it seem daunting to a small child. We cycled down Galleywood Road from the farm, now Plumtree Avenue. The first site was the demolished wall at the bottom of Galleywood Road. Then we cycled down the High Street. Firstly we could now see Carter's Bakery on the left. It was completely undermined by the force of the water and seemed to hang in suspension without visible support. At the junction with Pump Hill the wall at the edge of the road, near the large tree, had been demolished. The remains are still visible near the library. Further along the road towards the junction with Maldon Road the boundary wall of the Vineyard's estate had been demolished. Opposite the Blue Lion the force of the water had dug out the hard packed gravel to a depth of three feet exposing utility pipes. The rear of the building had been ripped off and furniture strewn across the slope. The BBC had just finished filming the damage to Manor House as we arrived. We cycled down Baddow Road and could see the flooding of the Chelmer valley. This was greater than I have ever seen since. It covered from where Meadgate School is now (there was no Baddow by-pass then) across to Springfield Lyons Estate, overtopping the barrier. (This barrier was raised in the 1960 scheme). We cycled down to the Army & Navy roundabout, which was then the small size roundabout created in the 1930s. That

was partly flooded, adjacent to the builder's merchant. Shortly afterwards an ITN News camera team arrived. They asked us to walk across the flooded Baddow Road. The water was about eighteen inches deep at this point on the Chelmsford side of the Army & Navy. Then an open top sports car was driven out of the timber yard, which was also flooded, creating a spectacular wake during its fifty-foot journey to dry ground at the Army & Navy. This was also filmed by ITN. I never saw myself appear on television as it took over 24 hours to restore power to the Rothmans estate in Great Baddow where we lived.

Jesse Pryke:
Shortly afterwards they began flood relief, as they did not want it to happen again. I think it was Biggs Wall who the Council employed to dig a trench right through the village to pipe the stream underground, replacing the old culvert. The stream is still visible in Baddow House gardens. It stays under the road and it is piped all the way down through the village to the rear of Manor Place.

Village hearsay states that where it went under the road originally there were shafts leading off the tunnel to various properties along Church St, up to Baddow Brewery. They were reckoned to be secret passages. Once we had a flood in the DIY shop on Church Street caused by water coming up through a hole in the floor, so perhaps our secret passage tunnels are only entrances to drains.

Conclusion

Hopefully we shall not experience floods of this magnitude again in the village. The guilty stream now runs in a new culvert and ex Parish Councillor Doug Shinn assures us:
Over the next few years there was some concern that the surface water drain, under the Vineyards' site, might likewise become blocked. The drain was old and certainly needed repair. Repairs were eventually carried out and we have had no further trouble. Details concerning these repairs are probably available in the records of the Parish Council.
Meanwhile many of the traditional village events such as flower shows and the recently introduced May Day Fair thrive, and long may they do so.

Photo 13-1   W.I. Pageant 1933

Photo 13-2
Young Winifred Collins in 1920
when she became the first
woman in the world to
broadcast on radio

Photo 13-3
Jubilee Party Fancy Dress 1957
The lady at the back is Pam
Ambrose, the Chef is Jason Taylor,
the TV is Robert Taylor

Photo 13-4
Mr. Wilsher stops
Rogue Refrigerator

Photo 13-5
Valley Cottage damaged
by flood 1958

Photo 13-6
The White Horse

Chapter 14 - Mischief and Misdemeanours

Introduction

A chapter on CRIME may seem inappropriate in a book about a village, and fortunately Great Baddow has been very law-abiding over the years. This was in part due to the presence of the old-fashioned village bobby. He knew everyone, including the habitual criminals. Consequently much potential crime was prevented or nipped in the bud before it got out of hand, (a lesson for today's forces of law and order). There were of course some criminal acts, but much of what people spoke about was really mischief and minor misdemeanours.

The Village Bobby

Bert Collis told us of his father, who was village constable for 20 years (1934-53):

> Father was the old fashioned Dixon of Dock Green type, what we now call a 'beat policeman'. When he retired I met Sergeant Pink, who was very well known in the Chelmsford area. He told me that when my dad retired he said to Superintendent Day, "How is it that P.C. Collis never got promoted (and posted elsewhere)?" He said, "We haven't had any serious crime in Great Baddow for twenty years. Why should I move him?" I think that sums it up. Dad just knew what was going on. People told him things. He cycled round the village and people would stop and chat to him. They would even say things that perhaps they didn't intend to. He was well thought of and after he retired from the police he became Clerk to the Parish Council.

PC Collis' treatment of Dougal Berry is a good example of how effective he was. Berry was the scallywag of Gt. Baddow. First he attended Approved School, then Borstal and finally prison:

> If there was a problem in the village my father said his bicycle always headed for Berry's house. I remember just after the war, the telephone rang and someone in Great Baddow said they had just arrived home to find their house burgled. My father didn't go to their house, but headed straight for Dougal Berry's where he caught Berry returning with the stolen goods.

But Dougal Berry bore no resentment to PC Collis and even wrote to him quite regularly. He recognised the constable was only doing his job, but said:

> "He was like a father to me. When I was about fourteen someone gave me an old clapped out motor bike. I was riding it up Galleywood Road, from the White Horse pub, when your dad was coming down on his bike."
>
> He stopped me and said, "'What are we going to do with you? This thing is not fit to ride, you're not taxed, and you're not insured; you haven't got a driving licence and you haven't passed your test. That's good for twenty years. Come with me."
>
> "I thought he was going to take me to the police station. He didn't, he took me up the hill to a farm. He asked the farmer for use of a field where I could ride my bike without doing any damage. I never forgot that, he was really good to me."

Mischief

Les Sparrow as a young lad admits to being one of the village pranksters.
Living in the Maldon Road Les would carry a stick on his way to choir practice. On passing the chestnut close-boarded fence in front of the bungalow called Causeway Lodge, next to the RSPCA shop in the Causeway, he would run a stick along the fence making a loud *brrrrrrrrrrr* noise. People used to come out to see what the noise was, but he was long gone by then.

Den Harvey was a prankster rivalling Les Sparrow:

> I used to sing in the choir but got into trouble. Years ago the organ had bellows, and when the organist played someone had to stand pumping it with the hand pump. The pump was in the room where the choir changed into their cassocks. If you pushed the pump down it used to take about half an hour to creep up ever so slowly. When it got to a certain height, the handle at the side of the organ would swing and bang, making a very nasty noise in the middle of the sermon. I didn't exactly get expelled, but I got told off!

During the war, Laurie Russell, a fireman, would take his fire engine out as soon as the siren went off. He was one of the first in the village to own a television, and on Saturday nights he would invite Den to watch the entertainment. But that invitation came to an abrupt end when Laurie discovered young Den had set fire to bracken at the place called the dump at the top of Pump Hill.

Den's grandfather was brilliant at making catapults and used them to shoot rabbits. But the first catapult he made for Den was put to an entirely different use and grandfather might not have been too pleased! For young Den remembers shooting into a hedge at a bird - he missed the bird, but the stone went straight through a lady's French window in Hampton Road. Her budgie died from shock, and his grandfather had to pay for a new window!

Dora Norrington's pranks were never ending. The 'Hospital Fields', as the local children called the fields past the Isolation Hospital, were an ideal place to play and Dora Norrington recalled a large oak tree there, dead in the middle which made a lovely playhouse:

> The tree grew by the footpath where an old bowler hatted gentleman called Mr. Graves took his daily walk. So it was not surprising that as he walked under the oak tree he was showered with handfuls of acorns, which must have sounded like bullets falling on his hat. He used to stand and look around and up into the tree but he couldn't see us. He couldn't understand where the acorns came from. We children nearly fell from the tree giggling but I don't think he ever found out what happened. He would walk into the next field and when he came back we would do the same thing.

As a young adult Dora worked with her mother in their grocery shop cum post-office at the corner of Baddow Road and Beehive Lane (which the Co-op has recently converted for use as an Undertaker's). In those days postmen walked to and from the sorting office in Chelmsford to pick up mail on a daily basis. On one occasion Dora decided to play a prank on the unsuspecting postman and gathering two or three bricks out of the garden, wrapped them, and placed them in his sack. Imagine next day Dora taking refuge in her bedroom after being chased by a very angry postman.

Every three months two postmen, who worked in the main post office, came regularly to check the books at the local Post Office. They spent the whole morning going through everything. One of them who had cycled to their shop had just got married. So while they were busy dealing with the books she tied some old shoes, and decorations, onto the back of his bicycle. She said:

> I managed to hide the 'extras' so he didn't notice until he was well on his way. Another wintertime I stuffed paper up every finger of a traveller's fur lined gloves, while he was doing business with mother.

Scrumping apples

The scrumping of apples has always been an attraction to children, and who can blame them. Large gardens and delectable apples go well together, and there were many such gardens in Great Baddow. Peggy Bradley and her sister were caught red handed helping themselves to fruit and were chased off by the Matron of the Girl's Home at 22, Beehive Lane.

In the early 1900's Una Matthew's father Aubrey Hockley and some of his school friends went scrumping apples after dark in the garden of Mr Amoss their young headmaster. On one occasion they were surprised to find Mr. Amoss waiting for them and were duly dealt with! We're not told how, but Mr Amoss was renowned for having a strong right arm and a collection of canes!

Bert Collis was the policeman's son, which had its drawbacks. He said:
> The other boys were rather suspicious of me. Whenever they were going scrumping apples, they didn't tell me in case I told my father. It was silly of them, because I was the only one who knew where he would be, so I had to go scrumping by myself. I never got caught!

Others were not so lucky. PC Collis was waiting for Den Harvey as he climbed over the wall of the Vineyards behind Ducking Stool Cottage with his jumper stuffed full of apples:
> PC Collis used to ride a bike and wore great big gauntlet gloves. He took his glove off and whacked me across my backside. I flew home.
> My mother said, "what is the matter with you?"
> "PC Collis caught me".
> She gave me another whack, and then made a pie with the ill-gotten gains!

Dora Norrington was a frequent visitor to her grandfather's garden in Baddow Road and for temporary apple storage made use of her capacious bloomers, as we would use a plastic bag! But a skirt quickly dropped over bloomers is far more user friendly when an arthritic grandfather hobbles down the garden, to find an innocent little girl admiring his flowers!

Great Baddow was a farming community fifty years ago and many farms were situated in the heart of the village giving easy access to mischief-making lads. One of Tony Horsnell's friends found that if a chicken was caught and turned on its back with its head tucked under its wing, it would remain like that without moving, appearing dead. Imagine the shock of the farmer's wife when she discovered six of her chickens in that state.

A horse trough has occupied the site on the village green opposite the White Horse for many years. One bonfire night, seeing it was empty of water, Derek Hurrell made good use of it by setting off bangers, the explosion of which resonated throughout the whole area scaring local inhabitants out of their wits.

Of course much mischief went on in and around school. Den Harvey was in trouble even before he started at St. Mary's school:
> A small yew tree grew in the churchyard opposite the school and I used to climb to the top and pull faces through the classroom window at my brother and sister and other children.

Alan Willis and his friend Philip Woods both attended the village school. Alan said:
> One day we had a competition to throw a stone over the school roof. Philip had first go and succeeded. I was not so skilful and threw the stone straight through a window. What a to-do! Mr Amoss the head came out and lined all the children up and asked the culprit to own up. He said that if I hadn't worn glasses he would have boxed my ears. I never knew who paid for the window.

Les Sparrow remembers one prank from school when he was the ink monitor:
> At that time my Dad had a motorcycle which had carbide lamps in which you placed lumps of crystal carbide. When water got onto the carbide it produced a gas, and then

you lit the lamp. Sometimes I would get some of the dusty carbide bits from home and as I was passing on the way to my desk I would drop a small lump of carbide into an inkwell. A few minutes later it would fizz up and be like Mount Vesuvius all blue and green in colour as the liquid oozed out. I got the cane for that and many other pranks; but sometimes I got the cane for things I hadn't done!

Hardly mischief, but bullying went on then as now. Bert Collis recalled:
Every school has its school bully and Dougal Berry was one such. A couple of years older than I, he and another boy's playground activity was to gather the smaller boys into herds like cattle and 'drive' them with a stick round the playground. As he was bigger than I was he pushed me and told me to "get in with that lot". I refused so he pushed me again. I punched him on the nose, which made him think twice!

Crime

Great Baddow was a quiet and peaceful village and crime was not a common event in days past, which is surprising with all the large houses and wealthy people. However, there were instances of burglary.

Richard Carter, Magistrate and farmer, was burgled four times shortly after he and his new bride moved into Manor Farm on the outskirts of the village:
On one occasion I had somebody called George Frost working for me. George was under the impression that I thought it was he who had burgled my house.
He said to me, "You think I burgled your house. If you tell PC Kinnock, (or who ever the local bobby was at the time) to meet me down the pub and buy me a pint of beer, I'll tell him who exactly *did* burgle your house".
Shortly afterwards a man was arrested wearing my watch, which had been my father's watch. George knew exactly what was going on, but had not been prepared to tell me. He didn't feel he stood much chance with me if he came up before the bench.

Dora Norrington has also experienced crime at first hand, at work and at home. She met a criminal in her mother's shop seventy years ago:
We had some rather unpleasant times. Once we had a man call who asked for some cigarettes and as I went to serve him he made a grab at me. He twisted my arm and said he wanted the money from the till. As we ran the Post Office he thought he was in for a nice sum of money. But I was determined he was not going to get it. He was equally determined to succeed. I brought up my other arm and punched him in the face. Luckily, at that moment, a customer came in, and he ran out. He ran to the Carpenters Arms, the public house opposite, and robbed them.
In those days, the counter was open in Post Offices, but my mother's Uncle Robert Jackson thought that we should have a guard round the post office part. He found an old fashioned fireguard, and suggested we could stand it on the counter. He fixed the guard round the counter and it towered above us. Then he put a desk in, where we could keep the stamps and postal orders. We were well set up. The rest of the shop was for the groceries, where we sold everything.

Living alone in her house on Baddow Road after her husband's death, Dora had an experience she will never forget. She was always very careful about her jewellery and always kept it safely tucked under her pillow at night. Some years earlier she had lost her watch and her husband had asked her sons to buy another really good one for her birthday, so the watch usually went under her pillow too. But on one particular night Dora tells us: After locking up and going to bed as usual I was woken up about three in the morning by a noise. My bedroom door was ajar and a light shone through. The door gradually opened and I saw a pair of trainer shoes appear. I shut my eyes and breathed as if I was sound asleep. There were two of them. They were talking in low voices. They went through my dressing table but there were just some cheap necklaces. They did take two silver vases that were a wedding present, which we kept either side of the fireplace. I still kept breathing deeply until they went out but I could hear them downstairs. Then I heard voices talking outside. I was tempted to go to the window and look but I didn't in case they looked up. They had a van, which drove off. I lay there for about ten minutes and then went downstairs. The chaos they had caused! They had taken everything they could lay their hands on, even a tea service. My televisions too, I had one in the lounge and one in the sitting room. There was glass everywhere. But the awful thing was that on that particular night I had taken my watch off and put it on the sideboard. It was gone! The first thing I did was to pick my way across the glass-strewn floor, and put the kettle on. Then I dialled 999. A policewoman and a detective came, then the fingerprint man! Apparently the burglars had tried to get in the house next to Mrs. Howes, but had been disturbed. They didn't get in there. Why did they choose me?

The police said that the burglars had tried to get in the back door but it was bolted at the bottom and locked. They couldn't get in there so they smashed a window, and climbed onto a table.

Dora now lives in a small bungalow away from the busy main road. One afternoon, quite recently, on a beautiful summer's day, she and her neighbours were disturbed by a young man:

My next door neighbour asked him who he was looking for.

"Mrs Scott's son", was the reply.

He was told Mrs Scott had gone to town. So he stated he would wait! My neighbour thought the lad was genuine. Shortly after I heard a scraping around my back door (which fortunately was locked). I was later told by the neighbour that the fellow had been through her wardrobe and taken her handbag containing her pension book, bankbook and money - every thing ready for an outing on the free bus day. He had come round and tried my back door, climbed up on my rubbish bin and dropped her handbag over into the next door neighbour's garden. He had taken everything out and was off. The police came up in a car and drove around, but they never found him. That was real daylight robbery!

A week after that there was another robbery four doors away from me. The couple had gone away on holiday. They had left a little window open upstairs. They had gone abroad and left all her jewellery in the house. A skinny little boy was pushed through a window. He emptied her jewel box, he took everything and got it all in a bag and opened the door and went out the back way.

The gentleman that lived next door knew the lad and said, "Hello, Edward's gone away." The lad was a friend of the boy who lived in the house.

The lad replied, "I didn't know. I have come round to play with him."

My neighbour said later, "I think he was about ten. He knew that he was stealing the things and that he was doing wrong. Whether others threatened him or not I don't know. He wasn't able to tell the police who the people were who forced him to steal. I think that they either threatened him or bought him chocolates or something. That's what the police think anyway". It's very unpleasant to come home from holiday and find all your jewellery gone.

In some instances, sharp eyes and quick reactions helped to foil crime. Jessie Pryke tells us about a very observant postman who, while working on his rounds spotted a car parked outside Baddow Court. This was a lovely old house, built on many different levels with wide staircases and lofty ceilings and had been empty for years. Highly suspicious, the postman reported the incident to the police who caught the burglars that very morning, selling lead to a scrap dealer. Apparently during the night they had stripped the roof of lead, leaving the car outside the house, thinking it safer to drive off in the busy morning traffic.

The police were also involved in another arrest when Peggy Bradley's father reported a suspicious salesmen trying to sell linoleum, which they said, "was left over from a job". Peggy was proudly driven in an open backed police car to look for them:

Peggy: "On another occasion I was in the front garden, where I had been planting some little plants. I saw a man come in the gate so I dropped my spade and came indoors. He said, "I have come to mend your bell."

I said, "I haven't got a bell". I had a little pusher outside, where there used to be a bell, before they put heavy knockers on the door.

He said that it was upsetting people's bells further down the road.

I said, "that's a tall one since I've haven't got a bell". I wanted to have a good look at him and see how he was dressed.

I said, "I don't know what your game is but I am going to ring the police now". He scuttled off. I rang the police and when they came I said that he had gone across the road. They cruised around. I gave them a description: he wasn't very tall, had very short hair, and wore jeans, a T-shirt and trainers. He had a round face and a little bit of a moustache.

They said, "wonderful".

In the Chronicle on Friday they were warning people about this con man.

They said, "there was a lady in Great Baddow who had a con man call. She sent him away with a flea in his ear!"

In modern times Neighbourhood Watch schemes have been introduced to encourage us all to watch out for potential criminal acts, all the more necessary since we no longer have a 'bobby on the beat'.

Old-Time Crime

Just to keep things in perspective Richard Hazelton, of Chelmsford Library, supplied us with copies of crime posters from the 19th century. An example is shown.

Here are a few old crimes to compare with today's misdemeanours:

1800. MOLL RAM AND MOLRAMS LANE
According to the story, Moll Ram was a woman who lived on the boundary of Gt.Baddow and Sandon in the early 1800s. She liked her ale. She preferred the company of the drinkers in the Royal Oak at Sandon to her own family. One evening her husband got home from work to find no wife, a dirty house and no dinner. He being somewhat angry set out to find her. That was not difficult as she was in the usual pub. He hit her, which no one objected to, since she was his chattel, then he dragged her out by her hair, along Sandon Lane and into what was then called Lovers' Lane. She was found dead in the ditch next morning. (We have no data on what happened to her husband).
It was felt that the lane, which was much frequented by courting couples, should be renamed Molrams Lane.

Many years later two women were walking along Molrams Lane after dark from the direction of Ladywell corner on Southend Road when they felt that someone was behind them, but on turning round they could see no-one. There was a strong feeling of evil and foreboding, which followed them for several hundred yards, with them feeling more and more terrified. At that time there were very few houses and no streetlights on the lane. Eventually they saw a light, and one of them said "Thank God", at which time the evil feeling left them.

1590. BADDOW MAGNA.

Thomas Bynder, Clement Tanner, Lawrence Lea. That upon Easter Tuesday they played at Futt Ball in service time. Alleged that they played not, but were absent from church and were minded to go to another towne to play.

[It will be observed that the Church apparently had the power to take cognisance of the playing of games during service-time on holy days and festivals besides the Sunday.]

How crime has changed!

£2 REWARD

Great Baddow Association for the Prevention of Crime, and Prosecution of Felons.

Whereas some Person or Persons did, last Night or early this Morning, break into the Hen-House of Mr. WILLIAM MUSSETT, at POND LANDS, GREAT BADDOW, and steal and carry away therefrom,

8 YOUNG FOWLS,

4 PULLETS

AND THREE HENS

Any Person or Persons giving Information that will lead to the Apprehension and Conviction of the Offender or Offenders, shall receive the above Reward on application to the Secretary. If more than one Informant the Reward to be apportioned.

Great Baddow, 26th November, 1842.   H. S. GILSON

Solicitor and Secretary.

[DUTTON, PRINTER, CHELMSFORD]

Chapter 15 - Footnote

Introduction

As a finale to our little book, we have included extra data on street names, which came from the study of the village, and a concluding poem that sums up the idea of local history.

Street Names

A regular comment made by residents is "What a good idea it was by our predecessors to name roads in Great Baddow after people who made their mark in the village". This policy has met with general approval.

As far as we can ascertain the derivation of a few of these names is as follows:

Tabors Avenue was named after James Tabor who owned Manor Farm in the early 1900s.

Spalding Way, named after the Spaldings of Meadgate Farm.

Paschal Way was named after Jane Paschal, who died in the village 1614. A plate in St. Mary's church provides details of her claim to fame.

Jeffery Road was named after Jasper Jeffrey, who endowed a school in Great Baddow in 1731.

Loftin Way, named after Mr Loftin who built the road in 1937.

Gilmore Way on the Baddow Hall Estate was named after Mrs Gilmore, who owned Baddow Hall.

Buckleys was named after Mr Buckley, a medical consultant who owned Noakes Place at the time it was demolished in the 1960s.

Amoss Road was named after Mr Amoss, the headmaster of Great Baddow School for many years.

Britten Crescent was named after Mr Britten, who lived in Baddow Lodge and who was a Parish Councillor around 1930.

Smithers Drive was named after Mr Smithers, a stockbroker who owned Baddow Court pre-war.

Molrams Lane was named after Molly Ram, murdered by her angry husband we believe.

Other roads have been named after buildings, eg:

Whitehouse Crescent after Whitehouse farm.

Meadgate Avenue after Meadgate farm

Lodge Avenue after Baddow Lodge

Lathcoates Crescent after Lathcoat's Farm (note the change of spelling)

Oldbury Avenue after Oldbury House.

Foxholes Road after Foxholes House, formerly on Pump Hill. (We also like the name of the flats in Foxholes Road called appropriately 'Reynard's Court')

Apparently the main roads in the village suffered name changes:

Baddow Road was at one time known as Baddow Lane Jim Hurrell's Great Aunt was frightened to go along it as a girl because it was so dark, trees overhung it like a tunnel. Previous to that it had been called the Hundreds Road. At the Blue Lion it split, the Maldon Road was known as the Dengie Hundred Road & the High Street / Church Street was the Rochford Hundred Road.

The Maldon Road was called the Danbury Road, as Danbury was the next place.

Church Street was called Southend Road.

On old maps pre 1900 one finds that Vicarage Lane was once called Workhouse Lane, with the workhouse about 400 yards along on the left going from the vicarage, not far from the Marconi mast.

Beehive Lane was Gravelwood Lane on the Chapman & André map of 1777.

Village Poem

The following poem forms a fitting conclusion to the book:

Memories

The jingling of harness in the half light of dawn
Stomping of boots on a cold winter's morn
Scrunching of wagon wheels out in the street
The steam from the horses, the spark from their feet
The rustle of movement as the village awoke
Silhouettes of chimneys with their ribbons of smoke.
Then scurrying figures hunched against cold
All at their work 'ere the day's very old
And later the chattering children apace
Socks round their ankles, red in the face
Some to work in the kitchen, others as maid
Schools for the lucky ones whose parents have paid.
Sun drenched hedges in the mid-morning hush
Alive with the song of the blackbird and thrush
Farm workers in fields with dinners on knees
New bread, and an onion and a small wedge of cheese.
Then the twilight shadows down roadway and lane
As the horses and wagons return home again.
Then with animals watered, stabled and fed
Time for eating by lamplight and by candle to bed
Those days have long past, modern life moves apace
Little time for a chat now as we keep up in the race.
Meadow and hedgerow now with houses abound
And traffic roars by where once horses were found
But of late there are changes, a stir in the air
Laughter, enjoyment and a new will to share.
There are smiles of approval from those who've passed on
We're a village again a hundred years on.

Les Sparrow

Composed by Les Sparrow to mark the centenary of the founding of Great Baddow Parish Council. His grandfather was one of the founder members of the first parish council in 1894.

Acknowledgements

The Oral History team is indebted to the village residents and former residents who consented to being interviewed on tape. They provided the bulk of information on which the book is based. The personal anecdotes give a vivid picture of village life in days gone by, fulfilling the overall object of an oral history.

Clive Barker	Peggy Bradley	Ruth Brooker
Richard Carter	Janet Chilvers	Harry Clayden
Bert Collis	Sadie Gemmill	Eileen Hance
Florence Hardwick	Den Harvey	Rosemary Hill
James Hodgson	Tony Horsnell	Bert Hunt
Jim Hurrell	Derek Hurrell	John Jackson
John Kemp	David Norman	Dora Norrington
Robert Norrington	John Parkinson	Mary Parsons
Jesse Pryke	Betty Spalding	Les Sparrow
Tom Steggelles	Kathleen Stevens	Philip Taylor
Jeanette Williams	Alan Willis	Colleen Yaxley

Thanks are due to the head and teachers from the following schools, who happily agreed to participate in the project. In particular, thanks to the pupils who told us of their likes and dislikes, about their families and leisure in 2002:

School	Head	Teacher
Larkrise School	Mrs K.Claxton	Miss Marilyn Hampton/Clare Adams
Meadgate School	Mrs L.Hughes	Mrs Leatherdale
Baddow Hall School	Mr.Guy Niven	Miss Susanna Roper

Appreciative use was made of data from the following, with their permission:

David Emery, who provided much architectural detail of buildings in the village, and about Gt.Baddow families, especially the landed gentry.

Alan Willis, who provided (via Great Baddow library) two comprehensive Great Baddow albums.
[Ed: A large content of the companion walking guides comes from David and Alan.]

Don Bright, who gave unrestricted access to his marvellous collection of old photos of Gt.Baddow.

Mrs Betty Spalding kindly lent the journal of her late husband Reg Spalding, (born 1894). This has been used a great deal, since it contains much unique information about farm life.

The following contributors provided written data, or allowed a member of the team to take notes concerning their reminiscences and knowledge of the village. They are in alphabetical order :

Alan Beedham for photographs and sketches of old Baddow at 3-10.

Reg Bush, (born 1911) provided much detail of years gone by in a talk to the Local History group of the U3A. A synopsis of this is included herein. He also supplied photo 7-1 showing his father at work, and 8-2 of Sandford Mill.

Dennis Byatt, provided much detail on the battle surrounding the Vineyards development in the 1960s.

Stella Caruthers re detail on Beehive Lane and Loftin Way.

Chelmsford Museum's Keeper of Art, Anne Lutyens-Humfrey, for permission to use copies of paintings by A.B.Bamford seen at 1-8, 6-10

Bill Clark, who provided photographs and architectural detail.

Country Life, from whose January 1911 issue detail of The Vineyards was gleaned, plus photos 2-9 & 2-10,

Mrs P.Crawford for 'A History of Manor Lodge 1788 - 1999'

Gillian Crowe, née Russell, who provided much detail concerning Russell's Barn and shop.

Iris Easter, who described the shops of her childhood.

Mrs H Ely, who wrote a newspaper article in 1965 about her formative years (provided by her daughter Colleen Yaxley).

Mr.J.C.Flack for details of his property development in Bell Street and of Russell's Barn.

Rob Galley for details of the Munnions.

Sue Gardner of New Road for details of Great Baddow in the 1881 census.

Pat Herniman, who has made a detailed study of the life of Thomas Hooker, Puritan preacher in Chelmsford, one time resident of Great & Little Baddow and founder of Hartford ,Connecticut, USA .

Mr.McIntyre for the history of Baddow Court.

Una Matthews, who provided details about the forgotten sport of Quoits, at which her father played for Essex and England.

Peter Newman, who provided a map of the village as it used to be.

Mr.Nutbeem re the Essex Carpet Centre.

Tony Pennack, who provided many photographs and notes about Baddow personalities.

Doug Shinn, who described some Parish Council activities in the 1960s.

Parish Councillor and former scout Andrew Sosin, who got distinctly wet in the floods of 1958

Flossie Steel, who has lived in Baddow Road many years.

Christine Goldstone, née Steele, who lent her project thesis on Great Baddow, written as part of her teacher training studies.

Alan Thomson provided much detail concerning Yews, Thomson's shop and former occupants.

Clive Turner provided a brief history of Gt.Baddow Tennis Club.

Christine Vernon provided much detail about her father, Mr Collins and his taxi service; her grandfather and his horse-drawn carrier service.

Roy Wall who provided notes made by his mother about village tunnels.

Stuart Rawlins, Editor of the Essex Chronicle for permission to copy photos 13-4 & 13-5 and to reproduce articles from the paper concerning the great flood of 1958.

Jane Allen, Kath & Don Brown, Stella Carruthers, Mrs Hougham, Ronald Larter and Muriel Plowright who provided general information.

Thanks to Chris Woollard and many other residents who have supported the project.

Many residents lent me their valuable photographs of the village to be scanned into the collection, some of which appear in the book. My apologies if I have left anyone out, or attributed the photo incorrectly. The detail of ownership of the photographs follows:

Alan Willis: 1-7, 1-13, 2-2, 2-6, 2-8, 2-12, 3-1, 3-2, 3-7, 3-9, 3-12, 3-13, 4-3, 5-1, 5-3, 5-5, 5-10, 6-7 to 6-9, 6-11, 7-5, 7-9, 7-11, 7-12, 9-4, 10-1, 10-4 & 11-7

Allen Buckroyd: 1-9, 2-14, 2-15, 2-17, 3-8, 4-4 to 4-7, 5-2, 6-1, 6-12, 6-14, 7-2 to 7-4, 7-6, 7-8, 7-13, 8-3, 8-17, 8-18, 9-1, 9-2, 10-2, 10-3, 10-5, 10-6, 11-5 & 12-4.

Richard Carter: 1-22, 2-5 & 11-4

Don Bright:. 1-1, 1-5, 1-6, 1-10, 1-11, 1-12, 1-14, 1-15, 1-17 to 1-20, 2-1, 2-4, 2-7, 2-16, 3-4, 3-5, 3-14, 7-14, 8-4 & 11-1. Many of these were originally taken by famous photographers Fred Spalding or Mr Hoy of Gt.Baddow.

Den Harvey: 8-6 to 8-8.

Jeanette Williams: 5-11.

Sadie Gemmell: 5-4.

Derek Hurrell: 1-3, 11-8 & 11-10

Gt.Baddow Women's Institute: 13-1 & 13-2

John Jackson: 1-4, 1-16, 3-6, 3-11, 7-10 & 11-9.

John Marriage: 7-7, 11-11 & 11-12

Dora Norrington: 4-1, 4-2, 6-13 & 9-3,

Martin Lee: 8-5

Tony Pennack: 5-6 to 5-9, 12-5.

Harry Clayden: 8-10.

Christine Goldstone, née Steele: 1-22, 2-3 & 6-2

Philip Taylor: 6-3 to 6-6, 9-5 & 11-6

Una Matthews: 8-12 to 8-14

Ann Whalley: 2-18, 12-2 & 12-3

Colleen Yaxley: 2-11, 8-1 & 8-15

Bert Hunt: 8-11

10-7 is from St.Mary's booklet

Pat Freeman: 6-12 & 11-3

Pauline Cutmore: 13-3

Thanks are due to Gt.Baddow Parish Council, (particularly Chairman Mrs Chris Shaw) who gave their wholehearted support throughout the project and for financial help to allow the project to get off the ground. Mrs Shaw kindly provided the Foreword to this book and Parish Clerk Ann Wood who from her own literary experiences advised about getting the book into print.

The Committee of the Baddow and Galleywood U3A deserve thanks for their support of a project that was somewhat ambitious for a group such as ours. They too backed up their faith with U3A funds, which were used wisely.

The Oral History team are deeply grateful for the Local Heritage Initiative Grant funding which has allowed us to get this book into print. They have also funded the resources necessary to carry out a programme of informal lectures based on the audio recordings, the text and photographs recorded in the book, plus a brief history of the village that is associated with the publication.

The Local Heritage Initiative is a partnership between the Heritage Lottery Fund, Nationwide Building Society and the Countryside Agency.

Lastly I wish to express my appreciation of the hard work carried out over three years (so far) by the Oral History team of the Baddow and Galleywood U3A:

Ann Whalley, Assistant Editor
Brian Barker, U3A Local History group co-ordinator
Pauline and Hugh Cutmore,
Vera Evans,
Sylvia and Norman Tingey,
Ken Nickol and Mike Nel.

The work of the team covered recruitment of suitable contributors, interviewing them, transcribing from audio tapes into the word processor, copying and pasting on personal computers to build up chapters, editing and re-editing umpteen times. Photographs have been taken, scanned, cropped, repaired and selected. Proof copies have been read and re-read. Copying on floppy disc and CD-ROM provided essential backup copies. Resolving of queries, research, fact-finding, fund raising, shopping for paper, tapes, and software also featured. Last but not least there was a considerable amount of tea and many pounds of biscuits consumed, which often saved our lives.

Publicity has been by word of mouth, via local publications and with the help of BBC Essex, in particular Angela Lodge, Steve Scruton and Dave Monk.

In the future we will continue the work by publicising the book and selling copies to relatives and the many new friends we have made during the project. No doubt we will be advised of the vast amount of data about Great Baddow we have omitted. However, we never claimed that this book would be the only history written about Great Baddow!

Allen Buckroyd, Oral History Team Leader and Editor.

Disclaimer

Reminiscences

Any Oral History relies on the long-term memory of the contributors, many of who are able with remarkable clarity and accuracy to recall events that occurred 60 or 70 years ago. However this ability is not a universal attribute and, moreover, two different people may view the same event entirely differently. The editing team has therefore endeavoured to cross check data wherever possible. However, we are unable to take responsibility for the views of contributors with which the reader may disagree.

Copyright.

We have also endeavoured to seek out copyright holders wherever possible to request permission to reproduce written or photographic material. All contributors of oral material (i.e. their speech on cassette tapes) have signed release notes transferring the copyright to the Baddow and Galleywood U3A Oral History team. Suppliers of written material were aware of the use to which their material would be put and were happy to hand over their notes and observations. Many people have supplied photographs with the same knowledge of eventual usage. We apologise if we have overlooked any instances where permission should have been sought.

Some photographs have been altered slightly, either by cropping, or by removal of obvious flaws caused by the passage of time. Their content has not been changed to alter their meaning in any way.

Sensitive Material

We have omitted material that in the opinion of the editorial team could be construed as hurtful or insulting to persons mentioned in the text, or their descendants. We apologise if we have overlooked any instances where an entry inadvertently causes distress to the reader.

Conclusion

It is hoped that the reader has gained knowledge and derived pleasure in reading this book. As far as we know it is the first book to be published about Great Baddow and its residents. If you enjoyed it, tell your friends and relations. If you did not, keep quiet please.

Comments and observations can be made verbally or by e-mail to the editor, the Oral History Team or to the Secretary of the Baddow and Galleywood U3A. Mistakes will be corrected in the next edition, if there is one.